WITNESSING

From the Rwandan tragedy to healing in South Africa

Pie-Pacifique Kabalira-Uwase

Kwela Books,
an imprint of NB Publishers, a division of Media24 Boeke (Pty) Ltd
40 Heerengracht, Cape Town, South Africa
PO Box 879, Cape Town 8000, South Africa
www.kwela.com

Cover design and typography: Wilna Combrinck
Cover photographs: atosan/iStock and Ivana Cajina/Unsplash
Author image: Verity Fitzgerald
Editor: Gillian Warren-Brown
Proof reader: Kathleen Sutton

Set in EB Garamond
Printed and bound by CTP Printers, Cape Town

First published by Kwela Books 2022
ISBN: 978-0-7957-1047-6
ISBN: 978-0-7957-1048-3 (epub)

CONTENTS

PROLOGUE

It was a cloudy morning in December 2006 and gusts of Cape Town's infamous south-easter shook the leaves of the oak trees flanking St George's Cathedral and rattled the sash windows of the historic Mandela Rhodes Building where we had gathered in the fourth-floor executive lounge. We, the class of 2006 Mandela Rhodes Scholars, had been brought to Cape Town for a private Christmas luncheon with Nelson Mandela, founding patron of the Mandela Rhodes Foundation (MRF). Only one of the fifteen scholars in residence that year couldn't make it back from abroad in time to be there.

Beneath our attentive silence was palpable excitement as we listened to a last briefing from MRF chief executive Shaun Johnson. After explaining the protocol, he remarked: 'We are lucky that Madiba was available for us today. We can never take his presence for granted, as you can imagine.'

He ended his briefing with a hint, clearly designed to heighten our anticipation even more: 'Two of you will have the significant task of entertaining Madiba and Graça. I won't tell you who, you'll find out when you get there!'

I remember thinking: just being here is more than I could ask for! For the second time in the space of a year, I was going to be in the presence of Nelson Mandela, whose life had fascinated me since I was a little boy. I had dreamt of meeting him one day; a second time was more than I could have imagined. And this time, it was going to be an intimate occasion, a small private function on the patio of Shaun's home on the Atlantic seaboard.

When I received the invitation, I had asked the foundation to bookend my trip with two extra days in Cape Town so I could visit my friend Eric, who, with his sister Erin, was now living in Retreat in the Southern Suburbs. I'd seen him only once in South Africa, but when we were growing up, the back windows of their home faced onto the back yard of my family's house in the densely populated suburb of Muhima in Kigali, the capital city of Rwanda.

Eric and Erin had left Rwanda for South Africa in 2002, and had at first stayed with family friends in Cape Town. But they soon moved out to live on their own, and like many African immigrants arriving in the major cities of South Africa, they struggled, barely making ends meet as car guards. When they eventually managed to get asylum papers and a chance to study, Eric realised he had a choice to make: continue his own tertiary education while they both battled for survival, or work to earn a living for them both. He decided to keep working while his sister studied. After a few months as a car guard, Eric got his driver's licence, which opened doors for him to get a job as a driver and a waiter with an events management and catering company.

Spending time with Eric was a joy. We shared memories of our childhood, the conversations we'd had through the windows of their house, how I had feared his parents, and envied him and his siblings as they were whisked off daily in their dad's bright red SUV to the primary school of Rugunga, then known as a school for children of rich and influential people.

'All that comfort, my friend, it disappeared in no time . . .' he said. 'And when that happens, you grow up very fast!' I understood from experience; there was no need for words to fill the brief silence between us. He continued: 'You know, sometimes I used to stand in the parking lot of a shopping centre here in Cape Town as a car guard and see how dismissively some of those people treated me as they parked their cars. I would just shake my head and think: you don't know!' I knew exactly what he meant, from my own time as a car guard in Durban in 2001 and 2002.

Eric and his family had been among the hundreds of thousands of Rwandans who had managed to cross the border into what was then Zaire. Waves of people had fled – when war broke out, during the genocide, and to escape feared retribution by the new regime. After living in camps for almost two years, the refugees were forcibly repatriated when the new Rwandan army – the victorious RPF rebel troops – invaded Zaire and dismantled the camps under heavy artillery and gunfire. Eric knew from the inside the bitter experiences many of our family, friends and neighbours had shared when they got back to Rwanda after surviving the forced repatriation ordeal. Refugee tents in flames, long, hard, barefoot hikes deep inside the dense, trackless forests, walking day and night, swollen legs, no food or water, screaming, hungry children, crying mothers, helpless fathers, dead bodies, mud stained with blood . . .

It was not hard for me to imagine the horror; I had lived in Kigali throughout the genocide in 1994. He told me how the family managed to make it across the border, and I shared how I had lived through the war. And then we told each other stories about our separate journeys from Rwanda to South Africa, and the shock of the new reality that hit us upon our arrival, beginning life again, one more time. I was humbled by his decision to drop his own studies to support his sister through tertiary education.

'I have no choice, I have to be the responsible one here,' he said. 'When she is done, it will be my turn to study.' I was struck by how firm his decision was and how peacefully he was living with it.

As he described how he was managing to get by in Cape Town, his phone beeped with an incoming SMS, telling him he was on driving and catering duty the next day, Wednesday.

'This is how it works, man! You have to be available, sometimes with only a few hours' notice. It is impossible to plan anything else and make money!' After he cooked dinner for us, we chatted deep into the night till we fell asleep.

On his way out the next morning, dressed in his uniform – a white shirt and khaki trousers – Eric stopped in the doorway, shoulders stooping slightly because he was almost taller than the

9

door frame: 'Enjoy your day, son!' he said, looking at me intently, a slight smile on his face. 'Yoh! So from here you are going to have lunch with Nelson Mandela? I still can't believe it. Life, man, life is amazing! That gives me hope that things will look up again!'

'Thanks! Enjoy your day too, son!' I said as he left. Although we were of the same age, we'd started calling each 'son' as a joke sometime in the past. Through the open door, a shaft of bright light shone into the small living room and tears welled up in my eyes, I wasn't sure why. Perhaps I was sad to see how my friend was living; it felt unfair. I was touched by his courage and positive outlook, despite his hardships. At the same time, I had butterflies in my stomach and a mixture of anxiety and excitement: in only a few hours, I would have another encounter with the great Madiba.

My fellow scholars and I had grown to know each other fairly well because, during the course of the year, we had met on several occasions for workshops as part of the Mandela Rhodes Scholarship programme. Each time, we would catch up, share jokes and experiences from the programme or our studies at various tertiary institutions across South Africa – in my case, the University of KwaZulu-Natal (UKZN). On this momentous day, the conversations rambled on as we were shuttled in two comfortable passenger vans from Cape Town's city centre, over Kloof Nek and down the narrow, winding roads to the beach house. Along the route, I noticed several police cars and members of the VIP protection unit.

We were guided through the lovely property, and greeted by Shaun's wife Stefania, and Luna, their beautiful six-year-old daughter. I felt nervous but tried to calm myself as I moved from the living room to the patio, carefully staying out of the way of the busy catering team. Suddenly, I was pulled up short by one of them who was standing still and tall, blocking my path. He was wearing exactly the same uniform Eric had put on that morning. For a moment, I couldn't believe my eyes. It *was* Eric.

'Oh my God!' he said. 'Do you mean this is where you . . .'

'Yes!' I said, interrupting him. 'This is where the luncheon is taking place! How is it possible that you are also here?'

Disbelief rendered us speechless. So we smiled. And hugged. Tears pricked my eyes as emotions swirled up. The moment was brief. He and his team were working non-stop, so he had to get back to his task. Beaming, he hurried away, and I heard him telling his colleagues in the corridor: 'That's my home boy!'

On the patio, the décor was striking: a large, purple heart shape hung from the ceiling, echoed by smaller hearts beside each name tag on the round tables. The patio was almost level with the sea and beach rocks formed part of the garden; the waves crashing over them, sometimes fiercely enough to scatter droplets onto the manicured lawn and impeccably maintained flowers. Out on the ocean, a small police boat patrolled, and at the house, stern-looking men in black could be spotted all over the place.

As I took everything in while chatting to my fellow scholars, I got my second surprise of the day: my name tag was placed next to that of Graça Machel. I was one of the two lucky scholars Shaun alluded to in the briefing! The other was Rachel Adams, who was to sit beside Mandela at the table next to ours. I felt even more nervous. How would I begin to make conversation with Graça Machel? I breathed in and out consciously and carefully to keep my nerves in check, secretly rocked by the prospect of 'entertaining' the illustrious lady for the duration of the luncheon. The all-too-familiar questions flashed through my mind: how did I get here? Me, the little boy from Muhima? How does a car guard in the streets of Durban end up next to Graça Machel, and a step away from Nelson Mandela? I felt gratitude, awe, mixed with disbelief – a part of me screaming that I surely didn't belong there.

I was zoomed out of my reverie by the arrival of Nelson Mandela, walking slowly and leaning on a supportive arm, smiling as always. Next to him was his wife Graça Machel, with her unmistakable elegance. Everyone, dignitaries included, respectfully remained standing as Madiba took his seat and Graça Machel was shown to hers on my right. Among others at the table were Shaun and Professor Njabulo Ndebele, then vice chancellor of the University of Cape Town (UCT), with Machel as his chancellor. Directly opposite me and in my line of sight was Mandela, fellow scholar Rachel to his left and Professor Jakes Gerwel, then chairman of the Mandela Rhodes Foundation, to his right.

When the staff started serving the food, another surprise: Eric was in charge of our table. I had mixed feelings every time he came to pour a drink or put a plate of delectable food in front of us. I was delighted to be there with him but felt a level of guilt about our roles. For a few moments, the dichotomy weighed on me heavily.

The guests began to strike up conversations, and Graça Machel turned her attention to me.

'You have an interesting name, Pie-Pacifique!'

'Thank you,' I replied, still feeling out of my depth.

'I was told you are from Rwanda and that you have had an interesting journey to South Africa. Please tell me your story.'

I was pleasantly surprised that she'd pronounced my name correctly in French – so Pie sounded like the beginning of the name Peter. Of course, she's been briefed about me, I thought, feeling a swell of pride. Then I hesitated for a moment, deciding where to start my story. I gave her a truncated version of my upbringing in Rwanda, and very little about living through war and the genocide. It was not because I didn't want to tell her. The memories of the genocide still haunted me and I had not done enough to confront them, so I merely mentioned that I had witnessed the killings. But when I reached the part where I left Rwanda, I had much more to say because my journey had included a few days in Mozambique, Graça Machel's home country. I spent a little more time on that, enjoying the fact that she knew the places I had passed through.

'So how did you manage to go to university when you were working as a car guard?'

In a more serious tone, I told her of the struggle that had culminated in what was then the University of Natal changing its financial aid policy to include refugees, which surprised her. Given her position as chancellor of UCT, I realised that she, and possibly Prof Ndebele, would have an interest in refugees' struggle to access higher education. As I recounted how I got into university, she frowned, asking if there was no national policy on that. I wasn't sure so she checked with Prof Ndebele, who said all institutions dealt with refugees differently, and that UCT adopted a case-by-case approach. Visibly displeased, she took out a pen and made a note in a small notebook.

Soon Shaun called us to attention, and everyone fell silent – everyone except Nelson Mandela, who appeared not to hear the signal and continued talking to Rachel. He was talking about people believing that they are superior to others. We all listened in as he spoke with great conviction, no one daring to interrupt him. Eventually, Prof Gerwel, perhaps one of the very few people who could, broke in to get his attention.

Shaun invited each of the Mandela Rhodes Scholars to introduce themselves. A few of my peers spoke before me; when my turn came, the doubts and nerves evaporated. I picked up on where Madiba had left off, his words still ringing in my ears:

'As you have mentioned, Ntate, it is a tragedy when one group of people believes that they are superior or even inferior to another. The consequences are too big for our humanity to bear. I have experienced it in the form of the genocide that took place in my own country . . .' The exact words I used in my brief speech are vague in my memory, but it was a sincere pledge not to be part of the divisiveness in the world that spawns apartheid, war or genocide, and to contribute to creating a different and better world. It was an extraordinary feeling standing in front of all the distinguished guests, but my eyes were focused on Nelson Mandela who appeared to nod as I directly addressed him. As I sat down, I felt a swirl of emotions that instantly made my eyes moist. I knew this was a seminal moment.

When we'd all spoken, another course was served and conversations picked up again before one of the scholars, Piet van Rooyen, entertained us on the cello, playing a beautiful piece of classical music with extraordinary skill. As tables were being cleared yet again, I marvelled at how precise and meticulous the service had been, to which I had paid special attention because my friend was in the team. I felt relieved that Eric was no longer a car guard, and that he didn't work for just any catering company; theirs was often chosen to serve the who's who of South Africa.

I mentioned to Graça Machel that the person serving us was my dear friend Eric, briefly telling her his story and how we had both ended up there by sheer coincidence. She listened intently, then sat quietly for a few moments before saying to Shaun: 'Shaun, I want you to promise me that Pie-Pacifique's story will be in a published book.'

'Yes!' Shaun replied, smiling with confidence.

Shaun Johnson was not only the CEO of the MRF. He was also an award-winning author and had been a renowned anti-apartheid journalist and later newspaper editor. He knew the ins and outs of writing and publishing, so he could confidently make such a promise. He chuckled and repeated, 'Definitely! We will make it happen!' And so the idea of my story becoming a book was born.

When the event came to an end and Mandela beamed his trade-mark smile as he shuffled out, still dignified in old age, his presence left us with a boost of energy to try to live in this world differently.

Sadly, due to health challenges and the resulting need to manage his workload, Shaun was unable to continue playing an active role in my book project. But he encouraged me enough for me to see it to completion.

It would take a lot of support from family and close friends, time, sweat and tears to go through the proverbial eye of the needle, and come out on the other side. The result is a text I often say has been writing me, rather than me writing it.

PART 1

Ordinary boy in Kigali

CHAPTER 1
A stranger in the house

A five-year-old boy stands in the courtyard in front of the one-bedroom house, impatiently waiting for his mother to get home from work. His little brother, three years old, is learning to copy what he says, trying to follow him everywhere, and imitating what he does. It is early evening, at the hour parents arrive home from work. The boys position themselves next to the avocado tree that stands alone in the mostly empty yard. When a sound comes from the corrugated iron gate that adults have to wrestle with to come in or go out, they run. Their mother, emerging from behind the gate, stands still as the boys embrace her, hurling themselves into her arms at full speed. She picks up the little one while the older boy tells her the disturbing news.

'Mom, you won't believe what we saw the *umuboyi* do! He came out of your room!' he says, the younger one echoing a few words of his brother's claim. In Rwanda, *umuboyi* means a male domestic worker. In the boys' experience, *umuboyi* was never allowed to go into their mother's room.

She sets about convincing them that the man is definitely not *umuboyi*, but their own father. She has to explain where he has been all the time, and reassure them that he is not going to replace *Oncle*, the male figure who visits often and with whom they have grown very close. She was referring to her brother, Henry, who visited the family often.

I was that older boy growing up in the township of Muhima,

while my father was in prison accused of treason. My mother told the *umuboyi* story so often that with only fragments of that event in my memory, I never forgot it. I grew up understanding how deeply that moment had marked her. Later, she also revealed that since he was unemployed when he came out of prison, she would give him money to spend on little treats as he bonded with us.

Besides the faint memories of my father appearing in my life when I was five, I fondly remember our playtime in the dusty streets of Muhima, built on a hill that faces two other hills of Kigali that were still green in the 1980s: Mount Jali and Gisozi. The three hills overlook the Nyabugogo valley, through which flows a river of the same name. As little boys, we would roll up our shorts, and tighten them around our hips. Our T-shirt sleeves would be rolled up to expose our budding biceps (which we believed to be tough!) We would form a line led by the tallest boy and, right hand on the shoulder of the boy in front, we would bunch our left hand into a fist and swing it, marching like soldiers and chanting:

Turi Ingariso – We are the boys
Za Muhima – of Muhima
Uwadukora – Whoever dares to touch us
Twamumena – We will break them
Twamumenamenamena – We will break break break them

We played soldiers, marbles, football and other games such as *agapira*, in which two teams vie to eliminate each other by throwing a ball to touch the opposite team's players until they are all 'out'. It was one of the few games boys and girls played together.

All our parents had equal rights in punishing us, so when my father was released from prison, he had to assume his role as one of the parents we feared and respected in the neighbourhood. And I had to learn to call him *papa*. It was through a moment of great anguish for me that the clearest memory I have of him as my father was formed.

I was with a group of boys who had run to cheer the *gendarmes*, the national police force, who often jogged in platoons around our neighbourhoods. We took some short cuts along the paths between houses so we could get to La Fraicheur, an intersection that had taken on the name of a bar that occupied one corner. There, we would wait for the *gendarmes* to pass, so we could run after them. On the way, there was a carpenter's workshop where one day men were working on a beam of wood that extended over the dirt path at about head height. When the *gendarmes* appeared, we jogged after them but they were running too fast – we couldn't keep up for long so we turned around and raced each other back. Trying to catch up with the boys ahead of me, I ran with my eyes on the ground to avoid stones and broken glass because I was barefoot. At the workshop, running at full speed, I smacked straight into the beam of wood. Its edge cut across my forehead and I fell hard, flat on my back.

As if in slow motion, confused, I saw my clothes turning red as the blood gushed down from my forehead. One of the carpenters knelt down, holding my back against his chest. Although there was blood running over my eyes, I could see people peering at me. Men, women and children I didn't recognise. I was scared. I don't know how long I sat there, hearing people talk over each other, arguing about what to do. And then suddenly, a man with a familiar face forced his way through the crowd and knelt in front of me. It was my father. He spoke, but I didn't hear what he was saying. As if his arrival signalled permission to cry, I burst into tears, holding tight onto his clothes. I don't remember much of what happened next, but what stuck in my memory were parts of a conversation he had with a man we met as we walked back from the Muhima Healthcare Centre, popularly known as *dispensaire* (dispensary). I can only remember that the man wore a white jacket. Looking at the bandage around my head, he asked: 'What happened to him?'

My father explained, and then he added: *'Kandi umuhungu wanjye ni intwari pe! Nta n'ubwo yarize bari kumudoda!'* – And my boy is so brave he didn't even cry as he was being stitched up!

The man replied: 'Wow! He is as brave as you are. And he looks a lot like you!'

I still feel a sense of pride every time I remember the moment my father said I was brave and he was proud of me. And now, when I look at the faded scar on my forehead, it reminds me not of the distress and pain, but of the feeling of having my father when I needed him.

So who was my father? That's a question I have asked myself for a long time. Every time I discover another piece of his life's puzzle, I have more questions.

I heard that he spent his early childhood in the commune of Ndusu. His father died when he and his little brother were young. His mother returned to her native and adjacent commune of Gatonde, where she remarried, her new husband agreeing to raise the boys as his. The new family grew as two more children were born, but they were so poor that my father had to skip some terms in his primary school to work in the fields. The story goes that he shone during a school play and touched the heart of the bishop of Ruhengeri, his native province in the north of Rwanda. The bishop arranged for Caritas, a Catholic charity, to pay for my father's secondary education.

As written records were rare when he was born, all official or administrative documents list my father's date of birth only as 1945. The most revealing (and perhaps most complete) document I have seen was a job application to the United Nations High Commissioner for Refugees (UNHCR), signed May 14, 1986, after my father was released from prison. It shows that he finished high school in 1964 and taught at a primary school for five years before studying at a church-related education centre, the African Catechetical Institute in Butare. He then taught at one of their institutes before jetting off to the Pan African Institute for Development in Douala, Cameroon, where he was based from 1973 to 1975. Upon his return to Rwanda, he worked at the social affairs ministry before becoming the *bourgmestre*, the equivalent of a mayor, for the Commune of Gatonde in December 1976, an influential position he held for five years.

Given his humble beginnings, for my father to have a wedding ceremony attended by some of the most powerful people in Rwanda was remarkable. Even the then governor of Ruhegeri prefecture, Protais Zigiranyirazo, aka Mr Z, the brother-in-law of Rwandan president Juvénal Habyarimana, was there. Before the wedding, Mr Z had been part of my father's delegation that went to ask my mother's family for her hand in marriage. At the wedding were at least three cabinet ministers that I know of, including Colonel Alexis Kanyarengwe, then interior minister. My father had become part of high society. And that is what brought about his demise.

When it was rumoured that Col. Kanyarengwe was plotting a coup d'état, he fled to Tanzania, but by association, my father was arrested for high treason in 1981. Later that year, he was acquitted by the Rwandan State Security Court but was rearrested in 1983. I was two and my baby brother was just six months old. My father was held in Kigali's Central Prison known as '1931' without charge or trial. Amnesty International campaigned for his release, and wrote in its 1985 report:

Eustache Kabalira had previously been tried and acquitted by the same court in November 1981 on charges of organising a campaign to destabilise the government. In August 1984, he told the court that he had been re-arrested in February 1983 and held by the security service for 19 months without charge. He asked to be released from prison while investigations into his case continued. This was refused, but the court said it would look into his case. Eustache Kabalira's action in bringing his own case to court to complain about his long-term detention without charge or trial was the first known legal action of its kind by an untried political detainee in Rwanda.[1]

---

1   Amnesty International Report 1985 (p83). Amnesty International Publications: London. https://www.amnesty.org/en/wp-content/uploads/2021/06/pol100021985eng.pdf

He remained in prison for a further twelve months before a short trial led to his release. It was not long after he re-entered our lives that my father came to my rescue and whisked me off to get stitches. As I got to know him, I embraced him as my father and learnt to admire him. He struggled to get a job, but was eventually hired as *Chef du Personnel* (chief of staff) of an Indian holding company that owned the biggest textile factory in the country. We moved to a bigger house and when I started Grade 1 at Sainte Famille Primary School in September 1987, he promised to buy me a bicycle as a prize if I managed to be top of my class. Owning a bicycle was one of my childhood dreams.

Apart from his role after my accident with the wooden beam, I have very few memories of my father. Those I have are mostly of him as a religious man, a devout and committed Catholic. At home, we had a rigorous prayer schedule, and on the first Saturday of every month he hosted long prayer sessions at home that included the full three rounds of the ordinary rosary, the Stations of the Cross, and the Rosary of the Seven Sorrows of Mary. Other regular features of these sessions were readings of apocalyptic messages believed to be from the Virgin Mary apparitions to young people. Those who attended would talk about the expected troubles of later days, the beast, the 'number of the beast' (666), and what believers would have to do to survive the impending doom: holy water, wearing heaven's chosen colours (red, white, green and black), stocking up on food, and more importantly refusing to have 666 stamped on their bodies. My father went on several pilgrimages to Kibeho, a popular site believed to be where apparitions of the Holy Family happened. It was into this environment that my sister was born. She was born premature, after my mother had spent months in hospital due to pregnancy complications.

My father's health was also fragile. Since his release from the second stint in prison, he was often sick. Sometimes, he called me to the main bedroom for minor tasks he was unable to do himself. I remember a day when he had difficulty breathing. He was wearing light yellow pyjamas and was sitting on the edge of the bed while

I knelt at his feet, cutting his toenails. He was breathing heavily, with long pauses between breaths. I stared at his chest, hoping to see it rise and fall. The silence was scary. Then one Monday, while I prepared for afternoon class, my mother arrived home with two other men. They and our *umuboyi* carried my father to the yellow hatchback that belonged to one of them and they took him to hospital. That was the last time I saw him alive. He died early that evening. It was May 29, 1989; he was just 44. I was in the second year of primary school. I have faint recollections of the funeral and mourning period. But the memory that stuck was of being in the cemetery in Kigali's Nyamirambo sector. I was terrified by the sound of the ground and stones falling onto the wooden coffin, which made haunting drum-like beats. At the same time, voices of men and women were singing a popular Catholic funeral hymn:

> *Twaremewe kuzajya mu ijuru* – we were created to eventually go to heaven
> *Niho twese tuzishima iteka* – that's where we will eternally be happy . . .

～ɔ～

A few months after my father's death, my mother used his pension fund payout and some savings to renovate our house. She enlisted the services of builders recruited and led by a young man named Charles Giraneza. During the building project, some of the exterior walls were going to be down, so my mother asked Giraneza to stay in the house with us, primarily to be our guard. Originally from the prefecture of Byumba, Giraneza had been forced out of school by poverty. He ventured to Kigali, where he used his entrepreneurial skills to create a building team. Most of his laborers were older than him. Giraneza also took a keen interest in my schoolwork. He insisted on me showing him my homework, and effectively became my tutor in the evenings. Giraneza spent a lot of time reading newspapers and listening to his tiny FM/SW/MW receiver. He often listened to Radio Rwanda, the local station, and also to news from around the world, in French and in Swahili. I often wondered how he had taught himself so much with only a primary school education.

Giraneza instructed me to read newspapers, listen to the radio and know as much as I could about Africa. He made me recite the names of all the African countries and their capitals. He taught me about heroes of Africa, such as South Africa's Nelson Mandela, Ghana's Kwame Nkrumah, and Burkina Faso's Thomas Sankara, who had recently been assassinated.

I was in third year at the Sainte Famille School when Giraneza started tutoring me. Because the school was oversubscribed, each class of the first three grades was divided into two groups. The groups would take turns, one attending class in the morning for one week, then in the afternoon the following week. Giraneza used the extra time I had in the day to teach me. He always made sure that I knew about major events in the world and where they happened. One day, he instructed me to listen to the radio in the afternoon because something important would happen and be broadcast.

'You have a quiz this evening. You must tell me what happened and why it is important,' he said. At 4 pm that day, ears glued to the FM receiver, I heard of Nelson Mandela's release from prison; like local football games, it was being broadcast in Kinyarwanda, Swahili and French. South Africa had been a focus of current affairs in Rwanda for some time: even at our primary school, where we began each day with a prayer and a short speech about what we were praying for that day, the teacher would often tell us we were praying for the end of suffering and the liberation of the black people of South Africa. Sometimes, we would recite an additional prayer for the cause. So even to us, the release of Nelson Mandela felt like a victory, and it was major news in the country. Giraneza had already taught me a lot about the horror of the apartheid system. The Berlin Wall. The Cold War. The different independence wars of Africa. Algebra. French. Geography.

One of Giraneza's builders, Mwubatsi, was kinder to my brother and me than the rest of them. He let us play with the cement mix he was using and took the time to teach us how to lay bricks properly. Mwubatsi was mostly a quiet man and looked focused but he smiled constantly, playfully encouraging us to learn more about building. I remember standing close to him, looking at the fingers of his left hand firmly gripping a brick. In his right hand was the trowel: he would scoop wet cement, spread it on the topmost layer of bricks on which he was going to place another, then he would scrape off any excess cement. I watched this repetitive set of movements for hours. Then Mwubatsi would let me and my brother try our hand at it, under his delicate direction, until the wall was too high for us to participate. When we did so well that he didn't have to redo it, Mwubatsi showed pride in us. We grew fond of him. It was his tolerance of our timewasting participation that helped me enjoy the renovations, though with obvious inconveniences. Constant dust, banging noises, wetness all over the place, and too many unfamiliar faces in our house were all overwhelming. But it became fun when Mwubatsi held our little hands and guided us through skills we didn't even know we would need. When the builders were not busy, waiting for a truck of sand or at the end of their day, they played cards. It didn't take long for me to learn.

When I began my Primary 4 class, I was excited. I had just turned ten on August 21, 1990, something I glowingly told everyone who cared to listen for a few days after my birthday. I felt grown up. The first term of the new grade started in September. It was a big jump. One major difference was that it was all one class, morning and afternoon, separated by a lunch break. I was also going to start the lessons I most looked forward to: French.

Giraneza, who was still living with us, was turning me into a little nerd: I knew a lot about geography, and was already reading basic French. By the time I started Primary 4, I was certain of a top-ten finish at the end of term one. In case I finished top of the class, I asked my mother, repeatedly, if she would buy me the bicycle my father had promised. She was unambiguous in her answer: no! According to her, that was a deal between me and my father.

'But I still expect you to be the best. I will reward you. But it will not be a bicycle,' my mother would say, making sure I heard the bicycle part well. That was when I knew life would be very different without my father.

CHAPTER 2
Rumblings of war

While I had my head in my books, everything in the country changed. We heard on the news that Inyenzi had invaded Rwanda. Inyenzi means cockroaches – that's what the government called the rebels that attacked the country on October 1, 1990.

Word was that the invasion had occurred through Kagitumba, the border post between Rwanda and Uganda, where the Rwandan Patriotic Front, known as RPF-Inkotanyi or just Inkotanyi rebels were said to be based. Adults were agitated. Giraneza had his FM receiver on all the time. He read newspapers, and instructed me to read them too. Radio Rwanda reported that the president had cut short an official visit to the US, returning to command the national defence against the rebels. Then, adults spoke of hearing gunshots at night around the mosque in Nyamirambo, a suburb near the centre of Kigali.

While everything was still so chaotic, news filtered through that the leader of the Inyenzi, Fred Rwigema, had been killed. That night, the city of Kigali was jubilant. My mother, who had been fearful since the news of the invasion had surfaced, instructed all of us to stay home. But that evening, I managed to sneak out and followed the sound of singing. There were shirtless men, sweaty from dancing, some men carrying coffins to 'bury' Rwigema, women crying with joy; the massive crowd filled the breadth of the tarred main road joining the neighbourhood of Nyabugogo to the city centre. I returned home late, knowing that my disobedience would have angered my mother. When I arrived, she was ready for me with a dry stick, and she let me have it!

'How many times do I have to explain to you that going out now is dangerous?' she hissed, emphasising certain words with an accompanying lash.

The following few days were terrifying: it was rumoured that the Inyenzi had infiltrated Kigali. First, gunshots in the city and near the main mosque in Nyamirambo, then Deogracias and Ruben, who lived in our backyard annexe, went missing. Deogracias had been our *umuboyi*, and my father had met Ruben in prison in the mid-eighties. After my father's release, he followed up Ruben's case, as he had promised him when they were inmates. Ruben was eventually released. Shortly before my father died, he had helped both young men to get jobs at his employers' textile factory. My mother frantically paced up and down, and made calls from our fixed line, trying to locate them. She was afraid that they were among the many people being held in the stadium at Nyamirambo, on suspicion of being accomplices of the Inyenzi.

A few days later, Deogracias and Ruben returned home. With hundreds of others, they had indeed been held on the stadium football pitch, closely watched by army officers. They told horror stories of people being beaten. They were scared, hungry and dirty. Both had no shoes. At the chaotic feeding station, they had used them to collect porridge or water – the only things provided to sustain them.

They told us they had been stopped by the Rwandan security forces and told to produce their identity cards, which showed that they were Tutsi – reason enough for them to be detained at the stadium. It was the first time I heard that Deogracias and Ruben were Tutsis, not Hutus. Soon after that, these words were hard to escape.

I knew they represented two of the three tribes of Rwanda, the other, a minority, being the indigenous Twa – often called pygmies. We would later learn in history at school that Hutus comprised more than 80 per cent of the population, and Tutsis 15 to 20 per cent, and that both groups had their origins outside

Rwanda. Hutus, who traditionally worked the land, had come from the region of the current Chad in search of fertile land, while Tutsis, who were cattle owners, originated from the regions along the Nile, most likely Ethiopia. Over hundreds of years, the three ethnic groups had cohabitated, evolved a complex spoken language, and shared cultural practices and spiritual beliefs.

We also learnt about how Rwanda's territory expanded under a leader named Gihanga. Since, successive Rwandan monarchs conquered neighbouring communities, it reached into the south of what is now Uganda, and into the eastern part of the current Democratic Republic of the Congo. I was enthralled by the story of the thriving, well-organised kingdom with leaders ruling different territories on behalf of the monarch. But after the Inkotanyi invasion, as the war spread and political tensions increased, the narrative changed; I was too young to understand the tragic consequences. Now it was no longer about the kingdom's efficiency, instead, the focus was on its oppressive practices. We were told that the monarch had to be from pure Tutsi lineage and that the Tutsis had made Hutus their slaves.

When we covered the colonial period in history, we learnt that Rwanda had been reduced to its current size and become a German territory when, in 1895, fourteen European nations divided up resources in colonial Africa. With the demarcation of its boundaries, many Kinyarwanda speakers found themselves no longer in Rwanda but in Uganda and the Congo. Nearly three decades later, after Germany's defeat in World War I, Rwanda, Burundi and the Congo became Belgian colonies, and in 1922, Rwanda and Burundi were combined to form an administrative territory named Ruanda-Urundi.

As the war escalated, the slant was that when Ruanda-Urundi was governed by the Belgians, they had favoured Tutsi children and educated them to be future leaders, that the colonial powers had insisted an individual's ethnic group should appear on his or her identity documents, and that some Belgian scholars had even asserted that Tutsis had a natural superiority to Hutus.

The rise of the Hutus was, to some extent, enabled by the missionaries, who established their own schools where there was no discrimination, and the schools produced the first generation of seminarians that became the new Hutu elite. They claimed that the natural superiority of Tutsis was a fallacy, and that since Hutus were the majority, they ought to be given control in a democratic system. This movement culminated in the 1959 Hutu Revolution: the monarch fled the country and violence against the ruling Tutsis began, driving many into exile in neighbouring countries.

After gaining independence in 1962, a Hutu leader, Grégoire Kayibanda, was elected but a north-south conflict developed between Hutus, with those in the north accusing the southerners of concentrating power. A coup d'état in 1973, led by Major General Juvénal Habyarimana, assisted by, among others, Col. Alexis Kanyarengwe, saw Kayibanda imprisoned. He died in detention in 1976.

Meanwhile, in neighbouring Uganda, many (mostly Tutsi) Rwandan refugees being subjected to increasingly oppressive treatment joined Yoweri Museveni's resistance army and acquired significant military power when they helped him take over the country in the mid-eighties. In 1987, these soldiers formed the RPF and tried to negotiate a return to Rwanda, but Habyarimana claimed the country was overpopulated and refused them entry.[2] Rwigema, who had become the deputy minister of defence in the government established by Museveni, led the first RPF-Inkotanyi rebel invasion of Rwanda and was apparently killed by the government's army – resulting in those celebrations in Kigali.

Now, while Habyarimana's army was fighting an invasion, his one-party state was also being challenged with the formation of new political parties. Before, every Rwandan citizen was automatically a member of the sole political party, the *Mouvement Révolutionnaire National pour le Développement* (MRND). Habyarimana's

---

2   Des Forges, A. Human Rights Watch Report, March 1999. *Leave None to Tell the Story: Genocide in Rwanda*. Human Rights Watch. https://www.hrw.org/reports/pdfs/r/rwanda/rwanda993.pdf (pp31–74). Last accessed 30/01/2022.

regime was said to be Hutu, and my parents' identity documents said they were Hutus . . . So why was my mother terrified? Why did our family need to be afraid? And what did all this have to do with my father?

My mother's answer was as complicated as was the world of conflict I was growing up in. Following the 1973 coup, Col. Kanyarengwe became minister of the interior in Habyarimana's newly formed government and he was the cabinet minister to whom all 145 *bourgmestres* were accountable. Even though they were all presidential appointees, Kanyarengwe, a native of the Commune of Gatonde, was apparently behind my father's appointment to lead the commune in 1976, and they became friends.

It was this political connection that placed my father at odds with the Hutu government when Col. Kanyarengwe was suspected of plotting a coup. In his absence, the government swooped on some of his friends and collaborators. They were indiscriminately arrested, some were tortured, and they were tried by the National Security Court in Ruhengeri. Even though my father was eventually acquitted, after his final release in 1986, he never got another government job, despite many applications.

Although the RPF-Inkotanyi was said to be a Tutsi group, their political head was Col. Kanyarengwe, apparently a Hutu. Inside Rwanda, anyone known to be associated with him, whether Hutu or Tutsi, was automatically considered an Inkotanyi member, supporter or sympathiser. And so, in the context of the October 1990 invasion, our family found itself involuntarily, by association, on the Inkotanyi side of the fence. At just ten years old, I found this complexity too overwhelming to grasp, especially alongside the Hutu vs Tutsi rhetoric we were exposed to. The media, sometimes through cartoon-like illustrations, portrayed the RFP-Inkotanyi in various demeaning ways: as cockroaches, or thin, dark-faced creatures with tails and large ears. How could these funny, helpless creatures have any chance of success against the mighty Rwandan Army, with its elite fighters known as commandos and Garde Présidentielle?

When we saw French troops alongside the Rwandan Army, the biggest thing for me and the boys I played with was how they resembled heroes we had seen in Hollywood movies screened in places that showed videos. Soon, the French haircut – cropped close to the scull but with the hair still visible because of the contrast with the men's white skin – became a thing to talk about. Apart from admiring the French soldiers we saw in Kigali, we thought those from Zaire were great because they looked dark, mean and ready for combat. What could go wrong?

After the initial turmoil in the wake of Rwigema's killing, life started to normalise. After a while, the markets were trading, we went back to school, and played street football again. The country was at war, but only in the north-east. We knew that because it was in the newspapers, because Radio Rwanda said so, and because more songs about the Rwandan Army victory against the RPF-Inkotanyi were being played on radio. Many of the songs spoke of the invincibility of the mighty Rwandan army. Despite this, I was aware of the adults' anxiety, and at home, my mother remained on edge and constantly told us to be careful, warning us never to talk about or comment on anything political.

CHAPTER 3
Games and ambitions

When I wasn't running around the neighbourhood, I snuck out to play football. The most popular spot was nicknamed 'Malaria'. It was a vast stretch of dirt street that led to a dead end, so hardly any cars interrupted our game.

Among the children I played with was the most celebrated *karere* ball maker. Bangira was better than anyone else at making balls out of plastic bags and other soft material, and made some money through selling them to us. There was another barefoot entrepreneur among us, who sold *amandazi*, known in French as *beignés* and in South Africa as vetkoek. Although I don't remember him being the best during our games, he was the only one I know who remained faithful to football. He went on to be a member of Rwanda's national squad that competed at the Africa Cup of Nations in Tunisia in 2004, Rwanda's only participation in the continental tournament.

Playing football in the streets of Muhima, much like anywhere else, came with risks. First, no one was allowed to play with shoes. Anyone who came wearing shoes had to remove theirs to be fair to those who didn't have any. We threw the shoes on the side of the 'pitch' or used them as goal posts and dusty pitch-side markers. And at the flip of a coin, one team would remove their tops. The other would keep theirs on so we could see who was on which side. I played goalkeeper and was always pleased that whichever side you were on, you didn't have to remove your shirt. But I had to remove my shoes like everyone else, so many times I would go home with just one shoe, which angered my mother, resulting in a hiding.

Sometimes, fights broke out. Like a fist fight I once had with my opposing-side goalkeeper over who should be called Thomas Nkono, after the iconic Cameroonian goalkeeper whose team went to the quarter finals of the 1990 World Cup. But the biggest danger was the bully boys. These were boys older than us. Most of them didn't actually go to school. They were stronger, and sometimes mean. But if we wanted to have game time, we had to be friends with them. On any given day, they would randomly walk up to a boy whose parents seemed to have money – it was enough to have a working parent to be deemed well off – and they would take the unfortunate boy's shoes, or even sometimes his shirt. But the worst thing they did was to make the boy owe them money. I would watch and feel sorry for their victims. It had never occurred to me that soon I would be old enough to be their target. And so one day, they came for me. I had no shoes, and they were not interested in my T-shirt. They wanted money.

'You. How much do you owe me?' one of them asked, pointing at me. I didn't answer. He walked towards me, held me by my shoulder. He lowered his head, bit my hair and pulled up. I screamed.

'Five. I owe you five francs.'

'No!' he retorted, speaking through his teeth. 'You owe me twenty.'

'Yes. Twenty!' I replied, eager to have the agony on my scalp end.

'If you don't pay me . . .' he said, pausing, pointing his finger at my face and moving it repeatedly as if he wanted to poke one of my eyes. '*Uzambona!*' – You will see me! That meant it would be worse next time.

So I had to find the money. I wanted to play, and for that I had to pay. That's when loose coins started disappearing at home. When there were no more loose coins, I snuck into my mother's bedroom to look for some. Then I started taking more than I owed the bully boys, using the rest to buy marbles, sweets, *amandazi* and *mbushi* (a tasty fried cassava dough). But I used most of the change to watch movies at Ezekiel's and La Fraicheur.

That's how one of the most embarrassing moments of my childhood happened. I stole 50 Rwandan Francs (RWF) and bought some sweets and fat cakes at school, reserving the rest to pay off the bully boys and to watch a movie. During class, the substitute teacher we had at the time called me outside. I was shocked to see Giraneza standing with her. He had followed me to school and I immediately knew why he was there. Giraneza simply reached into my pockets and took the change. The teacher instructed me to pull my khaki shorts forward to make them tight on my bum. I reluctantly did, while tightening my jaws and closing my eyes hard in preparation for the pain. She gave me a few whips with a fine stick. Fortunately, it all happened outside, and no one else witnessed it. But I feared more what would happen when I arrived home in the evening.

Embarrassed and scared, I had to reveal what I had been doing with the money. I finally spoke out about the bully boys and the hair-biting ordeal. The next time Uncle Henry came to visit, I was forced, at a family meeting, to quit street football and focus on school. They told me of countless stories of serious injury to footballers. They invoked a story of Uncle Silvain, another of my mother's brothers, who had been an amateur football player in his youth. He suffered a horrible jaw injury that took months to heal. Aside from injuries and other dangers, they were worried that football was taking far more attention than my schoolwork.

I still had the early morning playground games to look forward to. They were definitely one of the main reasons I enjoyed school and I often left home early so I could have enough time to play. Among the boys, football was the most popular: hundreds of us playing different balls at the same time, but somehow, although we were all dressed alike, we found our opponents and teammates. The energy, and the buzzing noise that could be heard some distance away added to the fun. The girls would usually play *agapira*, but they mostly used the space in front of the classrooms.

When one of the teachers blew a whistle, everyone had to stand still, silent. The second whistle meant we were to walk to our respective classes. This happened at 8 am, and at every break. Sometimes, learners who kept moving after the 'stop' whistle were rounded up and punished.

But it was all different on Proclamation Day, the last day of each of the three school terms. It was always a special day, and was usually held on a Saturday to give working parents a chance to attend. The best thing was that there was more time to play in the morning. The 'stop' didn't come until 9 am or later. After going to class and forming lines, we marched, singing, to the main ground, and joined learners from the whole school. Grade by grade, we made a large semicircle on one side of the main ground. Parents and other guests gathered in an elevated passage in front of the row of classes directly above the playground. They looked on as hundreds of boys in khaki and girls in blue congregated, leaving an open space in the middle. Standing with the parents above us would be the principal, who held a megaphone. After a prayer and a few speeches, the principal would call the top ten of each class, starting with Grade 1 and ending with Grade 8.

Before it was time for our class, our teacher, Immaculate, called my name in a hushed voice. The learners closer to her heard and turned to whisper: 'Teacher is calling you!' I gently elbowed my way through to stand in front of her. I immediately understood that she was preparing the top ten in our class to be ready for when our names were announced. But when it was my turn, I still couldn't believe it. Speaking in Kinyarwanda, the principal announced: '*Umwaka wa kane C: Uwa mbere*: Kabalira-Uwase Pie-Pacifique!' meaning P4 class C, the first: me! Teacher Immaculate gave me a nudge to start walking. I marched to the applause of learners, parents and teachers. For the first time, I walked to the middle of the semicircle to join the best – a walk I had fantasised about for three years. A teacher showed me where to stand and my classmates, from second to tenth, stood behind me when their names were called. I raised my eyes to look at the parents, friends and relatives of learners. I saw the principal. Then, as a tear flowed down my cheek, I spotted my mother in the crowd and she waved excitedly with both hands. Giraneza, standing beside her, just gave me a thumbs up. They had come to witness me coming first in class for the first time.

After receiving my school report from my teacher, my mother, Giraneza and I walked home. I lamented the fact that my father had already died – especially because it was my bicycle-worthy achievement. How I wished he was still alive.

Since my family's intervention to call a halt to my football craze, I was no longer playing as often, and my success at school gave my family even more reason to encourage me to stay away from the game. But besides football, there were other fun activities, such as pushing a car tyre, with a stick in each hand to guide it. The sticks met inside the tyre, at the bottom; sometimes we would connect the ends of the sticks with a plastic cup. We would use cow dung inside the tyre as a lubricant, to make the rotations smoother. Then we would run kilometres on the dusty streets of Muhima. Instead of tyres, we sometimes pushed bicycle rims, putting a stick in the curvature of the rim. A motorbike rim was even better because of being smaller and heavier, but those were hard to find.

All that running in the neighbourhood was before the main road through Muhima, which passed via the La Fraicheur intersection (now known as KN5 road), was tarred. When the tarring process was underway, we would run behind the road construction machines and trucks, or just watch the strange-looking machines at work.

La Fraicheur was not only a road junction but the place where two major sewers came together, passing under the road and effectively making the intersection a bridge.

Even once the road was tarred, one of Muhima's main problems remained: a smelly, open storm-water drain that also acted as a sewer. It was well known as a landmark and became known as Ruhurura. Built of concrete, the drain was at least two metres deep, and in some places much deeper because of the ground elevation.

It was more than two metres wide, and bridges, some distance apart, made it possible to cross from one side to the other. Ruhurura channelled water and sewage from the city centre on top of the hill, through Muhima and all the way down into the Nyabugogo valley. It passed through dense neighbourhoods, and right by the door of some of the houses. Although the drain was always running, it became a spectacle when it rained heavily: the storm water roared down from the city and, especially around the bends, made a thunderous sound. On those days, Ruhurura carried away everything that fell into it in a flash, offering a temporary reprieve from the stench.

Ruhurura was said to have killed children, and caused many accidents. Sometimes, while we were playing, a tyre, a rim, a ball or a marble fell into the sewer. We dreaded having to jump in to retrieve our toys, especially barefoot, which is what most of us were most of the time. As it was difficult to get out, whoever jumped in would hope his friends stuck around to pull him out.

When we weren't playing outdoor games, we would congregate Kwa Ezekiel – meaning at Ezekiel's – where we loved to watch Hollywood and Bollywood movies that were played on a VCR, and screened on a monitor. The cost was just RWF10 for children, and this is where I spent most of the change I scrounged from my mother's bedroom before I was found out. Ezekiel himself collected the money at the door and played the videos. He was tall, lean and strong, but he had a face deformity and sometimes, at home, my brother and I would compete to see who could inflate his cheek the fastest, to look like Ezekiel. There was no television broadcasting service in Rwanda at that time, so for those who enjoyed movies, the video screenings were prime entertainment. Before the afternoon and evening shows, the crowd crammed onto long benches in front of the elevated small screen. The first show, at 2 pm, was typically a super long Bollywood movie, and at 7 pm, a Hollywood blockbuster. The main features were always preceded by *actualité*, which had nothing to do with current affairs but referred instead to whatever was playing before the main feature. It would be either a memorable World Cup football match or music videos featuring popular singers such as Michael Jackson and MC Hammer. The small place was usually crowded and sometimes got so hot that people came out sweating, carrying their shirts in their hands or on their shoulders.

At some point another option became available: La Fraicheur, the venue, ceased to be a bar and began to show videos. But despite being much bigger than Ezekiel's, and being on a popular pedestrian route to town that was buzzing with barbers, shops and food vendors, the new place remained quiet. Kwa Ezekiel, less than 300 m away from the La Fraicheur intersection, was still the place to be.

I was regularly one of the boys outside who had no money, but who hung around hoping that Ezekiel or the doorman at La Fraicheur would take pity and let us in. Sometimes we stood outside for the whole movie. Sometimes, they would let us in at the beginning, or in the final minutes before it began, when no other paying customers were coming. They would instruct us to sit on the floor space in front of the front bench. I remember the first movie I ever watched, a popular Bollywood movie called *Disco Dancer*, starring Mithun Chakraborty as Anil. We didn't understand the language (Hindi), and no matter how many times we watched it, we didn't know he was Anil. We just called him Jimmy, mainly because of one of the songs. But we understood the story, identifying with the poor barefoot boy Jimmy, and sang along to the music, making up our own lyrics: *Oh rocky nata ah rocky, dunia he dunia roki!* we sang.

Bruno was one of the boys who was always at the movies; he was mostly known for his drawings of Chuck Norris, Jean-Claude Van Damme, Bruce Lee and other famous actors. He drew posters for the video houses, and always managed to put action onto the page using a pen. I remember spending hours imitating Bruno's depictions of Norris's moustache, the Van Damme splits and Lee karate postures.

Sylvester Stallone's *Rambo* and *Cobra* movies were always popular, as was *Commando* with Arnold Schwarzenegger. In fact, few knew their actual names. Stallone was Rambo and Schwarzenegger was Commando – even when they starred in other movies and portrayed other characters. Favourite scenes from *Commando* included holding a man upside down with one hand, then flipping a crashed yellow car onto its wheels and driving off. Van Damme's final blind fight in *Bloodsport*, and his double punch and holding position after his last kick in *Kickboxer* drove the crowd wild.

All the movies were in English, which was not a widely spoken language in Rwanda. Some had a French voice-over, which didn't mean much to those who frequented the video shows: although Rwanda was considered Francophone, French was spoken only in administrative circles, not in the street. But to us, language didn't matter. With no understanding of English, French or Hindi, we easily followed the (mostly predictable) story line: there was a good guy, whom we called *Type* (read in French), and one bad guy we called *De Bande*, shortened from *Chef de Bande*, who had to be defeated. And everyone else was on *Type*'s side or *De Bande*'s side. The details of the stories didn't matter. A disadvantaged guy, who the audience loved, would beat the odds and be the victor.

In 1992, with the advent of the national television service, Television Rwandaise, known as TVR, video devotees had something extra to occupy their viewing time. As most households didn't own a box, some of the video houses replaced evening shows with television, which was mostly in Kinyarwanda and French. They charged the same as they did for action movies.

Fear of the bully boys had pushed me into stealing loose coins, but the habit persisted; only now I used the change to watch videos, and to buy marbles or toffees. I didn't spend all the money though: I started saving to pay for membership at the Centre Culturel Franco-Rwandais. They had a children's library full of comic books I wanted to read. In the meantime, I had been borrowing from classmates who brought them to school. My mother discovered the small wooden box with a slit just big enough to fit coins through. I had found a broken one and hammered it together with nails. Upset that I had been stealing, she confiscated the box, promising to give it back to me when I mended my ways. My mother eventually returned it, and she and one of my cousins topped up the difference between what I had and what I needed for my own membership card. My first stop was at the children's library. When I walked down those stairs, I felt so proud. I showed my card at the door with enthusiasm, as if to say: 'Yes. It is real! I should be in here!'

Inside, there were white kids playing, and speaking French. Other Rwandan children were dropped off by their parents, who drove fancy cars. And they all spoke French fluently. That's when I realised I had stretched to a place I didn't belong. My mother knew it, and that's why she had resisted. The cultural centre was an exclusive club for expatriates and children of the rich. But I stayed.

I would finally read the whole *Tintin* series, *Lucky Luke* and other comic books. But that was not all. At the centre they showed movies on a big screen. It was such a shock every time I entered and saw the raked seating with comfortable red cushions, the sophisticated lighting, and a massive projector pointing to a big screen. It was so exciting. It was French. It was France. *Turtle Ninjas* and *Superman* were a hit on that big screen. There, I also watched documentaries and was introduced to the silent movies of Charlie Chaplin. I then entertained everyone at home by imitating his character, Charlot (The Tramp).

Later, I discovered that the centre had a big library for adults and screened movies for grownups. And one day, just one day, they would be mine too.

CHAPTER 4
My mother's plea

I must have been a handful for my mother: if it wasn't watching videos that kept me out late at night, it was catching locusts, in season, when they congregated at street lights. Or I would stay out late, delaying the inevitable, because I knew what was awaiting me when I got home.

But at school, once I had come top of the class, there was no stopping me. I only ever came second in one trimester of Primary 5, but I recovered and reclaimed my spot. Unfortunately, I didn't take that attitude of excellence home with me. Having tried a range of tactics, my mother sought the help of my teacher, Immaculate, who knew me well, or so she thought. That evening, my mother called me.

'Son, I know you are frustrated. We are poor. We have no video. We have no money for toys. I am sorry about that,' she said, sadness in her eyes. 'Every time you come first in school, I feel helpless, because I wish I could get you the bicycle, but I cannot,' she added, with a long pause. I knew she wanted me to change; she had never spoken to me so openly before.

'Today, your teacher was shocked when I told her of your behaviour at home. First, she wondered if we were talking about the same boy. She said you are the example in her class, so she could not believe me. I was embarrassed,' my mother said, noting, as she looked at me, that I had started crying softly. 'What do you want?' she asked gently.

44

I said nothing, for I really had nothing to say. After a long pause, she wiped a tear off her cheek, then asked me a question that, even as a small boy, was painful for me to hear.

'Is it because I am a widow? Do you want people to say the boys turned out bad because they were raised by a woman?' she asked in the loud silence. I didn't know what to answer. I was eleven, but those words have stayed with me to this day.

My mother was not a strict disciplinarian, but she never let anything, however small, go unpunished. When she needed to, she involved Uncle Henry, whom we respected and feared.

After I'd achieved top spot, Giraneza saw my determination to hold on to it and his regime of homework and other extra-curricular activities, such as reading, increased. Even when he and his team had completed their work and he no longer lived with us, he visited regularly to help me. Another big influence was Uncle Henry. He was the first male figure I had known as a boy. He owned his own consulting company. He drove his own car. His only son had a bicycle. To my mind, that meant they were rich. I wanted to grow up and be like my uncle, buy Fanta for children and help, like he did. But more importantly, I was determined, like my uncle, to create my own company. So early on, as I began to understand my father's history, I made up my mind that I didn't want a government job.

And the more I understood about my mother and her background, the more I was determined not to be one of her problems, but to make her proud. She was born in 1954 into a fairly wealthy family by the standards of the time: they had cows and many fields. Her mother came from Gahunga k'Abarashi, where the great Rwandan chief Rukara rwa Bishinge is said to have ruled. He is renowned for having fought colonisation, and being instrumental in the death of three white colonisers. My grandmother often swore by Rukara, or by arrow, a real battle arrow.

My mother was the last born of a family of ten children, one of only three girls. She grew up watching her elder brothers and sisters become successful. Most of them were educated, including

Uncle Henry who studied abroad. Other siblings decided to retain a rural life. From the family would come a nurse, a teacher and a senior accountant, who would later occupy a top post in the country's treasury.

My mother went to primary school near her home, starting high school in Zaza, in the north of Rwanda. She later enrolled in the then most prestigious school for girls, Ecole Sociale (School for Social Work) in Nyakabanda, in Butare prefecture.

'Back then, when we finished high school, there was a job already waiting for us. We just had to fill in a form and that was it!' she once remarked. It made sense. There were far more posts than educated people capable of doing the work. When she finished high school, her brothers decided that high school for a girl was enough. Uncle Henry often said that one of his regrets was not allowing my mother to continue her studies. They estimated that with high school and a husband, she would do fine. So when a *bourgmestre* came asking for her hand, with Prefect Zigiranyirazo as the future groom's family representative, all was set for a perfect outcome, beginning with a high-class wedding, officiated by the provincial bishop. I came as their first child on August 21, 1980.

But in 1981, everything changed. Since her husband had been arrested and was deemed a traitor, no one wanted to be seen assisting my mother. When she had to vacate the official house of the *bourgmestre*, she struggled to find builders willing to help her finish a small house on one of her husband's plots. She moved into the new house while the walls were still wet.

When I was growing up, she told me stories of how she had to keep awake at night, light a fire in the middle of the house, wrap the baby up to keep it warm, and sing lullabies long into the night to put it to sleep. When I first heard the story, it took me a few moments before I connected the dots: I was that baby.

My mother's direct neighbour was none other than Mukankindi, the sister of Col. Kanyarengwe. Both women were outcasts, one because of her jailed husband, the other because of her fugitive brother. They formed a strong bond and, according to my mother, they were practically co-parenting me. Her favourite story about Mukankindi is how she was called to help when my mother was giving birth to my brother.

In August 1982, when my mother was heavily pregnant, she was alone in the house with me – a toddler due to turn two in a week. When she went into labour, she was groaning in pain and, distressed at her cries, I shuffled close to her. She tells how she lamented the fact that I was too young to help, saying: 'If you were old enough, I would send you to call Mukankindi.' Apparently I imitated her, repeating 'Maanyindi . . . Maanyindi'.

Consumed by her labour pains, she didn't notice that I had snuck out and waddled to the neighbour's house, where I found Mukankindi. The story goes that I walked straight to her, grabbed her dress at the hem where I could reach, and pulled, trying to get her to follow. Instead, Mukankindi picked me up. But I pointed at our house and said: 'Mama . . . mama.' Unaware of what was going on, Mukankindi offered me milk. I refused, again saying: 'Mama . . . mama.'

When Mukankindi put me down, I cried, grabbing the hem of her dress again and pulling. 'Mama . . . mama . . . mama,' I said continuously. Then I began to cry, saying the word 'mama' through my tears. As I had never called Mukankindi 'mama' she was perplexed. She picked me up and decided to take me back to my mother, thinking that's what I was asking for. When she got there, she found my mother in labour, in agonising pain. She assisted with the birth of my baby brother.

After my father was released and fired from his *bourgmestre* post by President Habyarimana in late 1981, he moved to Kigali to look for a job. My mother joined him in 1983, while awaiting a transfer as a social worker. She was with him for only three days before he was arrested again and sent straight to prison with no charge or trial. Coincidently, when my mother's transfer from the commune of Gatonde came through, it was to the Central Prison of Kigali, where my father was being held. Unhappy about her being near her husband, politicians forced another transfer, this time to

Muhima Healthcare Centre, which is how we ended up in that part of the city.

Although my mother wrote letters to ministers and to the president asking why her husband was still in jail with no charge or trial, and organisations such as Amnesty International added to the pressure, it was three years before my brother and I found him in our home, and just three years before he died.

Since the war had begun in 1990, my mother had lived in fear. She was being kept out of any decision-making processes or meetings at work and was always excluded from promotion or other opportunities, such as bursaries, that would advance her career. She was treated suspiciously, even after her husband had died. Knowing she was being blocked, she eventually left the dispensary and got a job as a secretary in a government department.

Despite her feelings of vulnerability, my mother rose to other challenges that came with the times: when the war in the north of the country intensified, she welcomed cousins who had been forced to leave their homes. Although we didn't have much, she made sure we were comfortable welcoming them all. At some point, we had six cousins living with us. My mother, with the help of my uncle Henry, ensured that they were enrolled at high schools that were still open. The only one who didn't stay with us had been seriously injured when Inkotanyi rebels attacked the city of Ruhengeri in February 1993. After being hospitalised, he stayed at my uncle's house. His account of what happened was harrowing.

He was at home when the shooting began, some distance away. Then it got closer. Sporadic. Neighbours screamed and ran in all directions. He ran through the fields towards a small river. Inkotanyi soldiers, whom he identified by their military uniform and black gumboots, ran after him. He ran fast, but there were many of them and they caught up with him. They shot at him. He fell in the river and, as his head went under the water, one of them pointed a gun at him and shot an automatic round. He lost consciousness – he did not know for how long – and when he came round, he was floating. He heard the soldiers say 'he is dead', and then they left. He held onto branches floating in the water and crawled out. He then realised he was bleeding. He managed to get to the hospital of Ruhengeri where he received basic treatment before being transferred to Kigali. His injury was serious: a bullet had shattered his lower jaw on one side. Fortunately, it was the only bullet that had struck him. When he was discharged, he went to Uncle Henry, where he stayed for a number of weeks, living on only liquids and liquid food. His jaw was wired shut and he could barely open his mouth or chew. He spoke through his teeth for weeks. But he survived. Two of my cousins died that day.

Hearing of war far away is one thing. But when you see injuries, lose family, friends or people you know, and see others fleeing, it becomes real. I had played and joked with those same cousins who were killed. During school holidays, my mother used to send my brother and me to our grandmother, where we played, sang, and sat around the fire with our many cousins. My grandmothers' house was in the middle of the family compound, surrounded by the houses of her sons, as her daughters had been married and moved away.

We joined our cousins in their chores, taking the cows to their grazing, and occasionally to the streams so they could drink. At one of the water places, there was a spring of naturally occurring salty water that we knew as *amakera*. The water looked like beer, and the cows loved it. So did we!

We helped in the harvests, and sometimes ate young peas raw, an act known as *kunyogota*. We woke up before dawn to harvest tiny white mushrooms, *imegeri*, that appeared so rarely that they caused a frenzy in the villages. We set mole traps, and gathered wild sweet berries. We roasted potatoes, sweet potatoes and pumpkins in hot earth ovens we set up in the field. We enjoyed running in the black, volcanic soil of the north of Rwanda, and took views of the volcanoes for granted.

Through the death of our cousins, and having others living with us, we had constant reminders that nothing would ever be the same again. But, in the public domain, although the north-east of

Rwanda was still at war, and the political elite squabbled publicly in the media, sport, radio and television gave the impression that ordinary life continued as normal. And to some extent it did. We all followed the exploits of the football stars of the time: Valens Muvara, Nshizirungu Hubert (aka Bebe) and Gustave Mudeyi. Everyone associated cycling with Ferdinand Sebera, and the country's prize female international runner Marcianne Mukamurenzi was synonymous with speed. If anyone was running fast, people would say: 'Yoh! That one runs like Mukamurenzi!' There were car rallies that attracted crowds along the roads of Rwanda, dirt and tar, and rallies in Kigali were a major event. At sports venues, acrobatic gymnasts entertained spectators – their human pyramids being the most popular. This style of gymnastics was mostly associated with the famous Gatenga youth centre, and was apparently introduced by a heavily bearded white missionary named Carlos.

Those not directly impacted by the war simply got on with life. But no one could pretend the country was at peace: on the news, we heard that the negotiations to end the war had begun in Arusha. And before long, political assassinations started occurring. The killing, in May 1993, of Emmanuel Gapyisi, a senior politician, shook the country. Images of his funeral were broadcast on national television news. His assassination was the first major event showing the dangers of Rwandan political conflict. I couldn't help noticing the tension among the adults around me.

The next big thing was the launch, on 8 July that year, of Radio Télévision Libre des Mille Collines (RTLM) – named for the description of Rwanda as the 'land of a thousand hills'. The station was said to have been started by the rich and powerful of Rwanda, who put money together and then reached out to businesses, asking for contributions. For the first time on FM airwaves, radio was not only entertaining, it was exciting: people could call in and be heard on air. Also, for the first time, Rwandans heard presenters commenting on current affairs in animated, interactive conversation. They became instant superstars. The station had hit on a winning combination: talk shows interspersed with the latest musical hits – from Western rock to African beats such as zouk and Congolese rumba.

It was no secret that the station had a political agenda. It invoked the 'Hutu Power' slogan, which was used by extremist splinter groups of almost every political party, and it demeaned people opposing the regime and those perceived to be accomplices of the RPF-Inkotanyi. Most of the political commentary was about the victory of the Rwandan army and the inevitable victory of *Rubandanyamwinshi*, which referred to the majority Hutu, particularly the extremists. As with the theme of its commentary, the line-up of songs was dominated by those praising the Rwandan army, as well as Power.

In this environment of civil war and political turmoil, I began to prepare for national primary school exit exams because my dream was to go to seminary. I wanted the best, and seminaries had a reputation of producing the best intellectuals. But the competition was stiff. When I wrote the exams, I was top of my class, as I had been for the preceding three years. The publication of the results was a major event in the country. To see the results for Kigali, I had to board a taxi to the Nyamirambo stadium and look at the lists stuck on the walls inside. When I got home, I was extremely proud to announce that I had been assigned to the Groupe Scolaire Officiel de Butare (GSOB), one of the most prestigious public schools in Rwanda.

Shortly after, on August 3, 1993, the Arusha Peace Accords were signed. At home, there was a sense of relief, with high hopes that the war would be over. Although we didn't have a television at home, we found a way to watch the Arusha proceedings being broadcast. For our family, seeing Col. Kanyarengwe sign meant something: finally, perhaps being associated with him was no longer going to be a sentence.

I allowed myself to believe in a better world with Kanyarengwe as part of the transitional government. With what I was learning about my father's trials, originally directly as a result of Kanyarengwe's political choices, it made sense that, at the very least, the colonel would know who we were. I felt proud when I saw him on television, albeit in his capacity as chairman of the RPF, signing the Arusha Accords with President Habyarimana. I was twelve, but I knew not to brag about our family knowing Kanyarengwe, or rather being known by him. My mother had warned us repeatedly not to tell anyone.

On radio, particularly RTLM, the Arusha Accords were not well received. There was much criticism of the president; he was accused of giving too much to the rebels and the opposition. The Hutu Power songs and rhetoric were amplified. Historians were on radio explaining how Tutsis had oppressed Hutus for generations before the 1959 revolution, and that the RPF-Inkotanyi wanted to bring back the slavery, so giving them too much was dangerous. Hutus who opposed the government were called greedy traitors. The country was polarised. But the Arusha Peace Accords had been signed. The international community was poised to send troops to oversee the implementation. Still, my mother's plea was for us to stay out of harm's way.

CHAPTER 5
Rise of the militia

The political landscape changed very fast. Between October 1990 and 1994, many political parties were created as Rwanda moved from a single party to a multi-party system. As soon as parties emerged, they were usually known to be either supporters of President Habyarimana's MRND ruling party, or the opposition. Anyone in opposition was deemed to be a supporter of RFP-Inkotanyi. Unfortunately, the two camps rapidly began to mean Hutu vs Tutsi.

As political parties sprang up, Rwanda became awash with flags indicating which political party dominated the area. MRND was still the biggest. Then there was the Republican Democratic Movement (MDR), the Liberal Party (PL), and the Social Democratic Party (PSD). Across the country, parties held mass gatherings they called *mitingi.* Rwanda being a Francophone country, this was a fairly new word, but it caught on fast. (It was an adaptation of the English word *meeting.*) As politics was the buzz on every street corner, the Rwandan youth also became politicised and parties launched youth wing movements, mostly comprising unemployed youth, and those doing what were regarded as lowly jobs, such as porters – also known as *abakarani.*

Political parties often held demonstrations that disrupted the city so much that school and other activities were cancelled. One day I came upon unannounced demonstrations while on my way to school. Two groups clashed. It was most often the opposition-linked *Abakombozi* of PSD versus the government-linked Interahamwe of MRND. They would stone the houses of local party leaders affiliated to the other camp, and loot or vandalise stores. Then they would throw stones at each other. Sometimes, the *gendarmes* got involved; on that day, before I was even halfway to school, they used tear gas to break up the clashing groups. I was caught in it. The pain in my eyes was excruciating, and my nose and throat burned as I tried to breathe. I ran home, desperate for relief, for water to wash out my eyes.

Some of these youth wings, particularly the Interahamwe, were often the same young people one would meet in the video shows. During a demonstration, they behaved like different people. And as the militancy grew, the show of force became more and more daring. When they arrived at demonstrations and 'meetings', they would screech to a halt in cars driven dangerously fast. Many of the youth would be in uniform, in the colours of their party, or wearing themed kanga fabric fashioned to look like a military uniform, with a matching beret. They would carry guns or makeshift guns, strap themselves onto the vehicle with ropes and travel hanging outside the van or SUV, holding on with one hand, the other toting a weapon. Some adopted the names of movie stars, while others dressed like their heroes: for example, someone wearing a red ribbon around his head and dark shades was Rambo. Some painted their faces to look like Commando. Dangerous stunts, such as a racing SUV driving in a mad circle, with youths hanging off the side, barely holding on, as a show of power and invincibility, were common and somehow exciting. The admiring crowd would erupt in cheers when one of the youths lowered himself so his back was almost touching the ground. It was a miracle that no one left his skin on the tarmac or dirt road during those stunts. Neighbourhoods were in awe, some terrorised. The militia wanted to look intimidating and invincible. Hollywood movies gave them an image to mimic. It was terrifying. But it was also exciting – to boys and girls alike.

Soon, most of the newly formed political parties exploded into two factions. One was named 'Power'. This word was added to the factions that were *for* the pro-Hutu unity agenda: MDR-Power, PL-Power and PSD-Power. The rest of the label-less party, just because it did not adopt extremist views, was seen to be aligned to the RPF-Inkotanyi, and therefore pro-Tutsi.

The 'Power' factions rallied to defeat the enemy, considered to be the RPF-Inkotanyi, which was increasingly being called the Tutsi rebel group. It was not much of a leap, then, for the assumption to take root that *all* Tutsis were Inkotanyi (and therefore the enemy). Hutus who were not part of the Power factions were considered traitors. Indeed, anyone who questioned 'Hutu-Power' was branded *ibyitso*, and was considered to be an enemy of the state.

But the government continued to deny ethnic-based divisions. On one hand, it taught that Rwanda was an *inyabutatu* (tripartite) community, made up of Hutus, Tutsis and Twas, who should all live together in peace and strive for development together. On the other, it urged Rwandans to rally against their common enemy – Inkotanyi (read Tutsis).

It is in this context that a new party immediately gained traction: the Coalition for the Defence of the Republic (CDR) accused the government of being too ambiguous, and not doing enough to protect Hutu interests. CDR, whose members were called Impuzamugambi, was an unapologetically Hutu party. Songs were created, and newspapers written urging Hutus to unite against a common enemy. A new name for Hutus was *Bene Sebahinzi*, meaning descendants of Sebahinzi – a name derived from someone who cultivates the land.

The biggest claim of CDR was that the RPF-Inkotanyi were rekindling Tutsi dominance over Hutus. They reminded everyone what that meant: the monarchy, slavery and brutality against the majority Hutus. The 'Hutu Power' and Impuzamugambi urged Hutus to be vigilant, a sentiment reflected in the lyrics of a popular song: *Rubanda Nyamwinshi Murabe Maso*.

Col. Kanyarengwe and other Hutus in the RPF leadership were called the *slaves* of cockroaches, and all those related to or associated with them were called *ibyitso*. Although I was young, I understood that, by association, our family would be considered the enemy. We were not alone.

Silvestre Tabaro had been a member of the paracommando battalion, then the most elite government army unit in the country, and had even become an army instructor. But he was a native of the commune of Gatonde, and was therefore associated with Col. Kanyarengwe. As the army became politicised, tensions intensified, and Tabaro was pushed out. He settled for a post as a commune police officer for the city of Kigali. Instead of a black beret, he wore a yellow one, and his uniform was a plain, brighter green than that of the army. He rented our backyard annexe, and stayed there alone. Tabaro was firm, neat, humble, and well-mannered. He often spoke about respect and discipline, and I came to understand that it was part of his training, first as an army officer, then as an instructor who had to instil principles in others.

Tabaro was well liked; his fellow policemen who came to visit told us that everyone at work respected him because they knew of his paracommando and army instructor background. He rarely brought his gun home, but when he did, he always took care to hide it in the deepest recesses of his cottage.

My brother and I longed to touch it. The idea of a gun on our property was exciting; Hollywood movies had made guns cool. But Tabaro never allowed us even to see it and when we nagged him, he rebuked us: 'This is a very dangerous thing. Don't even think of touching it,' he would say, much to our disappointment. Tabaro's boots were always shiny, his uniform ironed. Often, I would offer to shine his boots so that I could touch them and be inspired. One day, I dreamt I would become a highly respected commando, which is what we called members of the paracommando, and go on to be a senior officer. Of course part of the attraction of being a 'commando' was its association with our movie hero, Commando.

Sometimes Tabaro's best friend Rugira came to visit him. He was shy, and was the lightest skinned man I had ever seen, his complexion contrasting dramatically with his very dark hair. The two men often joined us for dinner, which was served on a large platter from which six or seven people ate. Sometimes, when other family friends came to visit, or when we had several cousins staying with us, there would be two platters. Every day was an opportunity for communion, and on weekends the gathering was even bigger.

Besides Tabaro, we had other friends in uniform. They told us the Inyenzi-Inkotanyi were much stronger than the government allowed the country to believe, and that their progress was under-reported. Certain characteristics of these friends stood out for me, and this is how I remember them: Corporal David was a quiet, yet approachable officer; Serge was much chattier, and sometimes let my brother and me touch his disarmed and emptied gun; Dieudonné stuttered a little, but nonetheless enjoyed telling jokes. We knew Serge and David through my mentor Giraneza. During the school holiday, David's sister Chloe, who was studying nursing in Gisenyi, in the north-west of Rwanda, would come and stay with us. She looked very much like her brother, having the same light complexion. Her hair was long and slightly curly.

Another source of unsettling news about the civil war came from Giraneza's builders. Like Giraneza, some of them hailed from the prefecture of Byumba, where the first invasion had taken place. In the months that followed, there were many reports of people being killed by the Inkotanyi, among them family members of men on our building team. They said surviving family members had disappeared. Mwubatsi, the smiling builder who had shown my brother and me how to lay bricks, became sad and withdrawn when he heard that members of his family had fallen victim to the Inkotanyi.

It wasn't long after the war had started that we heard of internally displaced people in camps. The biggest camp was Nyacyonga, on the road from Kigali to Byumba. Because it was relatively close to the capital, many of the camp occupants went from house to house begging. The camp itself, sprawling over a few hills, was an extraordinary sight: tents upon tents spread over a deforested, hilly area, with thousands of people depending on food donations and what they could get from begging. It was mainly women and children who roamed the city, asking for food, water, clothes or money.

My mother would sometimes bring home displaced women who had babies, to give them scoops of flour, old clothes or water. Sometimes they would open up to us, telling us the horrors they had witnessed as they fled. Some had seen their family members being executed by Inkotanyi soldiers, while others didn't know where their loved ones were.

'Sometimes I feel sorry for people of Kigali who spit in our faces,' one of them said. 'They should pray that war does not reach the city because they might find themselves begging for food and water. And then they, too, will be laughed at like fools.'

Some of them insisted that the government was lying about winning the war. 'We left our fields just before harvest. Thousands and thousands of us, now begging. We were people before. If the government was winning the war, we would be back. People, listen and listen well,' they warned. While the government constantly claimed to be winning the war against the RFP-Inkotanyi in northern Rwanda, political party factions gained traction and there was fighting across the country. Soon, another phenomenon erupted: explosive devices. There were reports of an explosion at the central taxi and bus station in Kigali city centre, injuring many people. The device was apparently hidden in the luggage loaded on one of the taxis.

Then, grenades came into vogue. They were commonly thrown at popular stores in the neighbourhood, mostly in the evening, injuring people congregating there. These explosions created so much terror. Travelling on taxis became dangerous, going to the minibus or taxi station was a hazard, and staying out at a store could mean you would end up in hospital. Just a few metres from our house, the store of one of our family friends was attacked; fortunately he survived the grenade explosion. When it happened in the early evening, we were cooking on a charcoal stove outside. We ran inside and locked the door, leaving the pot on the stove. The explosion was so close that it shook everything. We only found out in the morning that the grenade had wrecked the store. The walls were pock-marked, sugar and raw rice were scattered all over the floor, and there were traces of blood on the doorstep. No one believed that the army or national police were using grenades. They attributed the explosions to thieves and rebel infiltrators. But if that was true, it meant that thieves had access to weapons. Life had changed in the city of Kigali.

CHAPTER 6
First casualty of war

I enjoyed my primary school years, liked my teachers, and relished the fierce but friendly academic rivalry I had with a learner named Esperance Uwayo, who regularly came top of her class. We would compare our marks to see who had achieved more.

Unfortunately, the memory that overrides these positive ones is far from happy. One ordinary morning, I ran to school barefoot as usual, and arrived early to play football. Our laughter was abruptly silenced by a loud explosion that sounded very close. Some children ran toward their classrooms. I looked around and saw dust, smoke and pieces of paper fluttering about in the air. I knew that's where the explosion had taken place. Without thinking, I ran down the path of the hill we called Bigogwe, because of its steep incline. It was one of several paths connected to the school and the main playground.

While I ran towards the blast, my school mates were running away from the scene, eyes wide, some screaming, clearly in shock. A small group of people was already congregated at the scene, which was along my path. They were gathered around a boy who sat on the ground.

'Mamayi wee . . . Mamayi wee . . .' he called out for his mother, revealing his terror and agony. Then he looked up at all the people looking on. A woman next to me cried. The boy, in his khaki shirt and shorts, sat down on the dirt right next to the path, one hand on the ground to balance himself, the other holding what remained of his leg. The foot had been blown off, blood was pouring out of the wound and pieces of flesh were hanging loose. The boy stared at his wounded leg, murmuring and breathing heavily.

'Mamayi wee . . . Mamayi wee . . .' A chill ran down my spine and a lump formed in my throat. I was trembling with terror, imagining my leg being blown off. I knew the boy had stepped on a landmine. Adults around him scrambled to help, exchanging opinions fast, arguing what to do. The boy kept calling for his mother, holding his bleeding limb, still staring at where his foot had been. More onlookers arrived, adults and children in school uniform.

That was one of the paths that I used, like hundreds of other children, several times a week. That mine could have taken the leg of any of the boys or girls going to school. That boy could have been Hutu or Tutsi. His parents could have come from any or neither of the political groups polarising the country. Yet, someone placed that mine there. Someone who knew well that it was most likely going to be a child, one of the hundreds of school children in khaki or blue, who would step on it.

It was a few weeks later that the boy returned to school. He was easily distinguishable from the rest of us because he wore long khaki trousers to cover his prosthetic leg. I often spotted him on the main ground playing with other boys from his class. They made every effort to include him, deliberately letting him limp and kick the ball. He had been injured, but he was back.

That day, it was also all of us who were injured. The military sent soldiers to speak at the assembly, telling us to be careful what we played with, and that we must always pay attention while we walked. Walking to school had become a thing to fear.

I looked forward to getting away from the neighbourhood when I started high school. I knew my mother and my uncle were very proud of my achievements, and of me being assigned to a prestigious public school, although they knew I had wanted to go to a seminary. One of the reasons was to follow in my uncle's footsteps. He had been a seminarian, but after spending time in Rome and in Germany, he had chosen not to continue on the path toward priesthood.

Despite this, I wanted to grow up and do everything he had done. Seminary. Studying abroad. My own business. A car. Another car. A nice house. And helping everyone else in my family, like my uncle did. But I was not granted a place in seminary. So, when I embarked on my journey to high school at GSOB, my goals were high.

My mother helped me to buy what I needed, but I only remember my maroon pyjamas. They were soft and fitted me well. To me, sleeping in pyjamas was a sign that I was grown up. After all, I was embarking on a life alone, away from my family. My mother travelled to Butare with me, where we completed my registration. Then we were given directions to my new residence for boys, Ryoha.

Ryoha, which mean 'be delicious' was a building erected during the colonial era. It had the feel of an old convent. From the outside, it looked like a fortress with tall, unscalable walls. It was a collection of long halls and offices, joined to form a rectangular shape. In the middle were basketball and volleyball courts, a lawn, a garden and a smaller structure where our lockers were. Some of the halls were dormitories with hundreds of beds and bunk beds. There was a study and exam hall, with hundreds of chairs, each with an extended armrest that acted as a study table. There was a large playroom with facilities for table tennis, and a big screen for movies and, on occasion, Rwandan television. There was a room where the balls for the various games, including basketball, volleyball and football, were locked up. That was also where other games and toys were stored: Rubik's cubes, board games such as Stratego and chess, puzzles, and even roller skates. We had to queue at a large window, waiting our turn to exchange our student card for whatever we wanted to borrow, one at a time. I had never played most of the games. On the rare occasions that I had seen the games, they were being played by white children in movies. Ryoha had what I imagined was a flavour of European life. It was another world.

Ryoha had just two exits. We used to joke that it could serve well as a prison. One exit was to the main entrance of the school. The other led to two important places. On the left was a full-size football pitch, with a well-marked multilane Olympic track around it, with stands for spectators. It was the school's own stadium that was known as Kamena Stadium. On the right was the restaurant with a large, full-scale kitchen. That's where we got our meals. On Thursday and Sunday mornings, there was extra excitement because the regular sorghum porridge was served with two freshly baked rolls. There was a tradition of creating a sandwich we called a *gauzette*: we hollowed out a roll and filled it with meat samosas that were sold by mobile vendors outside. *Gauzette* was one of the few things that showed those who came from well-off families because they had money to buy samosas every Thursday and Sunday. Another feature of Ryoha was avocados. Butare prefecture was known for its supply of massive and delicious avocados, and the vendors knew we had a weakness for them.

The rest of the school was so vast that it would take months for a pupil to explore every aspect of it. But among the many facilities was our own chapel, and a theatre, with benches to seat hundreds, and a sophisticated stage and backstage. There was also a semi-Olympic size swimming pool, which is where I could be found most Saturdays, swallowing plenty of water as I taught myself to swim. Past the pool, the road bent down to the Kabutare hospital, serving the school and nearby communities.

Beyond the school grounds was a swathe of greenery, and a wide area in which farming and agricultural research activities took place. There was also a small forest that seamlessly merged with the arboretum of the University of Rwanda, and the buildings of the university could be seen just beyond the greenery.

The school was widely respected and its learners were generally referred to as those who studied at Groupe. Established in 1929, it was one of the first secondary schools in Rwanda. In my class, hanging above the windows, were hand-painted portraits by graduates of the school. One of them was by a certain Melchior Ndadaye. When I started at the high school where he had studied decades earlier, he was President Ndadaye, the first democratically elected Hutu president of our neighbouring country Burundi, just a few kilometres south of Butare.

Burundi's history had, for generations, been intricately intertwined with that of Rwanda. I remember Ndadaye's election in 1993 being celebrated in Rwanda, particularly as a Hutu victory. Before I finished my first term at GSOB, he was assassinated, an act that was blamed on Tutsis. Even though it was in another country, the event was deeply felt in Rwanda, as if the countries were one. Just as his election had been celebrated as a Hutu victory, his assassination was felt as a Hutu loss; a provocation by Tutsis.

When I returned home from boarding school for my first holiday, everything seemed to be normal. The Arusha Accords were being implemented and the United Nations had sent troops as part of the UN Assistance Mission for Rwanda (UNAMIR). In addition, some 600 RPF-Inkotanyi soldiers were welcomed in Kigali. They were to be hosted at the National Assembly building, one of the most guarded locations in country, and were there to ensure the protection of the Inkotanyi members who would be deployed in the new transitional government. I remember hundreds of people lining the streets, waving and dancing as trucks carrying the soldiers drove through the streets. There was real excitement about seeing the RPF soldiers because the propaganda had depicted them as creatures with weird features, so everyone wanted a glimpse of them. But most importantly, their association with the transitional government was a sign that the war was ending. Welcoming them was an expression of hope.

The children of Kigali – mostly the boys – were always excited to see the UNAMIR soldiers in what we called *amajipe* (Jeeps). Even though I was a teenager, I was among those who ran after their vehicles as they drove by. The soldiers had camps in various places across Rwanda, but the one that interested us was near the valley of Nyabugogo. Groups of curious boys – I was among them – would congregate at the entrance to get a glimpse of the soldiers. Occasionally, they would give us fruit and other treats. We especially enjoyed their oranges; they were very sweet and had no pips.

Seeing the UNAMIR troops from different nationalities – among them Canadians, Ghanaians, Bangladeshi and Moroccans – gave hope to many Rwandans. For us kids, the exciting thing was that the soldiers looked just like the movie characters we loved and hero-worshipped.

Along with the phenomenon of white soldiers in Kigali came the introduction, by RTLM, of a white Belgian presenter named Georges Ruggiu. Thanks to Giraneza, I had learnt how to tune in to Radio France International on shortwave. But having a European voice on FM radio made it unnecessary: Ruggiu couldn't speak Kinyarwanda so he read and commented on current affairs in French. Among the educated of Kigali, he became an instant hit. Along with the music he played (much of it classical), his upbeat energy and interactive approach, Ruggiu was yet another feature that helped RTLM steal listeners from Radio Rwanda. When I arrived back at school after the Christmas holiday, the white man working at a radio station in Rwanda had become a topic of discussion.

But all that was of secondary interest to me. The volleyball rivalry between our school, the National University of Rwanda and the Kurubanda Seminary was far more important. This trio of teams in the academic capital of Rwanda attracted crowds whenever there was a clash between any of them. I was also particularly enamoured with theatre productions, a Rwandan traditional dance troupe, and a show by Burundian traditional drummers.

However, even in that faraway place of safety, the tensions of the political situation would sometimes creep into our environment. I remember two particularly tense and fearful days in February 1994 when two political leaders were assassinated. First, the shooting in Kigali of Félicien Gatabazi, a government minister and senior member of PSD, which had many followers in the south of Rwanda, where GSOB is situated, and the following day, the slaying of Martin Bucyana when his vehicle was stopped and he was dragged out and murdered by an angry mob. He was the leader of the overtly pro-Hutu-Power party, CDR. Rumours spread that he had been killed in Butare, only a few kilometres from our school, and the fear was that angry, vengeful mobs would come to Butare and avenge Bucyana. Our residence supervisors tried to calm us down. But they told us not to go into town unless it was absolutely necessary, or we were accompanied by an adult. School gates that were usually open were locked. There was a grim feeling as predictions of impending chaos spread. A few days later, everything seemed to return to normal and school activities resumed until it was time to go home for the Easter holidays.

The Gahigi family had recently moved in to the neighbourhood and my mother invited the woman of the house over as a courtesy. When Marcelline was sitting in our living room, she noticed a photograph of my father and recognised him.

'I know that man. He was a lecturer at the Institute in Rutongo,' she remarked. My mother was surprised. Then the conversation turned serious as Marcelline made a stunning revelation: 'He had a child with my friend. Viola is my god-daughter and she is about twenty now.'

Surprisingly, my mother was excited. She had known of the girl, but after my father's death, she had never encountered anyone who could help us meet her or her mother. Now Marcelline was going to make it happen. My mother had told me and my brother that she wanted to include the girl in our family, and had even considered bringing her to live with us. She had told us that my father also had a son, born about a year before I was. She knew his mother, who didn't want us to have anything to do with the boy, whose name was Régis. We'd heard that he had been adopted by a French family while my father was in prison.

During the first part of the Easter weekend, my mother spoke often about Marcelline's revelation, and looked forward to her facilitating a meeting with my half-sister and her mother.

After Easter Sunday, I had one more week of holiday before returning to Groupe. The situation in the country had calmed down enough for most of my cousins to go back to visit their families for the holidays. They had taken my little sister along, who wanted to see our grandmother. Only my cousin Erasmus had stayed behind.

We also had two guests: Chloe, Cpl David's sister, and Dianne, who had been living with us for a few weeks. She was an internally displaced girl from Byumba, in the north-east, where the war had first started, and her home village was in the area under the control of the RPF-Inkotanyi.

Dianne was shy, rarely spoke and looked sad most of the time, probably because she had witnessed the soldiers abduct her father, who was never seen again. 'He was still in his night shorts when they tied his hands and took him barefoot. That was the last time I saw him,' she had told us. She had become part of our home when Octave, a family friend, had asked my mother if she could accommodate her.

Others who were there that weekend were Tabaro and his friend Rugira, who was visiting for a few days. Since we didn't have a domestic worker at the time, Dianne and Chloe were helping my mother with some of the home duties.

Nothing was remarkable about that week. Until the evening everything changed.

PART 2

Genocide

CHAPTER 7
The long night

On the evening of Wednesday, April 6, 1994, Radio Rwanda abruptly stopped its normal programming and played classical music – usually broadcast only when there was national mourning. Curious, we switched channels to RTLM and were shocked by the announcement that the plane carrying the president had been shot down as it prepared to land in Kigali. President Habyarimana was returning from Dar es Salaam where he had been engaged in finalising preparations for the implementation of the Arusha Peace Accords. The RTLM announcer did not say if there were deaths or survivors. I went to bed knowing something big had happened, but it was not yet clear what.

When I woke the next morning, I heard my mother talking to our neighbour Gabriel's wife, who had come to our house unusually early. Gabriel was a strong, bulky man who had a pronounced limp. He worked as a security officer at an insurance company, and he, his wife and five children had moved to our neighbourhood a few months earlier. They rarely came to visit, let alone before 6 am, so that was the first abnormal thing about that morning. I heard concern in their voices as they spoke about the consequences of the president's death, which the RTLM had confirmed during the night, long before Radio Rwanda announced anything.

'Ayii weee! Umubyeyi w'igihugu bamwivuganye!' Gabriel's wife said – They claimed the Father of the nation's life! That caught my attention: I got out of bed and went outside to join my mother and her visitor. The morning was misty and eerily quiet. The only remarkable sounds were intermittent gunshots, but they sounded far way.

It was strangely unsettling to know that the president was dead, especially as he had declared himself invincible, earning him the nickname Ikinani. Many people believed he was indestructible. With him on the plane was President Cyprien Ntaryamira of Burundi, and Déogratias Nsabimana, popularly known as Castar, Rwanda's army chief of staff. Castar was a mythical figure: his name appeared in songs praising him as a mighty military leader. I was among the many people who believed Castar was the one winning the war; his death, along with that of the president, was a big blow to the army.

Everyone at home was fearful: it showed on their faces and could be heard in the strained tone of their voices. Chloe's perpetual smile was gone. Throughout the day, she expressed anxiety, wondering where and how her brother David was. Dianne was quieter than usual. Cousin Erasmus paced in slow circles in the back yard, his tall shoulders bent, looking down as if he was contemplating making a difficult decision. My mother's was the voice we heard most often that day, repeating the same instructions over and over: do not go outside. Occasionally, she would sing a hymn, but before she got to the end, she segued into another one in a fainter voice. I had never seen my mother so pensive and afraid. And rarely had our home been so quiet; it was usually filled with lively people who laughed and played when gathered together. But that day, it was grim.

Later in the morning, Tabaro, unusually wearing a camouflage jacket over his police uniform, came home with two colleagues. We all stood in the back yard, listening to Tabaro, his message punctuated by gunshots some distance away. Only my little brother, who had gone to visit family friends in Gikondo, was absent.

'Ikinani and Castar are both dead,' Tabaro said, in a stern voice I had never heard him use. 'Everyone listen carefully,' he continued.

'We are at war. War is here in Kigali. There is a lot of gunfire in Kacyiru. The city is blocked. No one leaves home to go anywhere. I will tell you more when I come back.'

My mother didn't wait for him to finish: 'My younger son is in Gikondo. Is there a way you can help get him back here?' she asked, sounding distressed.

That day, April 7, 1994, I saw another side to Tabaro: his military persona. His expression was dark and serious; he was carrying two extra magazines for his AK-47. After a quick meal, Tabaro and his two police companions, whom he seemed to command, went out again. We knew it was their duty, but by then Tabaro's presence at home had become not only reassuring but essential. We felt safe when he was home, and exposed when he was gone. I looked forward to his return for another reason too: he would always bring interesting and terrifying news. At thirteen, I found the thought of war strangely exciting, and I wanted to hear it all. To imagine it. To witness it. War was not just in the news and songs, or in the Hollywood movies. I could sense it getting closer and closer. And the weird sense of anticipation was exciting. I had no idea how close and how bad it would actually get, and that death, which we had only heard about so far, was about to knock at the door of our very own home.

Tabaro returned in the afternoon. He was driving a white civilian pickup truck in which he brought my brother back from Gikondo. When my mother saw him, she put her hands on her head in disbelief and stood still for a few moments, a slight smile on her face. I had not registered the danger my brother was in, so at the time I did not understand why my mother reacted like that. My brother wore a grey jacket with matching trousers that had belonged to me. He'd had his own, identical suit: we had worn them for our joint first Eucharist celebration. As we outgrew them, he gave away his, and I gave him mine.

After dropping my brother, Tabaro, still with his two police colleagues, left in a hurry; I didn't even know he could drive. I briefly wondered where he had got the civilian truck from. My brother

73

had heard a lot more shooting than we had throughout the night. He said no one in the family he was visiting had been able to sleep because of the heavy gunfire that sounded very close. He also told us of the roadblocks from Gikondo to Muhima, and that there were very few cars on the road, mostly military vehicles.

Before he left again, Tabaro told us he'd personally seen the body of the prime minister, Agathe Uwilingiyimana, who had been killed that morning. He had also seen the bodies of ten Belgian UNAMIR troops who had been killed in Kigali main military camp. He repeated his warning: 'We are at war. No one goes outside.'

We knew that Tabaro was still well connected in the army, so we took what he said seriously and obeyed his instructions. That evening, he and his colleagues returned, armed with AK-47s, and they sat with us in the living room. Also there was Fabien, who had come to ask Tabaro for information on the situation. Fabien had briefly been our tenant in the back annexe, and when he moved to Cyahafi locality in another part of Kigali, he had recommended Tabaro to take his place.

Others in our home that evening were Rugira, Erasmus, Dianne and Chloe. My brother, exhausted from not having slept the night before, had fallen asleep in one of the rooms, lying across the bed, feet touching the floor, still in his full suit and shoes. At about 6:30 pm, Fabien decided to go home, and Tabaro and his companions escorted him.

While they were gone, my mother, Rugira, Erasmus and I played cards in our living room. As the electricity had been off for a few hours, we had a paraffin lamp on the table. Chloe and Dianne were cooking on the charcoal stove in the back yard when we heard a commotion coming from there. Our dog, Bobby, yelped in pain. A moment later the two girls came into the living room, followed closely by two government soldiers in uniform, their automatic rifles poised and ready to shoot. The soldier in front ordered everyone to remain seated. Dianne and Chloe stood still as statues. My mother stood up and walked towards the soldier, as if to greet him.

But before she reached him, he asked: 'Who is Mme Kabalira?'

'It is me,' my mother answered softly.

'Bring your ID document!' the soldier ordered. She reached for her handbag, which was on the dining table, and handed him her green identity card.

'Ni ikinyagatonde, ni ikingiki dushaka.' – It is from Gatonde, this is the thing we are looking for, he said. *'Jya imbere tugende wa nyenzi'* – You are the one we are looking for.

By then I had gone to stand next to my mother.

'Tujye hehe' – Where to? Before she had even finished that short question, the soldier slapped her hard across the face. I had never seen anyone pointing a finger at my mother, let alone hitting her. My heart jumped and a chill ran through my body. Instinctively, I grabbed my mother's hand and pulled her towards the door.

'Mama, tugende. Tugende badakomeza kugukubita' – Let's go, Mom, so they don't carry on beating you, I pleaded, scared that she would be slapped again. She walked out slowly with me, saying nothing. Outside, we turned towards our main gate. I was in front, my mother following me, and the two soldiers behind her. As we reached the gate, we met Tabaro and his two police friends coming back.

'Murajya he Mukecuru? Muri iri joro mu ntambara?' – Where are you going, Ma'am? At night, in a war?' he asked, clearly surprised.

'Baranjyanye, ngo ndi inyenzi' – They are taking me, saying that I am a cockroach.

'Uwo ninde se ukujyane?' – Who is taking you?

Tabaro hadn't seen the soldiers, who were inside the dark yard. I slipped out and crossed the narrow pathway separating the neighbours' house from ours, then climbed onto the ledge surrounding the base of the building; on this side it was their back wall. When they saw the soldier behind my mother, Tabaro's colleagues acted quickly, pinning him against our corrugated iron fence, and rebuking him as they took his gun. I don't know what happened to the second soldier.

Tabaro climbed onto the ledge with me and paced back and

forth. He pointed his rifle at the sky and shouted: 'Other soldiers are at war, fighting, and you are busy killing innocent people calling them Inyenzi!' He discharged two bullets one after the other. I froze at the blast of the AK-47; my ears ringing. The acrid smell of gun smoke was very strong. For a moment, my mind suspended what was unfolding, and I found myself excited by the blue and yellow flash from the nozzle of the rifle. Tabaro was fighting for us.

Then other shots rang out, but not from Tabaro or the policemen. Tabaro ducked. I stood still, not knowing what to do. I stared at my mother in front of me, framed by the gate, also frozen. A soldier came from behind her, forcefully pulled her back into our yard and pushed her to the ground. Tabaro ran to her. There were more shots but I couldn't see where they came from. Tabaro's colleagues ran along the fence towards the street to escape the bullets.

Then I was suddenly alone and terrified. Through the open gate, looking into our yard, I could just make out the soldier pointing his gun at my mother, preparing to shoot. Tabaro jumped on his back, but at that moment the soldier fired. My mother lay on the ground. A man grabbed my T-shirt and pulled me to my right. The last thing I saw was Tabaro wresting with the soldier who had just shot my mother.

It was Gabriel who had grabbed my shoulder and pulled me towards the entrance of his house. There were more gunshots when we reached his yard. Inside the house was Dianne, sitting on one of the couches, sobbing. I sat down for a moment, my mind racing. Then I sprang up and ran out. I stood on the ledge where I had been before and peeked at where I had last seen my mother lying, thinking she was dead. She wasn't there. I sobbed, calling into the silence: *'Maman?'* No answer. I called again a few times. No answer. 'Tabaro?' Silence. 'Rugira?'

'Aaaaah . . . ahhhh!' I heard Rugira groaning. I called again; more groaning. His voice was coming from our yard, on the other side of the corrugated iron fence. When I called again, a shot was fired. I called my mother again. Instead of her voice, another shot rang out to my left. I could not see who was shooting and where. I panicked and yelled louder: *'Maman!'*

The third shot went straight through the corrugated iron fence, whizzed past my head and hit the stone wall to my right, creating a flash of sparks. At that moment, I saw Gabriel cowering on the ground next to me. He grabbed my hand and pulled me to the ground. We waited a few moments in silence. Then he quickly stood, grabbed my arm and ran back towards his house, dragging me along with one hand. Once in his yard, he smacked me on my butt and back, saying: 'You little idiot, don't you see that you are about to get us all killed?' He then pushed me into his house where his wife, Dianne, and his daughters were waiting. Gabriel told one of his daughters to put cushions on the floor to make a bed for me and Dianne, who was still sobbing quietly. He then locked the front door and put the key in his pocket.

Everyone in the house was whispering, except Gabriel, who issued instructions in a low voice: 'Sleep, and switch off the light now,' he said, as he left the room. Dianne and I reluctantly lay down on the cushions that had been covered with a thin sheet. The sofas around us made it feel as if we were lying in a hole. She blew out the paraffin lamp.

I stared into the dark at the ceiling, straining to hear if something moved or someone spoke on my right, from the direction of our home. Time stood still. It was dead quiet. And then *boom*! A loud explosion I knew well to be a grenade shook the table that had been pushed aside to make space for us, and the windows rattled. A moment later, bits and pieces fell on the corrugated iron roof above us. I snapped into a seated position. Dianne grabbed my knee and didn't let go, uncontrollably murmuring my name: 'Piyo, Piyo, Piyo, Piyo, Piyo . . .'

I waited for Gabriel or his wife to come into the living room, but no one came. Moments later, it was quiet. I lay down again, sobbing. I still hoped to hear a voice. Nothing. No one. No sound. I don't remember drifting off to sleep.

In the morning, I sprang up as soon as I opened my eyes and

immediately thought of the last time I'd seen my mother, the silence filled with Rugira's groaning, and the grenade. Dianne and I looked through the window of the metal door, waiting for Gabriel to come and open up. My brother appeared, looking distraught. He was still wearing his suit. His words tumbled out while Gabriel opened up.

'Tabaro is dead. Rugira is dead. We can't find *Maman* anywhere,' my brother announced. He was holding a RWF100 note with a hole in the middle, and a watch with black leather straps and a golden face.

'I found these in the front yard. The hole must be from a bullet. I don't know where the watch came from,' he said casually, as we ran home together, leaving everyone else behind. For a moment, I wondered why my brother was showing me those things then. I later understood that what I was about to see, he had seen hours before.

As we approached our gate I saw the devastating impact of the grenade: part of the corrugated iron roof of our house had been blown off. When I went through the gate, the first thing I spotted was Tabaro's boots, his feet pointing upwards. His right hand was under his back in a completely unnatural position. There was a little blood on his chest near his right shoulder. As I stepped over his legs that were blocking the way, I saw that his eyes were closed. The top of his head from his hairline had been blown off. He lay right in front of our outside latrine.

From where he was, I could see Rugira, in his white shirt, also lying face up. He had no visible wound. Just a little trail of blood flowing from underneath his back, past his shoulder and trickling below our tap that was also dripping, a drop every few seconds. Rugira must already have been wounded when I heard him groaning in response to my calls.

When I was calling, had Tabaro already been shot dead? Did Rugira see his best friend die? Their bodies were less than two metres apart. Standing between them, I looked through the window of our guestroom that had been destroyed by the grenade. I could see the sky through the iron sheets that were now pointing upwards. Pieces of the ceiling were on the floor and parts of the two beds were hanging from the ceiling that was still suspended. One of the walls was riddled with holes. I burst into tears. That's when I saw Chloe, standing at the edge of the back yard. She looked at me and Dianne, who had followed.

'You are still crying,' Chloe said in a sombre voice. 'For us, tears have dried up already.' As I walked towards her I saw that she had a wound on her left foot and on her shoulder. Erasmus was also injured from the blast, where shrapnel had pierced his back.

When I entered the main passageway of our house, there was my mother, walking slowly ahead of me. I rushed to her; fresh tears flowing. The destroyed room was to her left, letting in so much daylight that the usually dark passageway seemed unfamiliar. My mother looked at me, slightly dazed, then turned to look up through the open roof. She had one of her kanga wraps around her shoulders, and a cloth in her hand. I saw that the right side of her face was badly swollen and she had a fresh wound on the edge of her eye that was still bleeding; from time to time she dabbed it with the cloth in her hand.

She then walked out to the back yard. The others were surprised to see her – we learnt only later that she'd been hiding under her bed, unconscious some of the time. As if she had commanded us, we all remained still and silent as she slowly turned towards the side of the house where the bodies of Tabaro and Rugira lay. She seemed rooted to the spot and stared at them for a long time, hardly blinking, still using her cloth to dab the wound.

After a few moments, my mother took a few steps back towards the door and said in a soft voice: 'Piyo, go to Cyahafi and tell Fabien and the family. Let your brother go with you.' As we left, Chloe was covering the bodies with bedsheets.

It was about 7 am when we ran to Cyahafi. There was no traffic and no one walking in the street. We jogged together, impatient to deliver the message and return home. But we slowed down as we approached a young man lying on his back on the side of the road, immobile. As we got closer, we realised he was dead. There were stones scattered around him, and wounds on his face. We realised he had been stoned to death. He was wearing a multicoloured nylon tracksuit jacket and blue jeans. He had only one shoe on. There was no one else in sight. My brother and I were scared. We walked quickly along the extreme edge of the opposite side of the road to put as much distance between us and the body as we could. When had he been killed? Before that day, you would not have seen a dead person in the street. Or if there was one, the scene would have been buzzing with people in shock yet still curious, and no doubt the *gendarmes* would have been there. But not this time. It was eerily quiet on that long, straight stretch of tarred road. Once we had passed the scene, we started running again.

When we got back home, the bodies of Tabaro and Rugira were being loaded onto the back of a City of Kigali pickup truck that had been brought by Tabaro's fellow policemen. They also took Erasmus and Chloe to hospital, so their wounds could be treated. Dianne went to help them.

Three days later, the afternoon sun still high in the sky, cousin Erasmus and Dianne entered the small gate of our yard. The first question was: where is Chloe? Before they even sat down to rest, Erasmus and Dianne quickly reassured us that she was fine. Erasmus had bandages around his abdomen and shoulder. Red blotches showed through the bandage; they were either blood or Mercurochrome antiseptic. Most of the wounds on Erasmus's back were still exposed, but were daubed with the red liquid.

Their accounts of the scenes at the hospital were sickening. There were numerous badly injured civilians and soldiers, some of whom died on the veranda of the emergency room that was already full. The injuries they described were horrendous: missing limbs, machete cuts on the head. Some people's clothes were soaked in so much blood it was impossible to tell the extent of the injury. The stench of infected human flesh and drying blood was overwhelming.

Tabaro and Rugira had been taken to the morgue but it was full, so their bodies were offloaded outside, where the corpses were piling up. 'They kept bringing bodies while we stood there,' Erasmus said, clearly upset by what he'd seen. They were told the bodies would be loaded on a truck and buried in a mass grave.

While Dianne, Chloe and Erasmus were waiting to be attended to, a military vehicle bringing injured soldiers had screeched to a halt in front of casualty. Among those who had brought their injured comrades, Chloe spotted one of the army officers who worked with David, her brother. He had bad news: David had died in one of the first battles with RPF rebels in Kicukiro, one of the neighbourhoods of Kigali. A device had fallen in their trenches and exploded, ripping off half of his face and head. The officer offered Chloe, whose injuries did not need urgent medical attention, a lift to Gitarama province, which was still far from those territories the rebels had attacked. From there, she would manage to join the rest of her family in Gisenyi, in north-western Rwanda. Chloe briefly discussed it with Dianne and Erasmus, who agreed it was for the best. They said goodbye to her, all three in tears.

Over the next few days and weeks, when any of us remembered something about that awful night, we would share it with the others. My mother told us that when the soldiers came, she immediately thought they were looking for the Gahigi family, who were Tutsis. I was surprised when she revealed that she had been hiding them since early that evening: Marcelline in my mother's bedroom, and the rest of the family in our front cottage. Although my mother thought it was a possibility, she felt shocked when the soldiers were, in fact, looking for *her*.

When I thought my mother was dead, she had actually passed out: the soldier's bullet that I feared had killed her had grazed the skin next to her eye. When she came round, Tabaro was wrestling with the soldier, so she ran to the house, locked the door behind her and hid under her bed. Her wound was bleeding, and again she passed out.

Chloe and Erasmus explained about the grenade: when Rugira had been shot, they'd hidden under the beds in our guest room.

One of the soldiers demanded that they open the door, but when they didn't move, he smashed the window and threw a grenade inside. It fell between the beds and exploded, flying fragments injuring both of them. As they struggled to get up from the rubble, they heard my brother pleading with a soldier not to shoot him. He had slept through most of the terrifying events, waking only when the grenade exploded.

That's also what had roused my mother's attention, and she, too, from under her bed, heard my brother pleading: *'Papa, oya, papa. Ntundase ndi umwana.'* – No Papa, don't shoot me. I am a child. As she tried to crawl out from under the bed, she passed out again.

Knowing only that his life was in danger, my brother unlocked the back door and the soldier went to the room where the grenade had exploded. Threatening to shoot, he ordered Erasmus to sit in the living room and, paying no heed to Chloe's desperate pleas, forced her and my brother into the next room, where he ordered my brother to sit still, and Chloe to take off her clothes. He and some other soldiers took turns sexually assaulting Chloe in full view of my eleven-year-old brother. It took him a few days before he could bring himself to share Chloe's ordeal with us.

It was only after the genocide that we heard Marcelline's experience of that night. During the commotion, she slipped outside and, followed by our dog, hid in our stormwater drain. As Marcelline crouched there, she realised there was a soldier behind her. He ordered her to slide through the drain, under the fence, onto the neighbouring property, and did the same himself. Then, before inexplicably disappearing into the darkness, he ordered her to sit under an avocado tree in our neighbour's yard. With Bobby beside her, she saw the explosion, but too terrified to move, stayed there until morning. From under the avocado tree, Marcelline spotted some policemen in the street and alerted them to the shootings and grenade explosion. Then she went to find another hiding place with her family, who had escaped detection while hiding in our front cottage.

The minutes before the soldiers stormed into our living room are engraved in my memory forever. They were the last moments of *normal* at home. I even remember what Chloe and Dianne were cooking: *igitoki n'ubunyobwa* – plantains with crushed nuts.

In everything that happened that night, the most terrifying moment for me was at the very beginning: the soldier slapping my mother. I still shiver when I remember the sound. We never found out how many soldiers had come for my mother, how they knew who she was or who had sent them.

The bodies of Tabaro, Rugira and the unknown young man on the way to Fabien's were the first of many I was to see over the coming months. It was the morning of April 8, 1994.

Over the next few days, neighbours came and went. Some offering condolences, others sharing rumours of names on lists – lists of people to be killed because they were considered 'cockroaches'. Some men offered to redo the part of the roof that had been destroyed by the grenade. They forced the corrugated iron sheets back into place and used old iron sheets to temporarily cover those riddled with holes. They placed heavy stones, bricks and used tyres on the patched part of the roof to defy wind and rain.

Octave, a family friend, offered to take us to Gitarama in his small hatchback vehicle. My mother refused to go. 'If they want to kill me, they will come and find me at home. I don't want to die in the bush following the very people who were sent to kill me,' she said. With the small wound near her eye still fresh, my mother no longer smiled. I have never fully understood why, but she was determined to stay at home.

My mother eventually agreed to let us go, but the small hatchback could take only five people at a time. Dianne and my brother were among the first to go, and Octave promised to come back and fetch the rest of us. Erasmus, whose injuries were getting worse with infection, was evacuated to Ruhengeri. My despondent mother and I remained alone in the capital city, waiting for Octave. He never came back, and we had no way of knowing why.

CHAPTER 8
Blood flows in the neighbourhood

I was thirteen in April 1994. Thirteen years and eight months. No matter how much my mother tried to keep me indoors, I could not stay still when there was a commotion. An explosion, a gunshot close by, people shouting . . . I wanted to go and see what was happening. My mother did manage to lock me inside the house a few times, but the thing was that she couldn't go outside for fear of being accosted by the soldiers. I had to go out for basic necessities, and there was no way of knowing what would be happening along the way. Most of my errands took me to or through the La Fraicheur intersection. It also happened to be where most of the horrors I witnessed took place.

The La Fraicheur building that had once been a bar was now a branch of the main Pentecostal Church in Kigali. When war broke out, it was closed – like everything else, including schools.

In the few days since it had begun, we could hear gunshots intermittently day and night, near and far. On a few occasions, the sound of bombs rumbled for a while, and then stopped. I could no longer remember what day of the week it was because most days were the same. But as one particular morning unfolded, it was unlike any other.

It began with a tear gas device exploding in the La Fraicheur church. White smoke rose above the brown gate of the church, which was less than 70 m from our home. There were people standing in the road a short distance from the church, watching. I went to join them, and the sharp smell of the tear gas burnt my nostrils. Outside the church gate, which was locked, men with all kinds of traditional weapons were waiting, agitated. Machetes, sticks, clubs and axes in hand, they were impatient to catch men who were coming out of the church, overwhelmed by the tear gas. They emerged a few at a time, coughing, screaming, wiping their eyes, some covering their noses with a piece of the clothing they were wearing. Some burst out, running, but they were caught by members of the Interahamwe militia, who danced jubilantly, some jumping up and down as if warming up for a football match.

In the group of onlookers, men, women and children were all standing still, silent, eyes fixed on the scene in front of the church. I could not count how many men came out of the church: 10, 12, 15, 17? But I heard some of the Interahamwe making sure that every one of them was flushed out. Some of them went into the church to search for anyone who might still be hiding inside.

Some militiamen ordered their captives to stand along the wall of the church, on one side of the road. Others were still jumping up and down, and a few sharpened their weapon blades on the tarmac or the stone walls of the stormwater drains along the road. The scraping sound of the machete blades being honed created a macabre accompaniment to the different tones of the voices: the militias' barked orders acid with hatred versus the supplicating pleas or calm resignation of the churchmen, assumed to be Tutsis, who stood in front of them. At some point, the churchmen started singing Christian hymns, like a choir.

In the group of onlookers witnessing all this was a woman whose name was Odette. I was standing next to her and noticed that she was crying. Sobbing, her right arm trembling, Odette was taking very small steps sideways, back and forth, restless, evidently disturbed. Her younger brother was one of the Interahamwe militia, machete in hand.

An argument seemed to be taking place between the militia and one of the churchmen. I later learnt that he was one of the born-again men, but he was a Hutu who had been hiding with Tutsis inside the church. The militia were urging him to move out of the group. They were going to kill them all, but promised to spare his life because he was Hutu. But he refused to abandon his group, and they all continued singing together, some holding hands. Most of them wore no shoes.

It was very tense. There was still a lingering smell of tear gas in the air. No cars, no motorbikes, and no pedestrians going any-where. Just shocked onlookers mesmerised, as the victims were led towards a more open area of the intersection, in front of a line of shops adjacent to the church. All the shops had already been loot-ed. Some people were watching the unfolding scene through gaps in the fences of surrounding houses.

All the Interahamwe militia were in civilian clothing and armed with traditional or unconventional weapons. There was nobody in uniform around.

The churchmen, no longer singing, were ordered to sit on the tarmac. They complied. Moments later, the carnage began. The In-terahamwe hacked the men with machetes and axes, hit them with hammers and clubs, and stabbed them with sharp sticks. Blood splashed all over those being killed and over those killing them; some flowed onto the road. A few of the churchmen screamed, but most of them made no sound. I repeatedly heard the sickening thwack of machetes cutting through or crushing skulls and bones. The churchmen lay on the tarmac, huddled on top of each other. There were fewer voices as the militiamen moved around and on top of the bodies, cutting through them as if cutting down an un-wanted bush. A few minutes later, all the churchmen were lying on the tarmac, clothes soaked in blood. The Interahamwe militia continued to trample on top of still bodies, hitting and slicing here and there, indiscriminately.

I was so scared that my body was tremoring. Some of the onlookers were silently crying, while others covered their eyes with their hands, unable to watch what was unfolding yet unable to move away.

A few minutes after the hacking had begun, it all went quiet: the men on the ground motionless, blood gushing out of their wounds and flowing in a stream down the road. The militia continued to walk in the blood and to step over the pile of dead men, hacking the odd one they suspected was still alive. Others, weapons still wet with blood, cheered them on. This went on for a while. With all the victims dead, the militia just stood there, surveying to see if anyone moved.

Then, just as it all seemed to be over, one of the churchmen believed to be dead stood up and tried to run away from the scene. The militia shouted: 'Catch him, catch him!' The man managed only a few metres before being caught by three of the militiamen. He was a tall man wearing a long-sleeved blue sweater. Restrained by the arms of an Interahamwe on each side, he was pushed back towards the pile of dead men. He tried to fight but was wrestled to the ground by the men holding him, while another man came along with the wheel rim of a car. Lifting it with both his arms, legs apart to stand firm, he brought the rim down with huge force onto the man's head, which was already resting on the tarmac. The rim smashed the man's head, his skull crushed. The militiamen who were holding him on the ground jumped back as blood and pieces of flesh spattered on impact. The Interahamwe erupted in cheers. As the sound of the skull being crushed hit my ears, my jaw tensed and my neck stiffened involuntarily. Some of the women standing in the crowd screamed, holding their heads as if protecting themselves against the blow destined for the man on the ground. Some of the militia lifted his lifeless body and tossed it on the pile.

La Fraicheur was unrecognisable: no cars, no vendors, no bicycles or motorbikes. No buzz of stores on one side of the road and vendors on the other. At the intersection was a pile of dead men, their blood flowing across the road into the pile of garbage that had accumulated since its collection had been suspended when the war reached Kigali. The militiamen roamed around, walking in the blood, weapons still in hand, as if they were waiting for more to do. More people to kill. I stood among onlookers who stared at the scene, not daring to get any closer – as if there was a line on the road not to be crossed. Some were sobbing. I stood frozen, tense, unable to make sense of it all.

At home, I tried to find words to describe what I had seen. My mother was shocked. She raised her arms, wrapping them around her head as if to protect herself. Then loud cheers and whistling I had come to associate with the militia erupted from the street. My mother tried to stop me, but I ran while she was still trying to find words. As I reached our gate, I saw a man, arms in front bound at the wrists. He was walking ahead of a jubilant group of Interahamwe. As I rushed to the street to see more of the scene, I heard Gabriel's wife exclaiming: *'Oya weee. Ni Mugabo disi. Oya Mana!'* – Noo. It is Mugabo. God no!

I knew of Mugabo. He was the father of Bazi, one of the boys I frequently played street football with. Mugabo walked tall with firm steps, his head held high, eyes wide open and fixed in front of him. He walked neither slower nor faster than his captors, who in fact seemed to have fallen into step behind him, moving at his pace. He had thick black hair, uncombed, with dust on one side of his head.

As they reached the small crowd where I had earlier stood witnessing the massacre of the churchmen, people in the street silently moved out of the way as if to create a passage for him and the militiamen walking in the middle of the road. Mugabo could now see clearly, metres ahead of him, the pile of dead men. Blood was still running from under them into the rest of the street. The militia who were standing around the scene, still holding their weapons, pranced in celebration. Mugabo had to walk the rest of the way with his eyes fixed on the bloody scene, fully aware of the imminent death that awaited him. Although I have often wondered what was going through his mind as he marched to his place of execution, the absolute composure of his tall and elegant frame was impossible to miss, and it has stuck in my mind to this day.

At the scene of the massacre, Mugabo stood still for a moment. One of the militiamen shoved him towards the dead men. He lost balance, and involuntarily stepped up onto the pile of bodies, followed by a few of the militia. They forced him to sit on top of the dead men. One of the militiamen raised his machete and hit him on the head a few times. Blood gushing from his wounds, Mugabo fell on his back, kicking the air with his legs. He did not scream. He did not beg for his life. He did not cry out.

After a few minutes, Mugabo, still alive, could be seen struggling to sit up again and again. Finally, he managed to raise his body and sit up straight. One of the militiamen darted forward and swung a machete at his head. Mugabo fell back, facing up. But a few moments later, he managed to rise up straight, wrapping his arms around his bent knees. His head slowly arching down as if first looking between his feet, Mugabo raised his eyes and fixed them in front of him, as if he was looking at the horizon, the silent crowd of onlookers in his view.

The militiamen let Mugabo stay up straight, but he fell on his back. Moments later, he rose again, fresh blood gushing from his head, running down his face and onto his torso. Mugabo assumed his earlier posture: arms wrapped around his knees, eyes fixed on the horizon. The militiamen continued to jump up and down, weapons in hand, triumphant, mocking him as he moved his head up and down.

Odette, standing next to me in the small crowd, had been sobbing the whole time. She sent a small child to call her younger brother. He was one of the militiamen celebrating around the pile of dead bodies on which Mugabo sat, defiantly refusing to die. Odette's brother came running, his crimson-stained machete in his left hand. The machete's tip was dripping blood onto the tarmac and on his plastic boots. His trousers were also spattered with fresh blood. Odette, struggling to speak through her gasping sobs, battling to draw breath, pleaded with him: 'Please go kill Mugabo. Please go and end his suffering.'

'No! We won't kill him! He must suffer! That is what cockroaches deserve!' said her brother.

'Please, I beg you as your big sister, please go and kill him. Please,

I beg you, go and finish him off.' Odette beseeched her brother, hands pressed together, palm against palm, shoulders slightly bent, as if praying to him.

He was grimly withholding his power of death, with a clearly sinister sense of pride. He and his fellow militia would decide how long Mugabo would suffer. Shaking his head with a stiff smile on his face, Odette's brother said nothing more. He turned and loped back to his fellow militiamen, who were all silent though still moving around, their feet paddling in the slowly congealing blood that had begun to pool on the tarmac. Moments later, there was silence all around as one of the militia finally stepped up onto a few bodies to get within reach of Mugabo, who was sitting upright, still holding his head up as if looking into the distance. Mugabo did not react to the approaching man, who prepared to hit him one more time. Odette buried her face in her hands as the young man slowly lifted his machete and brought it down fast and hard on Mugabo's head, repeating the movement. The sound of the blows assaulted my ears as the machete cracked through Mugabo's skull. Chills sped through my whole body, I was shivering with fear; my mouth dry.

Then, silence. Mugabo slowly fell on his back, his legs straightened out, and his arms fell to his sides. He didn't move again. Odette lifted her face from the palms of her hands to look towards the scene. She sobbed, releasing a barely audible sound of gratitude through her dry lips: *'Urakoze, urakoze, urakoze weee, urakoze'* – Thank you, thank you.

Bazi was my age. I had just witnessed his father fighting death with everything left in him, as he was mercilessly murdered on top of dead bodies. Murdered because he was a Tutsi man. That morning, even just looking like a Tutsi would have been enough for him to suffer that terrible fate.

The bodies remained at La Fraicheur for a day and a night, in full view of all who passed by. They were only removed the next afternoon, loaded onto a truck by prisoners in their pink uniforms – shorts and short-sleeved shirts. The blood that had flowed down and spread across the road was still thick, turning darker. The smell of decomposing flesh and blood tainted the air. Even days after the bodies had been removed, the blood remained, a distinct blackening red layer that covered the entire breadth of the road. Everyone passing by had no choice but to step on it.

That distinct smell of death poisoned La Fraicheur for many days. It would not be the last horror I witnessed.

CHAPTER 9
The silence of death

We were surviving day by day. The price of vegetables from the few merchants still operating had almost quadrupled. To generate money, a friend suggested we could buy and sell a new kind of home-brewed beer. It was a concoction of water, sorghum flour, tea, sugar and other ingredients I didn't know. Due to the shortage of bottled beer, as well as traditional banana and sorghum beer, this very sweet brew was becoming popular. It got people drunk very quickly.

The beer was being brewed in a home a few kilometres away. As a test, I bought five litres, but my mother quickly instructed me to stop selling it because she wanted to avoid attracting the attention of the militia. She also did not want me walking too far from home to buy stock. She gave what remained of my five litres to Gabriel, who shared it with other neighbours doing patrol duty.

There were roadblocks across the city and all men were obliged to take turns at manning them. Their stated objective was to prevent surprise night attacks by the RPF, but although they were ostensibly protecting us, my mother was cautious and minimised contact with them. Her distrust partly resulted from derogatory remarks Gabriel had made about her to some men he was with. He was overheard saying: 'Look how tall this Hutu woman is!' (Height was seen to be a Tutsi characteristic.) My mother later said it was a matter of time, that she would not be surprised if Gabriel let the militia kill us. He had saved my life the night the soldiers came for my mother, but his remarks kept her on edge.

Her decision that I should give up my plan to sell beer was challenged a few weeks later when Serge, one of the officers Giraneza had introduced to us, came to see how we were coping since the war had come to Kigali. He was shocked and angry about the deaths of Tabaro and Rugira, and wanted to do something to help us. After much persuasion to get my mother to agree to it, he offered me a job. He had been planning to use his work transportation to bring bottled beer into the city from areas where it was still available. Since he was in the army, it was possible for him to get passage to prefectures that were still relatively peaceful. I would be in his make-shift bar, managing his stock and money and he would pay me a small amount every week. My mother gave her consent, provided that I would not be sent on any errands from the bar.

A few days later, this became my routine: wake up, get ready, walk about 300 m to the small room that had once been a shop but was looted and abandoned when the war broke out. It was beyond the La Fraicheur intersection, which was about halfway between our house and my new workplace. I would spend my days selling the popular Primus and Mützig brands to civilians and soldiers, and leave before sunset. Some days there would be nothing to sell because the stock would take a while to arrive. It always came with rumours from the battlefront, much of which made little mention of the government winning. Instead, it was stories of increasing struggle, and defiant RPF rebels who, in places where they were not advancing, were stubbornly staying put.

The RTLM and most of the people claiming to have seen them painted a picture of the rebels that still made me struggle to imagine them as normal human beings. They were cockroaches or snakes, and the RTLM, which was still on air, frequently described them as dark-faced creatures with long ears, sharp teeth and tails. Despite knowing that Kanyarengwe was a real human, with family photographs with my parents, the first image I had in my head of the RPF soldiers was the creatures they described.

The RTLM station would often broadcast where Tutsis or

'unwanted' Hutus were hiding, encouraging the militia, and their neighbours, to go and do the work. That meant to find and kill them. By then, we knew that when the war reached Kigali, somebody had sent soldiers to take my mother. The fact that we never found out who it was compounded the fear. It would only be a matter of time; our turn would come. Fortunately, our neighbours, most of whom had no knowledge of my father's history, had not yet turned against us.

My mother was completely homebound, and as I had a strong compulsion to go out whenever there was a hint of trouble in the streets, she was desperately concerned for my safety. As her instructions, warnings and pleas fell on deaf ears, eventually she gave up trying to stop me.

From the road running past our home or, in the opposite direction, from the makeshift bar where I worked, I had a partial view of La Fraicheur. When there was a commotion, it usually only meant one thing: people were going to be killed there. On one such occasion, an army officer was pushing a man in a grey suit in front of him. It was someone I knew: Muturanyi. As usual, barefoot and wearing only shorts and a T-shirt, I hurried out and manoeuvred my way through the scattered crowd to get a good view of what everyone was looking at.

This soldier was not just any soldier. He was an army officer I had seen several times, including before the war in Kigali. I didn't know his name, but he had made a massive impression on me. I admired how clean and shiny his boots were. I had never seen anyone looking better in military uniform. It fitted him perfectly. His face was always clean, his haircut neat. He often kept his beret folded under one of his shoulder straps. He was tall and walked with confidence. He was the very image of what I wanted to look like as an army officer in the future. Every time I had seen him, I had seen my future self.

That afternoon was the first time I heard his voice. As he pushed Muturanyi towards the middle of the La Fraicheur intersection, they were exchanging words. But it was Muturanyi who did most of the talking. Once in the middle of the intersection, the soldier simply ordered him to sit. He had to say it twice, and as Muturanyi slowly sat down, he pleaded: 'Why are you going to kill me? Please, son, please forgive me. Why are you doing this? Please forgive me.'

Muturanyi kept talking, faster and faster, as he bent down, begging, pleading for his life, asking for forgiveness from a soldier who had no expression of anger, fear or sympathy on his face. He seemed composed, confident in his step, sleeves rolled up to expose muscular arms. He held an Uzi submachine gun.

I had seen Muturanyi many times since I was in preschool. His house, one of the closest to the central prison, was a landmark. When giving directions, people used to say 'Kwa Muturanyi'. He had a boy my age or slightly younger: his son or perhaps grandson. Muturanyi's Peugeot was always parked outside their house, and I had seen the boy on a bicycle. A car for the family and a bicycle for a child were enough for me to conclude that they were wealthy. I thought of Muturanyi as one of the richest people I knew. But that day, in his white shirt and grey jacket with matching trousers, this man was being forced to bend his head and fold his tall frame and beg for mercy from a young soldier who didn't seem to care. Muturanyi's only sin was that he was a Tutsi.

'Sit down!' the soldier ordered again in a harsh tone. Muturanyi bent further, to sit on the ground in the middle of the tarred road. As he went down, he kept his pleading eyes fixed on the soldier's face, still asking: 'Why? Why are you going to kill me? Please forgive . . .' He sat on the tarmac. As if he had accepted that the soldier was not going to forgive him, he dropped his head to his right shoulder, saying, in Kinyarwanda: *'Mana yanjye wee!'* – Oh my God.

And with those words, the single bullet from the soldier's Uzi penetrated the left side of his head just behind his eye. I was standing only a few metres from the two men, so as Muturanyi fell on his back, I saw an opening on the right side of his head, blood gushing out where the bullet had exited. As if in slow motion, fragments of tarmac were sent flying by the bullet ricocheting on the road. I noticed my dry mouth filling with a metallic taste I had come to recognise: a taste that filled my mouth every time I was extremely scared.

The silence that followed that gunshot seemed eternal. That silence. As if everything around me was suspended in the air; the only thing that interrupted that near complete silence was the thrumming that filled my ears, along with shivers that ran the length of my body, again and again.

It was over. Muturanyi's last words calling on God were ringing in my ears, imprinted in my memory forever. The soldier, composed, looked at the body for a few moments. He slowly turned around, eyes still fixed on the man he had just killed. Then he turned his head away and with sure steps, walked away. He didn't interact with any of the people scattered around the scene, silent. The same tall, well-built frame, clean, dark face, well-pressed uniform, assured grasp on the gun . . . the man I had admired for so long became a source of tremendous fear and the object of intense hatred.

At that time, I no longer wondered why he had killed Muturanyi. It had been said, sung, and shouted in the streets and on a radio station too many times: all cockroaches, all snakes, or even more explicitly, all Tutsis must die. Only this time it was a government soldier who shot Muturanyi, not the civilian militia. That was a rare sight.

The sounds of gunshots and occasional explosions were so regular that they were no longer surprising. When we heard a gunshot or an explosion, we paid close attention to see if it was far or close, or if it was an isolated shot or a series. If it was a series of explosions and gunshots, we locked the doors, huddled silently in one room that had no window, and waited for it all to quieten down. I would often have the occasional thought of the worst case: the bomb falling on us. How different would it be, compared to the 'grenade room'?

We waited for our family friend Octave, who had offered to come and evacuate us, but he didn't come back. Was he all right? Had his car broken down? Were the roads closed?

As the days passed, it seemed like a very long time since the war had started. We lost track of time. All days were the same: weeks didn't exist as there was no Monday, Wednesday or mass at church to mark a Sunday. We were getting used to it, no longer wondering if it would end the next day or the day after. With no credible news, we had no idea who was advancing or retreating, or who was truly winning the war. Witnessing people being killed was no longer an extraordinary experience. There were days when there were no dead bodies in the streets, and days when a string of killings caused a commotion in the neighbourhood around La Fraicheur, which had become the place of executions.

I had learnt to identify the sounds of various weapons: AK-47, G3, R4, FAL, Uzi and others. They each had a distinctive sound, and most of the time my guess was correct. When I confused any of them, it was typically the G3 and FAL, which, apart from being different in colour (G3s were painted green and the FAL was black), they looked similar in every other way. Even their bullets seemed to be the same size.

Whenever gunshots were fired close to us, I began to tell if a shot had been fired in the air or shot to kill someone. What was disturbing was that I was accurate most of the time. It had less to do with my hearing or guessing ability than the fact that there were so many killings that a gunshot nearby probably meant someone had been killed. And I, the curious thirteen-year-old, would run to see what had happened every time.

So, early one afternoon, when a single gunshot rang out, I knew it was at La Fraicheur, guessed it came from an AK-47, and that it had just killed someone. I ran to confirm my guess. From a distance, I saw a crowd gathering on the lower part of the intersection. As I ran towards them, a second shot was fired. I was close enough to see a young girl who had been sitting on top of the garbage heap violently pushed backward, her arm swinging open unnaturally fast as she fell on her back. Dead. As I got closer, I noticed the body of another girl on the garbage heap, her leg touching the tarmac. She was the victim of the first shot I had heard from home. Tragically, I had guessed correctly.

Both girls were light skinned, with dense black hair. I could not distinguish who was older or younger, nor could I see enough of their faces to recognise either of them. But I could see they were young, Dianne or Chloe's age.

There was a tall young man who was being held by two of the militiamen. He stood barefoot, watching as the militia rejoiced at the killing. He must have watched as both girls were shot right in front of him. Then, shortly after shooting the second girl, the militiamen forced the young man to sit on the road. He was thin, and appeared very weak. His hair was thick and untidy. His eyes were wide open, and so was his mouth, looking distressed. He offered no resistance, overwhelmed by the menacing men who hurled insults at him. *Inyenzi* (cockroach), *Inzoka* (snake), *Inkotanyi* were just some of the words shouted at him. One of the men pointed a gun at him and fired a single shot, killing him instantly. The silence that I had come to recognise hung in the air for a few moments as the young man fell on his back and his legs straightened. Thumping in my ears, like distant thunder, interrupted that silence. The silence. Then I heard murmurs from onlookers saying that the three young people were *abavandimwe* (those who come from the same womb, which simply means blood siblings).

The militiamen jumped up and down in jubilation. One of them pointed his gun in the air and fired a single shot in celebration. One man in the small crowd of onlookers commented loudly: '*Nibapfe nabo abacu barabamaze!*' – Let them die, they too finished ours. He ended his comment with a sound known in Kinyarwanda as *kwimyoza*, which is made by abruptly sucking air into the mouth without separating the teeth. A sound of disdain.

As the militia danced, one of them remarked sarcastically about the beauty of the girls. He then picked up a stick from the garbage and used it to push up the skirt of one of the girls, exposing her thighs and part of her underwear. The other men cheered him on as he pushed the skirt higher, then tried to pull down her underwear with the stick. He failed. But he had done enough to expose her pubic hair, which contrasted sharply with her light skin.

The whole scene was so disturbing that my stomach churned.

One of the militia exclaimed loudly, as if announcing to all present: 'Look how God created you so beautifully. Even when dead, you are still beautiful.' The man with a stick continued his attempt to undress the girl. That was more than I could take. I felt nauseous, and a wave of shivers moved up the right side of my back as I saw her intimate parts being exposed; my jaw tensed and a noise like distant, insistent thunder thrummed in my ears. I felt my neck stiffening, and something in my head tightened up. I felt a compulsion to swallow, though my mouth was empty and dry. Like a dying fish, I gulped painfully on nothing, fighting my tears so they wouldn't show. It was the first time I'd seen a girl being undressed, ever. I couldn't take it: I scrabbled back a few steps, then turned and raced home as the man began to expose more of the girl's genitals.

As I ran, I heard another gunshot I guessed had been fired into the air by the same mob, followed by loud cheers from the militiamen, who were wildly jubilant, celebrating.

CHAPTER 10
La Fraicheur

Before the war in Kigali, La Fraicheur had always been busy, buzzing with people and motorbikes negotiating the sharp bend on a significant incline. At night, vendors lined the road and many people in the neighbourhood came to do their street shopping, transforming the intersection into a minimarket. Now, a crowd at La Fraicheur meant only one thing: death.

So late one afternoon, when I came to the intersection and found a gathering, I had no doubt that something terrible had just happened. As I walked forward to look, one of our neighbour's children, who was about my age, screamed at me: 'Don't step on that!' – pointing at my bare feet. Scared, I started hopping away to avoid whatever he was pointing at. It was a little bundle of what looked like parts of a brain, drenched in blood. I recoiled, a shudder passing through my body. As I caught my breath, my ears still ringing, the boy said: 'It came out of Ezekiel's head when they were being taken to the hole.'

He told me that Ezekiel, the video man, had been discovered in the ceiling of a house nearby, where he and a few other men had been hiding for weeks. They were immediately shot dead in the yard of the house where they were found. Then the militiamen carried their bodies to a nearby mass grave, blood and pieces of their injured bodies dripping all along the way. I almost stepped on the bloody substance that the boy was convinced came out of Ezekiel's head. I stared at it again, as if I was staring at Ezekiel's body itself. My stomach knotted as I tried to grasp how Ezekiel, the popular Ezekiel, had left a piece of his brain in the middle of the road, just because he was a Tutsi, or even perhaps just because he looked like one.

While the boy was telling me the horrifying story, loud cheers I had come to recognise erupted behind me. As I turned, I saw a section of the crowd slowly parting to give way to the militiamen and their victims: some adults and a toddler. Among them was an elderly couple I would automatically have called grandparents. They were very tall and thin. With them was a younger man and a child who must have been no older than three. The toddler was clinging to the older woman's African print clothing that covered her all the way to her feet. The frightened toddler held the old woman clothes so tightly that it was difficult for her to walk. They moved slowly and the militiamen were in no hurry, jumping up and down, whistling, some singing, while a mix of terrified and apparently indifferent onlookers stood and watched.

This time, I recognised two among the militiamen pushing them. One was Mukarani, a tall, strong man who worked as a porter at the charcoal depot a few metres down the slope from the La Fraicheur intersection. I had seen him many times before, carrying bags of charcoal that dusted his clothes with black powder, making him look dirty, untidy and poor. In times of peace, Mukarani was one of the many young people who would spend a whole day near the La Fraicheur charcoal depot, waiting for someone to buy something, anything they, themselves, were unable to carry. But in the time of war, he was not a porter. He commanded fear, and he probably knew it.

The other familiar face was Mwubatsi, the good-natured builder I had come to know and admire, the man who had taught me to mix cement and lay bricks. But that afternoon, almost three years after I had last seen him, he had changed. He was wearing civilian trousers, dark brown leather shoes, and a military camouflage jacket. He was carrying a brand-new AK-47, proudly holding it with one arm as if it was weightless. His eyes were bloodshot, and the expression on his face was different from the person I knew. This was not the Mwubatsi whose brick-laying hands I had admired many times as he held my little hands in his, showing me how to place a brick perfectly on top of wet mortar in the top corner of an incomplete wall, chest-high for the nine-year-old I was then. That afternoon, Mwubatsi was helping to prod people I knew were going to be killed by this mob of Interahamwe he was part of. He was the only one with a gun; the rest carried knives, machetes, clubs and other traditional weapons.

The frightened victims walked, staring forward. They were forced to climb onto a garbage heap that now extended to the other side of the large, overfull skip where the girls and their brother had been killed days earlier. As the militia pushed them up, Mukarani, the porter, suddenly turned his attention to the child. He looked at the little boy, hesitated for a moment, then grabbed his arm and pulled hard, trying to pry him loose from the elderly woman's skirt. She did not react. The toddler resisted, but Mukarani was too strong. With his right arm, he violently shook the toddler, who finally let go. Mukarani shouted in a scary voice, shaking the little boy once for every word he said: *'Aka kantu se kari gukoriki hano!'* – What is this little thing doing here? The terrified toddler did not cry or make a sound. Holding the child in one hand, Mukarani raised him in the air above his head, as if to prove to the silent crowd that he could manage the weight with ease. Then he ran back up the road, so fast that some bystanders had to leap back to make way for him, and disappeared between the many houses.

Mukarani had just snatched the little boy from the grip of the very mob he was part of, so violently and so fast that they seemed to have no reason or time to object. They forced the elderly couple and the young man to lie down on the rubbish heap. Mwubatsi stood over them. He seemed to be preparing himself to 'do the job'. I was standing close enough to watch what he was doing, just as I had a few years earlier. First, he lifted his gun to firmly hold the handguards with his left hand; with his right thumb, he pulled down the selector lever to the middle position, which I knew to be fully automatic fire. His straightened index finger was near the trigger, the rest of his fingers firmly holding the grip. He slowly and deliberately positioned himself between the people helplessly lying at his feet, towering over his victims. I could hardly believe that I was watching the man I had known to be kind and gentle with children getting ready to pull the trigger and kill.

The rest happened very fast. Mwubatsi pointed the gun down, twisted his upper body to the right and then opened fire, swinging slowly towards his left side as if drawing a semi-circle, spraying bullets with the nozzle of his gun. His arms shook and smoke puffed rapidly out of the side of his gun with each round fired. The bullets shattered the heads of the elderly people by his feet, killing them instantly. The younger man, injured from Mwubatsi's first round of bullets, was still alive. In the brief, harrowing silence that followed the round of fire, the young man crossed his arms over the top of his head, as if to protect himself from Mwubatsi's bullets. But the movement only attracted the killer's attention. Mwubatsi pointed the gun at him and opened fire for a second time, shattering bones in both his arms and skull. Debris flew high from each round, falling to the ground and scattering all over the place. One piece fell from the air and rolled down in front of my foot. It was a piece of bone impregnated with blood. Silence. The excruciating since that seemed interminable.

My scalp tensed; my dry mouth filled with the familiar metallic taste; my body shuddered, my eardrums vibrated. I stepped back and hopped from side to side, as if not knowing where to place my bare feet.

As I turned to run home, I saw Mukarani calmly walking back down the same path he had taken with the child endless moments earlier. What had he done with the boy? I realised the porter had snatched the toddler from the jaws of death. At least for the moment, the child did not succumb to Mwubatsi's bullets. I have always wondered what happened to him, hoping that by some miracle he survived.

Like Mukarani, before the war Ngenda and Mugenzi spent most of the time at the La Fraicheur intersection waiting for work. They had been roommates in a backroom at the nearby charcoal depot. After the death of Tabaro, and soon after we had cleared out his belongings, the two men came and asked my mother for accommodation. They didn't really ask; they just told her. Then they moved in – for free. There was no way to argue with them.

Mugenzi's dark-skinned face was almost always without expression. He spoke rarely and always seemed discreet. Ngenda, however, looked bitter. He wore a long, black coat in all weathers, and had a long sword in a leather scabbard, almost always hanging at his waist. My mother was advised by our neighbours not to argue or even talk with them; they were dangerous and, in fact, they had been seen in mobs killing people. So my mother followed their advice and allowed Ngenda and Mugenzi to occupy the annexe. They would be gone all day and come back late at night.

One night, they came back with a shy young girl named Umulisa, and some friends carrying many bottles of beer for the celebration: Ngenda had a bride. The next morning, Umulisa was left alone when the two men went about their business. Her eyes always looked sad and she cried a lot inside the cottage, sometimes even outside while cooking on the charcoal stove or washing clothes. When she arrived, she had only one outfit and some African fabric. My mother gave her some more fabric, and later, Ngenda brought more clothes for her. No market or store was open, so it was easy to think he had looted, or simply taken them from someone else.

A few days after Umulisa arrived, we heard screams and cries in the evenings coming from beyond the locked door of the annexe. We could only imagine what was happening: Ngenda beat Umulisa often, but always when his friend Mugenzi, whom I rarely heard talking, was not there. Although my mother was frightened of the two men, she often tried to speak to Ngenda to intercede for

Umulisa. But he always ignored her. He would stand and stare at her in silence, gnashing his teeth, then just walk away without responding. In the morning, the bruises on Umulisa's face were obvious. She still smiled, spoke to my mother, and sometimes even made a few jokes.

She told us her parents had been killed, but that she had been spared by the militiamen who killed her parents because one of them would take her to be his wife. That practice had become known as *kubohoza* (liberation). She told us that many Tutsi girls had been 'liberated' by the Interahamwe militia, who were often the very people responsible for the killing of their families. It was Ngenda and friends who had eventually caught her. She would cook, wash his clothes, clean the cottage and wait for him and his friend to come back. Until one day, things happened differently.

It all started at sunset when Ngenda arrived with other militiamen, saying they had discovered that his friend Mugenzi was in fact Tutsi. Ngenda stood outside in the back yard, facing the cottage. He called Mugenzi, who had spent most of the day inside. He silently walked out of the cottage. My mother watched it unfold while standing in the doorway of our house. I was restlessly moving every which way, trying to make sense of what was happening. I had never seen Ngenda's sword out of the scabbard; that day, he held it in his right hand. I could see the shiny blade reflecting the light from the lamps and torches some of the men carried. For a moment, I feared that they were going to kill Mugenzi right there. But they did not and Mugenzi didn't fight them. It was as if he had been expecting them. When they told him to step forward and go with them, he obeyed without resistance. They said he had fooled them for too long, and that they had finally discovered he was *inyenzi*. Mugenzi said nothing. He was taken away, never to return.

The next morning, Umulisa told my mother that when Ngenda returned late that night, he told her Mugenzi hadn't even begged for his life: 'He didn't make a sound. He died silently like a sheep.' Umulisa sobbed as she murmured repeatedly that Mugenzi was a good man.

One day, while doing household chores, I heard her tearfully tell my mother: 'My husband . . . he is a monster. *Igisimba*. What kind of man kills his best friend?' I missed much of their conversations as Umulisa would often speak in a whisper or be choking with tears. I felt sad and angry. Later, if I asked my mother what she had said, she would rebuke me, saying: 'That's not for you to hear.'

My mother would often hug and console Umulisa, and they shared their fears. 'He calls me his wife. But how long before he and his friends take me to the mass grave and kill me too, just as they did Mugenzi?' I overheard her say. My mother told Umulisa that she was also living in fear, knowing that the person living in her back yard could easily become her killer. Ngenda was, after all, one of the Interahamwe participating in the killings. We had been attacked by uniformed soldiers who killed Tabaro and Rugira. Thankfully, they hadn't returned. My mother hoped that the militia would never ask or discover who my father was, or connect with the people who had sent soldiers to us on that first night. We had no way of knowing how come Ngenda and friends didn't realise we were on a kill list. Being in a war zone had moved to another level of danger for us: we were living next to a man who could use his sword on us if he discovered who we were. My mother had resigned herself to the possibility of imminent death; fighting to get rid of Ngenda would only attract the kind of attention she wanted to avoid. We had no way of guessing how it would end.

One afternoon, under a cloudy sky, I was walking home early from the makeshift bar because there was no stock to sell. After heavy rain, the air was fresh, and the roaring of the stormwater in Ruhurura as it flowed under the La Fraicheur intersection was all I could hear. Few people were out in the streets, but some children had congregated and were looking at something. Seeing dead bodies had become so common that if people hovered around looking at something, it made sense to assume it was something else. My curiosity drew me towards the small crowd, which I soon realised was focused on the corpse of a man wearing a rain-wet green top and dark trousers, lying face down on the tarmac.

I could not tell how he had died as there was no visible injury. But there was something unusual: on his back, there was a hand, cut off at the wrist, and placed palm down. It took me a while to figure out that the hand, an adult's right hand, was not from the body on which it rested. Who was the man? Whose hand was that? Who had put it on the man's back? Was the person whose hand it was still alive?

It would be years later that I had a chance to reflect on that hand, on all it might have done in life – for good or evil. It could just as easily have been my hand, or the hand of anyone. Of a Hutu. Of a Tutsi. Or any other man on earth.

In itself, it was just a hand; similarly, a nose was just a nose. But so many had been killed for the shape of theirs. Hutus with long, sharp noses were killed. Tutsis with slightly flat noses survived. I was told that my nose was too flat to be a Tutsi, but that my arms, hands and fingers were too long for a Hutu. Comments were made that members of my family were too tall to be Hutus. But for those who found it important to define it, we were Hutus.

Fear and paranoia had emptied the area around La Fraicheur; only a few merchants braved various dangers and set up their vegetable and fruit stands. Instead of setting up in the open by the roadside as they used to, they set up in a sheltered corner of the intersection, closer to the walls of shops that had long been looted, but their doors were locked.

As La Fraicheur and Ruhurura were on my route to anywhere I usually went, I observed all that happened. After another heavy rain, for example, some people used the opportunity to tip garbage that was piling up into the raging Ruhurura, so it could be flushed down to Nyabugogo valley.

The valley was a dead zone. On one side, the hill of Muhima where we lived was still in the hands of the regular army, largely controlled by the Interahamwe militia. They hunted down and killed Tutsis, those who looked like Tutsis, and Hutus believed to be sympathetic to Tutsis. On the other side of the valley, Mount Jali and the hill of Gisozi were in the hands of the RPF rebels. Bombs and heavy machine-gun fire had been flying over our neighbourhood for many weeks in both directions, while on the ground, people were being massacred using all sorts of weapons. But as the weeks passed, the sound of guns and rocket launchers became less and less common during the day. So did the killing scenes.

The few merchants who managed to conduct business at La Fraicheur often had loud conversations among themselves and with some of the adult customers. That day, after the storm, they talked about the rain being welcome. One of them made a comment that has stayed with me ever since: 'We are lucky there was enough rain to wash away all the blood. Now the air will smell fresh.'

La Fraicheur had long stopped being just a set of converging roads. So much blood had been spilled on that tarmac that such a comment was logical, and its absurdity could almost go unnoticed.

CHAPTER 11
Aerial killers

Days were long, and nights were longer. Some were quiet, others were eventful. But they all had something in common: fear. Death lurked everywhere. As the weeks passed, fewer people went out, so the streets were mostly deserted. Mercifully, the incidence of public killings had dwindled.

Some days, we would huddle in the corner of my mother's room, hands covering our ears but still hearing as bomb launchers spat deadly bombs from Gisozi, flying over our densely populated neighbourhood on their way to hit military positions on top of the hill. The sound of the mortars would sometimes be so close that we were almost sure they would fall not far from our house. Sometimes, we heard them whizzing through the air, then, after a few seconds of silence, we heard the explosion. I would wonder how bad the devastation was.

Occasionally, the thought of American movies about the Vietnam War that were often shown at Ezekiel's crossed my mind. Sometimes, I caught myself feeling a sense of excitement I could not explain, and a disappointment that, unlike the assault rifles I was beginning to recognise by sound, I had no clue what weapon was in use when I heard the bombs. Was it the 12-tube beast, or the long twin tube I once spotted on a trailer behind an army truck? What were their names? Katyusha? Bitube? What did the bombs look like before being loaded? Could one man operate it or did it require several? I was disappointed that my curiosity would probably never be satisfied.

We would often hear people talking about destroyed civilian houses and people killed in their own homes. But some of them hit their targets with amazing precision: I remember one day when the RTLM radio station was bombed. I was at home, tuned in to the station at the time; my mother had told me to listen so we would know if they had announced her name or my father's, and were sending the militia. My mother hoped that if they mentioned our family, we would get to hear it first and hide, run or prepare. I was never sure what we would do if they came for us.

The day a bomb hit the RTLM studios, there were two presenters on air, a man and a woman. There was a bang, then noises that sounded like objects falling, followed by a break in the broadcast, filled with weird scrambling noises. And then I heard the female presenter calling to the male presenter, who responded inaudibly, both with panic in their voices; then the signal was cut off. After the station was off air, my mother seemed relieved. At just thirteen, perhaps I was too young to appreciate the extent of the danger we were in.

At that time, we thought the greatest threat for us came from the Interahamwe, but in another part of Kigali, the RPF attacked the neighbourhood of Kicukiro, forcing many people to flee their homes. Among them was my cousin Albert, who came to our home. Albert and his twin sister Albertina were just a few months younger than me, and they had three younger siblings, two girls and a boy. Albert was the only one left with his mother. Somehow, he managed to get to us. He told us he had been separated from his mother a few kilometres from their home when they were running for cover while they were being shot at. It was not long afterwards that we received the bad news: his mother had been killed by the Interahamwe militia. We were told that she'd asked to be allowed to pray before being shot. She was Tutsi.

Albert stayed with me and my mother. Some evenings, Albert and I would sit next to the upper road and stare at Mount Jali, waiting for bullets to be fired from the top of Mount Jali, targeting a military installation. The trajectory of the bullets was sometimes directly above us. First we would see dots of fire moving through the sky from the top of the mountain, then disappearing from sight before flying over us on their way to their target at the top of the hill of Muhima. Sometimes we would hear them whizzing through the air above us. As the flying bullets appeared, we would count them quickly before the sound of the machine gun finally followed, like thunder after lightning; we heard it at almost the same time as they became invisible. Often it would happen so fast that we would each come to a different number and argue about it, resolving to pay attention and get it right at the next round. Sometimes there would be a next round, sometimes, to our disappointment, none.

What we had not realised was that we were in the line of fire. We had always assumed the bullets from the Inkotanyi rebels would always fly above us. Until the day they started hitting our house and those of our neighbours. One hit our roof, cutting through the corrugated iron. Another one lodged itself high on the long side wall, just below the roof line. We would then search for them. I was once lucky to spot one that had hit the tarmac and ricocheted, remaining intact. It was as long and as thick as my thumb, narrowing to a sharp point, with twisting lines engraved around the middle. But even then, while I fantasised about seeing what gun they were fired from and how it worked, it never occurred to me how much danger we were in. The fact that we were often under the path of those bullets didn't worry me. Until one day . . .

⁓

Mark was a longstanding member of the prayer cells that my father had helped to start before he died. He had six children, four boys and two girls. His wife had died of natural causes some time before the war broke out in Kigali. One morning, Mark sent one of his children to call my mother to attend a rare funeral. The funeral of his teenage daughter.

His youngest daughter had woken up in the morning, leaving her older sister Lilianne in bed. When the little girl went back into the room to ask why she was oversleeping, Lilianne did not respond. Seconds later, the girl saw some blood on the sheets and shouted for her brothers and her father. They found a wound at the back of Lilianne's neck where a bullet had entered, lodging itself in her head while she and her little sister slept. The bullet, shot from Jali, had drilled through the dry earth and mortar, emerging on the other side of the wall with enough speed to pierce Lilianne's neck. When we arrived at their home, Mark was showing people what had happed. Lilianne's body was still on the bed where she had been sleeping when the bullet hit her. Her father believed that she had died peacefully, with no suffering.

As I stood outside Mark's house and stared at the bullet hole in the wall, I realised any house exposed to Jali was in the line of fire. The bullet that had killed Lilianne was one of the very bullets Albert and I had often enjoyed spotting and counting as they flew through the air overhead. Even then, I don't recall feeling fear.

Lilianne was laid to rest in a small ceremony near their home on the same day. As there was no possibility of getting a coffin in those times, her body was wrapped in white sheets and lowered into the ground in the presence of some family, friends and neighbours who were all overcome with fear and sadness. It was a funeral different from what I had seen before. It was not in a cemetery, but in the nearest open space among houses built so close together that there was no visible boundary between them. The grave was narrow and shallower than usual. The few people present sang funeral hymns with reservation, as if they didn't want someone to hear them. Those who could participated at the ceremony standing against the nearest wall for cover. As long as they could see the grave, they were part of the proceedings. An interment without a coffin, and a funeral without mourning or vigils. It was a different time in every way.

What happened to Mark's family could have happened to anyone, on any day. And the Inkotanyi rebel soldier who pulled the trigger on the mountain of Jali would never know that on the other end, there was an innocent teenage girl sleeping, whose life would end. Harm intended or not.

Because my mother was still trying to stay under the radar, I did our grocery shopping. On one of the days that she sent me to buy vegetables at the La Fraicheur intersection, some of the stallholders, mostly women, were sharing tales of being shot at, ducking for cover, and hiding in bushes on the side of the road while making the dangerous journey to bring their produce into the city. Several men and women who were listening admired their courage. It sounded adventurous and deadly. But there was an unspoken sense of resignation about it simply being the way things were. Every now and then, one of them would crack a joke that made everyone else laugh, while talking about coming within a hair's breadth of death. It was real and potentially deadly. But they laughed at it.

I had already bought the vegetables but I stood nearby listening to their stories. What would it be like to encounter the rebels? Hearing their tales made Jali and Gisozi seem a long way away.

While I was listening, I stood on a little concrete bridge over a deep gutter, alongside a girl, perhaps a little older than me, who had on a worn-out grey and white dress. I had seen her every now and then, but we had never interacted. As we stood side by side, listening to the stories, the girl jerked forward violently, grabbing her right thigh and screaming in agony. She fell to the ground on her back, hands still clutching her leg. People around started shouting, their words a confusion. I was the closest person to the girl, but when she fell, I had no idea what had just happened.

'*Baramurashe, baramurashe!*' – They shot her! They shot her! I heard, as people scattered from the scene. I saw that the girl was pressing her hands to a wound from which fresh blood flowed, then dripped off her fingers onto the road. She groaned and screamed in pain and terror, kicking in and out with the uninjured leg. She had just been shot. This time, I hadn't heard the sound of the gun, or the bullet whizzing. As more people scrambled to help her, I desperately tried to understand what was happening. Were we under attack? I was afraid, but also relieved that it seemed to be just one shot. Judging from where we were standing, it could only have come from one direction: the Gisozi hill. Could the rebels see the movement of people from such a distance? Was it an aimed shot or a stray bullet?

Some adults carried the girl down the few steps from the road to the flat area in front of the stalls. More people frantically gathered around as she sat in a pool of her own blood. Some were debating what to do next. But we were all still within sight of the Inkotanyi rebels' territory. The agitation of the small crowd could well attract more attention. Fighting the pull to stay and watch, I decided to run back home.

This became one of the many stories I told family and friends, especially those who knew the little bridge I was talking about. The more I spoke about it, the more frightening the memory became, as if with each time I told the story, I was getting more sensitised to the danger I had been in. I began to feel the full extent of my fear while obsessing about what could have happened. The bullet had missed my back by mere centimetres, flying past my lower back to hit the girl's leg.

Strangely, it was long after the war that I felt the full terror of the quiet, flying bullets that could have struck anyone at any time of day or night.

The days were marked off not by dates or days of the week but by incidents such as the girl beside me being shot. It felt like the war had been going on forever. Serge, the owner of the bar, was no longer coming. Even though there was still beer from the last time he had brought stock, there were so few clients that opening the bar was becoming pointless. Had everyone run out of money? Days inside the small room lit only by the daylight through the door became long and boring, and seeing familiar faces became rare. I still went, and called it work though I was not paid a salary. The owner just decided how much to pay me whenever he came. At that age, any amount seemed like a lot of money to me. But since he hadn't come back for a long time, I was careful not to take any of it. I just used enough to buy the few essentials we needed at home, and kept a record of it.

Soap, sugar and bread became rare and very expensive. The price of charcoal, which we relied on for cooking, skyrocketed. For food, we had the amaranth vegetable, yellow maize flour and the only meat we could afford: cow hooves. We ate sparingly. One meal a day. Every day, we were reminded of the deadly times we were living in.

One day as I walked home from work, the setting sun made clouds at the edge of the sky glow yellow, ochre and red. The time before the war was no more than a fantastic memory. It had been months; the number of people moving about on the roads in our part of the city had dwindled even further, and cars were rarely seen. Had more people left the city, fearing the war might get worse? Were people simply staying in their homes for fear of being hit by random bombs and flying bullets? Whatever the reason, that kind of silence in the streets was evidence of the shift in our lives.

I had walked from the bar all the way to the path leading home without seeing a single human being. In fact, I was shocked to hear a car roaring round the bend coming from the lower bend of the La Fraicheur intersection. Amused, I stopped to see if the vehicle would come up the sharp bend and continue along the top road where I was standing. It didn't turn. Instead, the dark khaki SUV continued towards the dirt road leading to the makeshift bar I had just left.

Now rolling very slowly, the car stopped in the middle of the road a few metres from the deserted intersection. The rear door opened. A young man jumped out, shirtless, barely managing to remain on his feet as he stumbled onto the dirt road; he must have been pushed from inside the vehicle. A man in civilian clothes jumped out after him. AK-47 in his left hand, he grabbed the young man by the arm with his right hand and pulled him towards the edge of Ruhurura. From where I was, I could see that the shirtless young man was wearing long pants, but no shoes. I stood still, numb, as if indifferent to what would happen if the Interahamwe in the vehicle noticed me. They didn't. The young man barely resisted as he was shoved against the pavement, tripping against the concrete barrier and falling into the adjoining two-metre-deep open sewer, which was almost empty.

I had a sense of déjà vu; I knew what the sequence of events was going to be. The man pushing the youth stood with one leg on the road, the other on the pavement. He held his AK-47 firmly with both hands and pointed it down the drain. As the sound of the full automatic round brutally broke the early evening silence, I knew the young man had become just another victim of the merciless mobs. The man fired a couple of single shots as if aiming at the same point. Then silence. That silence. That eerie silence that followed death. Only this time, I don't remember the tension on my scalp, shivering or the metallic taste in my mouth.

The militiaman casually turned and climbed into the back of the vehicle, seemingly impervious to what he had just done. Then the vehicle moved forward and disappeared around the next bend as if the brief and fatal stop had never happened. Nobody intervened. No crowd gathered around the scene. No one was even walking past. There was nobody in sight. Nothing else happened. I was still, staring at the pavement for a long time, numb, as if the rapidly disappearing daylight was taking away my sense of self with it. I had no urge to run home, or to go and see what damage the bullets had done; I was certain the young man was dead. It had been just another thing happening in a long, monotonous day. Only this time, there were no witnesses. Except me, standing about sixty metres away staring into the distance at absolutely nothing. Still and alone. Moments later, I took the few steps down onto the road and went home.

The following morning, on my way to the bar, I walked past the spot where the SUV had stopped. There were a few people standing on the edge of Ruhurura staring at the bottom of the hole. With some hesitation I stopped, stepped up onto the pavement and looked down. The young man was lying on his back on the concrete surface of the sewer, which was littered with stones, dirty plastic bags, and rotting old clothes. His lifeless body was riddled with bullets, most in his chest. There was little blood around him. His head was slightly turned to his left, arms on either side of his body, legs apart. I realised he was much younger than I had thought when I saw him pushed out of the vehicle the previous evening.

Watching people kill each other, or staring at a hand on the back of a dead body, were not things a child should have to witness. No matter who eventually won the war, these memories would remain. The souls of young witnesses like me would be scarred, probably for life. And the future of many children, like those beside me as we stared at men doing unspeakable deeds, would certainly be profoundly affected. All as a result of a war that someone would one day claim to have won. But how could there be a winner? How could a war, causing so much physical, emotional and spiritual destruction, tainting the innocence of children and making men, good and bad alike, kill fellow men, produce a winner?

PART 3
EXODUS

CHAPTER 12
Nowhere to run

'I will be surprised if Inkotanyi are not here by morning!' said an Interahamwe in civilian clothes. He had a new bandage around most of his left arm, soaked with blood at the elbow. The small crowd of men and young boys listened attentively, standing in the middle of the dirt road in front of the bar where I worked. The man was clearly in pain; he was using his AK-47 as a crutch, holding the nozzle in his right hand like a baton, the gun's stock on the ground. Another militiaman walked towards us, limping. He had a bloody bandage on his knee. 'I don't know what is going to happen, but Inyenzi will be here before the night ends,' he said, in the same pain-filled tone as his companion.

The late afternoon sun was setting when the men were dropped in front of my shop. They were both clearly shaken. One of them was close to tears, but he wouldn't cry. Men, these men with guns, they don't cry. They told the small crowd how they had encountered the Inkotanyi in Runda that morning, which was just a few kilometres from Kigali. They and the military personnel they were with had had to flee. 'They were too many. Even the army guys ran,' one of them said.

The Interahamwe had terrorised the city for months but the tide was clearly turning. Hearing sporadic shooting was common; boastful militia were too. Members of the army were occasionally to be seen, but I had never seen anyone with a gun admitting that they were afraid and that they thought the city would fall.

I ran home and told my mother. She seemed indifferent, and simply continued preparing the food. As night fell, there were no gunshots. But something was different: more human voices outside. Albert and I stepped out to see what the growing commotion was. The discovery was shocking: a long line of cars and groups of people, their belongings on their heads, leaving. The line of cars was rolling very slowly, with all the lights off. Even the brake lights had been disabled on most of them. Gabriel, the patriarch among our neighbours, was clearly agitated. He paced up and down and issued instructions to our neighbours, all trying to figure out what was going on. He approached one of the cars, a small hatchback. The driver rolled down his window, revealing a military uniform with three stars on his shoulder board. A captain. The small car was packed full, people and luggage occupying every bit of space inside.

'*Mon Capitaine!*' Gabriel said in a respectful voice. 'We see many people and soldiers going down this way, would this be the mass evacuation? Us too, should we get ready and go?' He asked in Kinyarwanda mixed with French. The officer hesitated, staring ahead as if wondering why the car in front of his was not moving. Then he replied with a question, as his car started rolling forward ever so slowly.

'*Ni nde wababujije guhunga*?' 'Who's stopping you from running away?'

'*Merci, Mon Capitaine! Bonne chance!*' said Gabriel, his last word spoken at a window that had already been wound up. He turned to those gathered around and shouted that we should get ready to leave and meet on that spot so we could go together. 'Wake up those who are sleeping,' he added.

My mother was no longer indifferent, but she *was* undecided. Do we go? Do we stay? She stepped out of the house to go and see for herself. At the road, she spoke to Gabriel, who was very clear with her: 'We are all going. If you stay, you will be alone here.' My mother knew that once Gabriel left, she would be exposed. Gabriel had harassed her numerous times, like the day he had commented on her height. My mother never knew if he had said it so he didn't appear suspiciously protective, or if he meant what he said. But on that night, it didn't matter. He was key to the tenuous sense of security we had. Now, he was leaving.

'We have to hurry and go with Gabriel,' my mother ordered. We rushed home and started packing in a panic. I packed whatever I thought was precious, including my school reports. Then I put on layers of clothing. My mother instructed me to add pots and a few kitchen items to my bag. I took the small pots, as the bigger ones were full of the boiled cow hooves with yellow maize my mother had cooked. We had no time for dinner. A bag each, Albert and I agreed to take turns to carry the rolled mattress we would all sleep on. My mother locked the house, and out we went. On the road, we stood for a few minutes waiting for other neighbours and Gabriel to show up so we could follow the crowd. They didn't appear. They had already left.

My mother led the way, and we followed everyone. Cars were moving more freely than earlier, still with all the lights off. We had no idea where we were going. We just followed everyone on the road. It was already a few minutes into the march that we realised how treacherous it was going to be. Before we even reached the market of Nyabugogo, a few men approached and snatched the mattress off Albert's head. He fought them, but he lost his balance and let go. As my mother turned to see what was happening, they were disappearing in the dark. She cursed at them. *'Mwa big-oryi mwe murakarindangira. Ntimubona ko twese nyacu tubisize? Apuuu!'* – You are stupid, may you lose it. Don't you see that we're all leaving all possessions behind? she said, the last words certainly to the wind as the men had already disappeared into the distance. We marched on.

At Nyabugogo, shots were fired from Jali. We ducked on the road but there was no cover. We saw men pushing their people into a stormwater drain near the road so they could walk inside, doubled over, but at least hidden from view. The shots were few and far between. Then, as we passed a petrol station, a much larger gun started firing. We could see the red-hot bullets flying ahead and above us from Jali towards Mount Kigali, an adjacent hill. But they were not just fired at random. There was a rhythm to the shooting – the basic musical rhythm of Rwandan traditional dance.

Ta! Ta! Tatata!
Ta! Ta! Tatata!

I caught myself thinking the Inkotanyi soldier who was shooting was having fun. My mother murmured as we huddled in the drain: 'They are celebrating'. Long stop, start, stop, start, crouching and waiting to see if everyone else was moving, we kept walking until we were past the major intersection known as Feux-Rouge. The 200 m straight stretch took us a long time to cover. Once we were away from the view of Jali, we walked upright, following everyone along the winding road towards Giticyinyoni. We were almost out of town, but not yet.

As we approached Giticyinyoni, the crowd on the road became denser. We could still hear shots, but far behind us. Most people walked in silence. It was so quiet we could hear the sound of steps on the tar road. Occasionally, adult voices urged their families on, or a child on a mother's back cried, interrupting the silence. But at Giticyinyoni, some five kilometres from Kigali, it was different.

Giticyinyoni is a major T-junction, where the main road heading to Ruhengeri and Gisenyi starts at right angles to the Kigali-Gitarama road, which continues to Butare. As we got there, dawn was breaking. People were moving very slowly as the crowd accumulated at the junction. My mother kept her watchful eye on us as she guided us onto a small dirt road leading to Nzove that everyone seemed to be following. It appeared to be the only way out of Kigali, which meant the major tarred roads had been closed off.

The crowd was completely still by the time the daylight was bright enough to see people clearly. Around us, there was nobody we recognised. We walked a few more metres, still forcing our way through the crowd, until we found a spot in a field on the side of the road where we could put down our luggage and wait, like everyone else. There were people everywhere, some standing, others sitting on top of their luggage. Women carried babies on their backs, others tethered young children with ropes or kangas that they tied around their waists, to avoid children getting lost in the throng. We heard that the dirt road had been blocked by Inkotanyi rebels a few kilometres ahead. We were all waiting because the army was moving to the front to fight off the rebels and clear the way.

Minute after minute passed as we waited for people to start moving. The crowd dispersed along the dirt road and in the mush of the Nyabugogo riverbed. The small river was only a few metres from us, flowing to join the major river of Nyabarongo, also not far. My mother, Albert and I sat in the green grass. Some of the leaves were light brown and dry. The cool morning breeze blew through the vegetation, but the rustle of moving leaves was drowned out by the multiple conversations of the groups of people resting in the valley, waiting. It was calm.

The three of us occasionally engaged in casual conversation, interspersed with moments of silence, each of us observing the people in our field of view. Suddenly, out of the corner of my eye, I saw a kind of brawl erupt. People fell, others ran, all screaming. I turned to see. Everyone was running.

'Inkotanyi. Inkotanyi!' someone screamed. Instinctively, I picked up my bag and looked to my mother. But there was no time. The whole crowd was running every which way. People fell. Others screamed. I lost sight of my mother and Albert. I ran towards the road. A man suddenly dropped his luggage and fell, face down. I thought he'd tripped. I turned round to scan the crowd for my mother: just people running. I saw the man still on the ground, blood running from beneath his face onto the yellow dust on the side of the road. From the totally unnatural position – one arm under his body and the other stretched over his head – I realised he was dead. People jumped over him. We were being shot at. There were more people on the ground, some crawling, others completely immobilised.

Gunfire: this time, I heard it. It was a long round of automatic fire. I crossed the road. Turned round again. No Albert. No mother. I ran alongside the road, which was on my left, still dragging my own luggage. On my right, a slope of greenery. People were climbing and running up the hill. Drivers revved engines and hooted impatiently, but there was no way through because of the running crowd. They moved slowly. I stopped again, unsure what to do. I turned around. In front of me, the driver of a red Toyota Stout raved and hooted. It was so overpacked and overcrowded that the back was almost on the ground and the front slightly raised. I looked over the pickup truck towards where I thought I had left my mother and Albert. I couldn't see them. I was pushed against the truck, which was trying to roll forward. The front right wheel rolled over the front of my foot. I was wearing solid leather boots, but my toes hurt. I tried to pull my foot from under the tyre, but I couldn't. I screamed, crying, and hit the bonnet a few times. Gunshots intensified. People ran. Some crawled. Others were shot and fell. I was pinned.

About two metres to my right, a slender old man in shorts fell. He struggled to stand, only managing to sit in the grass on the side of the road, his back against the hill. With both arms, he lifted one of his legs. He had been shot, the bones shattered in the middle of his shinbone, his detached foot was hanging. His mouth open wide; his eyes looking all around. No one stopped. No one attended to him. Everyone was running. When I freed myself as the truck moved forward, the pain receded quickly and I ran back in the opposite direction from where the old man sat. Suddenly, across the road, I saw my mother and her luggage on the other side of the road. She was struggling to climb from a ditch onto the dirt road. When she started towards me, she screamed: *'Zamuka ku mukingo tuve mu muhanda hariya mu rutoki!'* – Climb the cliff, let's leave the road and go into the banana plantation!

We helped each other up the cliff. Other people were doing the same. Then we ran into the banana plantation. I heard several other rounds of shooting, I still couldn't tell where it was coming from. As we ran, clutching our luggage, we had to avoid tripping over or stepping onto dead and injured people scattered along the way, and dodge other people running in the opposite direction. Confused, I heard more shooting.

As we ran through the greenery on the hill, I heard the whooshing sound of fast bullets, very close. In quick succession. I was sweating and nearly out of breath. My mother yelled: *'Bari kuturasaho! Manukira hariya!'* – They are shooting at us! Go down that way! We ran along a path zigzagging along the hill, downhill to our left, then up the hill again. There was a small path ahead of us. We turned left onto it, following its twists and turns. We heard more shooting, but not as close. It was behind us. We ran fast and started going downhill again. We could see people running on the dirt road we would rejoin some distance ahead. But this time, they were all running in the same direction.

We kept going down. Fast. Many people were doing the same. My mother fell, and her luggage rolled away. It was a dangerous path down. She cautiously pushed herself forward on her bottom, managing to pick up her luggage, and we negotiated the steep slope down to the road much more slowly. It seemed as if we were no longer being shot at. We rejoined the road and kept walking as fast as everyone else. No more shooting. That stretch of road in the sector of Nzove was quieter, the crowd less dense and moving fast. Fewer people running.

It started raining, just a shower. My scalp was hot from the plastic bag on my head. I was sweating. In the chaos, we lost Albert. No time to find him. We walked quickly, along with the rest of the crowd. The shooting ordeal was behind us but we knew it could happen again. I saw a dead body on the side of the road, a man in dark clothes. It looked as if he had been there for a while, drying mud all over his body. There was another one closer to the centre of the road. Some people were nearly tripping over the body because it was difficult to see through the hurrying crowd. Apart from the bodies, the road was littered with clothes, pots, paper, bags, rolled mattresses, and a spot where there were some RWF100 notes caked in mud.

We kept walking. One army officer in full uniform was holding a young woman clamped to his side. She was limping heavily, with a flood of fresh blood on her right thigh wetting her kanga. She had been shot, most likely in the chaos we had just left behind. The officer had no gun. Had he lost it? On the left side of the road was a burnt bus. There was no smoke. It was clear that whatever had happened there had taken place many hours before. In front of the bus, along the road, was a dead woman. I saw no obvious injury on her body, which was facing away from the road. More bodies. More lost goods. More injured people being helped to walk along. More hurry. More fear. It was not over yet.

We kept walking. Up ahead, to our left, a body of a small boy. The sight of that body frightened me. The familiar taste of fear flooded the back of my mouth. My stomach knotted as I noticed the boy's body was completely twisted. As we got closer, peering through the sea of walking legs, I saw that the lower part of the boy – legs in shorts, and bare feet – was facing the road. But his chest, one arm, and his head were facing away from the road. As we drew level with the body, I noticed that most of the abdomen was missing. The little boy had been cut in half, with only traces of blood on the grass on the side of the road between the upper and lower parts of the body. How did that happen? But there was no time and nobody to ask. We pressed on.

CHAPTER 13
The eyes that haunted me

Up ahead, to our right, a dirt road branched off from the main Nzove dirt road. The rain had stopped, except for a few drops here and there. At that small intersection, there was another gruesome scene. Dead men lying in what looked like a circle. In the middle sat a woman. She was still alive, held upright by the bodies of dead men. Her legs, hacked off at the knees, were resting on top of a man's body in front of her. She was facing the road, the crowd walking by in front of her. Her amputated stumps were pointing towards the crowd too, revealing flesh and drying blood.

As I walked past her, I saw her eyes – very white eyes. They were the only feature distinguishable in her very dark face, which had no expression at all. Her mouth was closed. Her head was covered in the way of Rwandan women: a piece of cloth wrapped round her head, covering her hair, and knotted at the back of the neck. She looked as if she was observing the crowd from the side of the road. Occasionally, she seemed to turn her head, following a person or a group in the moving crowd with her eyes. No one paid her any attention in return; everyone was hurrying past.

I was not sure why I had slowed down when I approached, but I was not the only one. I was confused about my own feelings, but I wondered why nobody was attending to her. Why would the Inkotanyi rebels cut off her legs? Why had they killed all the men around her and left her alive? As if in slow motion, her eyes tracked back in my direction. Although I was walking right in the middle of the road and there were people passing closer to her, it seemed to me that our eyes met. My eyes fixed on hers, hers fixed on mine. I tensed up in fear. I am not sure how long that lasted. A few seconds, perhaps. As I walked past her, she slowly turned back to her left; perhaps to fix her eyes on someone else. I twisted my head over my right shoulder to keep looking at her while I walked. As I began to fall behind, I looked forward and caught up. Then as if pulled by a magnet, I looked over my right shoulder again to see the woman, but I had already lost sight of her. There were too many people moving on the road, and I had walked some distance already. The image of her bright white eyes on her expressionless dark face was stuck in my mind. What would happen to her?

Death. Death lurking everywhere. We had just left behind a city in which the Interahamwe militia had massacred thousands of people. A city in which seeing a human being killed in the street had become a normal, everyday occurrence. And soon after we left the city behind, we realised it was not a rumour that the RPF rebels, too, killed innocent civilians, including the elderly, women and children. They indiscriminately shot at a crowd. It was a reality we had just experienced in Nzove. Just how many people fell on that dirt road may never be known. And that is if anyone will ever ask.

We marched ahead, at times keeping on the road snaking between hills on both sides, like the river Nyabarongo that we spotted every now and again. At times, we took shortcuts, paths that saved us time and some distance. A few hours later, all signs of danger were behind us. No more corpses, nothing littering the road. A few injured people were being carried by their loved ones. A crowd of people of all ages, walking quickly, most with luggage on their heads, some with children struggling to keep up. But there was no sign of fatigue. It was the first day of a long walk; the first night in the open was almost upon us. We had survived a mass shooting and witnessed scenes of brutal massacre. The memories were still crystallising in my mind. But one was dominant: the woman's white eyes.

We went with the flow of the crowd. Along the way, we spotted people we knew; a former neighbour, a colleague of my mother's, an old acquaintance. It was while we climbed up the hill of Muhondo that chance intervened. Our neighbour Gabriel and members of his family were going up Muhondo at the same time. They were sitting next to the path when we caught up with them. In that moment of pause, my mother shared her concern about losing Albert. But before long, we had to move on, and joined Gabriel's group. By the time we reached the top of the hill, the sun had begun to set. The main dirt road was flanked by coffee plantations. As we offloaded our luggage on the side of the road and prepared to set up for the night, I heard a familiar voice calling my name from behind me.

'Piyo!' the voice said, in an amused tone. It was Albert! He was safe! We hugged, overjoyed to be together again. We quickly set about deciding where to sleep. Gabriel's helper was carrying a mattress, which we placed in a coffee plantation close to the road. We laid it horizontally so we could all rest our upper bodies on it. Apart from the three of us, there was Gabriel, his helper, and two adult family members. (Gabriel had sent his wife and children to Gisenyi, where he would join them.) We got a fire going and cooked. Many other families were around us, huddled near their fireplace, talking softly. There was even some laughter now and then. I hardly remember that night, but I remember everything that happened when we woke up.

Two AK-47s had been abandoned right by our sleeping space. We didn't see or hear anyone leaving them there. I had no idea where Gabriel had left his green G3. But when he saw the AK-47s, he was excited. He checked them. They were both loaded. The adults in the group discussed what would happen. The women wanted the guns to be left alone. My mother suggested that they be handed over to the next military people we came across. Gabriel insisted we should keep them.

'If we're in another ambush, we get to fight,' Gabriel said. He wasn't really consulting the rest of us. He was dominant. It seemed natural, as if it was the only role he really knew when dealing with people. He had helped to protect us during the war. When he mentioned protection, all the other adults relented.

We got ready to go. Gabriel would carry one of the guns. Who would carry the other? His relative said he knew nothing about guns. I was the next option, and was excited about it. But my mother was not enthusiastic.

'He is only a child, Gabriel. He can't carry a gun.'

'He has to learn how. Haven't you seen children with guns?' he concluded, handing it to me. I didn't hesitate. Guns fascinated me. I took the loaded magazine off, placed it in my luggage, put the strap over my shoulder, nozzle facing the ground. As we started walking, Gabriel and my mother argued silently.

But soon after we took to the road again heading north, Albert disappeared again. Was he behind? Was he ahead? I ran ahead to see if I could spot him, but I didn't. We stopped for a few minutes hoping that he had fallen back. My mother was worried but we had to keep going. At our next temporary camp for the night, Rwankuba, we found many people already set up for the night.

There, I excitedly took the gun apart, cleaned it, reassembled it, and pulled the trigger with an empty chamber a few times. My mother was visibly displeased. People walking by saw me with a gun but no one flinched. The reality was that I was a thirteen-year-old boy with no prior training on how to handle a gun. I had never shot a live round before. But I was excited to have a gun I called mine.

We settled next to the main dirt road, above which was a very steep hill, with winding paths through the trees on the tricky slope. On top of the hill, there was a high school bearing the same name: Rwankuba. The school grounds had turned into a temporary camp, and some classrooms were temporary shelters. My mother suggested that I do a tour of the camp to see if I could find Albert. I climbed the steep slope and looked everywhere, but I didn't find him. Walking back, I could see down to the site where my mother and Gabriel's group had set up camp. Not far from their site, men were struggling to kill a cow. One of them used an

AK-47, but he had to shoot the beast several times before it was down. A small crowd gathered as the animal was taken apart piece by piece. When I reached our spot, my gun was gone. My mother was very happy when she told me she had convinced Gabriel to get rid of them. She suspected that he had sold them. That night, we ate some boiled meat with potatoes.

The following day, we got back on the road, passing the major centre of Rushashi. As we continued on the dirt roads of rural Rwanda heading north, the crowd thinned out. We slept in the open once more before parting ways with Gabriel's group, which continued towards Gisenyi to join their families, while my mother decided we would go to the house of the *bourgmestre* of Ndusu near Vunga. He had been a family friend, and had maintained his friendship with my father after his release from prison.

Not long after we arrived, it was as if the *bourgmestre*, his wife and my mother had exhausted all topics of conversation. The living room was well lit and I could hear the roaring power generator somewhere on the large compound. The *bourgmestre* had briefly apologised that we had been left waiting at the gates for hours. But he showed absolutely no interest in anything else. The silence felt awkward at times. I thought he would want to know something, anything about our journey. The capture of Kigali? The deadly ambush of Nzove? The thousands marching through his commune on their way to somewhere? The years that had passed since he last saw us?

The best thing was that I got to take a wonderful hot bath. It had been a while since I'd had the chance, so I relished every moment. The next morning, I woke up to the smell of freshly baked bread. The *bourgmestre* had a bakery in his back yard. The following day, he arranged transport on the pickup truck belonging to the Ndusu Commune and we were in the city of Ruhengeri in a matter of hours. A short walk later, we were at my maternal grandmother's compound in Cyuve.

I was seven years old when I met my grandmother; it was at my grandfather's funeral. She sat in a dark corner of the volcanic stone house as mourners, in a queue that moved very slowly, came to offer their condolences. I remember wanting to see her face, but when I entered the poorly lit room, I was scared of my grandfather's body. I had never seen a dead person, and didn't understand the concept of death. At first I could only see the shape of his feet under the sheet that covered him but as I moved along in the queue to look at his face, I felt tense and scared. I was obsessed with the idea that he might suddenly wake up, like the ghosts I had seen in a Michael Jackson music video. So I hardly glanced at my grandfather's face before I rushed out.

When we returned to stay with my grandmother during the holidays, my brother and I had a great time hearing her many stories and playing and dancing with our cousins. But nothing was more mysterious than my grandmother's eternal fire in her kitchen rondavel. I never understood how that structure didn't burn down. There was flammable material everywhere: the ceiling, for example, was used as storage for dry wood and maize meal. The fireplace was in the middle, with three stones on which the pots of different sizes rested, the fire raging under them. When the cooking was finished, we sat, ate and listened to my grandmother's stories. And when it was bedtime, she would simply put a smaller stone in the hot ash in the middle of the three main stones. That was called *kuvumbika*. The following morning, all she had to do was remove the small stone from the ash, throw dry grass in its place, and blow on it a few times. The fire would be revived, first with choking smoke until the grass caught alight and there were flames, to which she would add firewood. My grandmother would do the same thing in the evening. That fire seemed eternal.

My grandmother could no longer stand straight, but she hardly used a walking stick. She never wore footwear. Despite her age, her steps were firm. I only worried about her when she needed something in the main house at night while we were in the kitchen. She would pick a short piece of wood from the fire, extinguish the flame but keep it red hot on one end. Then, holding the other end, she would shake the piece of wood rapidly, and the burning end would light her path. What worried me was that she would take it inside the house to act as a torch. I was terrified she would burn herself or that something would catch fire.

Equally memorable were the early morning gatherings before the cows set out for grazing. My grandmother often got the fire in front of her compound going and aunties and cousins joined to enjoy the warmth and tell stories. At sunrise, everyone would scatter to their chores. My favourite activity to join was herding the cows, two of which I remember well: Rukungu and Gapyisi.

Gapyisi was brown with big white patches, some on her face. She was slimmer, more agile, taller, and definitely had more personality than Rukungu, who was the oldest cow and had brought most of the herd into the world. She was brown, with darker brown colouring around her eyes and near her horns, fatter, slightly shorter, quiet and majestic in her movements. She was definitely commanding. Rukungu was the ultimate matriarch. She would only make a small gesture and the rest of the herd, including restless Gapyisi, followed. It was as if all the other cows sensed what Rukungu wanted them to do.

Visiting my grandmother's place had been a once-a-year break from the buzz of the capital city, mostly during the long July/August primary school holidays. But all that seemed like a long time ago.

This time, when my mother and I arrived at the compound, it was no holiday. The compound was almost deserted. There were more cows than humans. Most of my uncles, their wives and my cousins had already left. Although Uncle Henry's wife had gone to Zaire with her family, he had remained, along with my uncle Darius and his sons Aubrey and Erasmus, who'd been injured by the grenade in our house. They had stayed precisely because my grandmother had refused to leave without the cows.

Was she genuinely just worried about the cows? Did she think she was too old, and therefore would not get very far anyway? Was it that she didn't fully comprehend what was going on? She continued to resist, but after a few hours, my uncles finally managed to get us moving, cows with us.

My mother, two uncles, two cousins, my grandmother and I moved at the pace of the cows, on a path that meandered through isolated, mostly flat green fields. Some of the cows tried to graze as we walked, but one of my cousins would chivvy them into moving again.

Suddenly, we heard a popping sound in the distance, coming from somewhere in the various shades of green below the volcanoes. The sound was foreign to that environment and we all turned our heads to see where it was coming from. But there was nothing to see. A growing whistling sound broke the silence. I knew it was a bomb. Uncle Henry shouted: *'Mwese hasi! Mwese hasi hasi!'* – All down, all down down, as the whistling sound increased and passed over us, then dwindled away. Then just as everyone was trying to take cover on the ground, there was a loud bang a few metres from us, near a banana plantation we were approaching. I was behind a large, black volcanic rock, lying on my right side. As I looked to my left, I saw my grandmother, still trying to get down on the ground, looking to the cows as if waiting for them to do something. 'Stay down! They can see us! Leave the cows alone! Get down!' my uncle yelled at her, before leaping up and taking giant strides to reach my grandmother, who had just managed to sink to her knees. He helped her lie down, and lay down next to her.

We stayed down for about a minute; the cows scattered to the left. We had lost sight of them. Then, just as we were standing up again, a second popping sound interrupted my uncle, who was trying to tell us something. We knew it was another bomb coming. The whistling sound began almost immediately and got louder as the projectile approached. This time, it landed much closer, kicking up black, damp volcanic soil as it exploded, making a hole. The force of the explosion was fortunately dampened by the softness of the moist ground in that area.

As fragments and soil rained down on us, I realised I was not scared. Instead, I was excited, stimulated, as if I wanted this to go on. It was surreal. The *Rambo*, *Commando* and American Vietnam movies I had seen had scenes like this in them. Fantasies coming true. Now it was happening to me.

The inexplicable excitement quickly dissipated when I saw my grandmother; her tense and shaking body told a different story. Her eyes were wide open, her lips taut over her closed mouth, and her face was frozen in an invisible mask of utter terror. Her fragile body was still on the ground, leaning against a heap of earth covered by some dry grass; she was lying face down, supporting herself on her arms, palms on the ground and elbows sticking out above her back. Her brown woollen beret had fallen off, revealing her shiny, bald head, which I had never seen before (my grandmother kept her beret on almost permanently). All dignified women elders I had ever seen kept their heads covered; an exposed head was as undignified as being naked. In that moment, I felt embarrassed for my grandmother. In the very same fields where she had walked and tilled for decades, she was ducking, shaking helplessly on the ground, stripped of her dignity, with no knowledge of who was trying to kill her or why. Then I felt scared.

My uncle shouted more instructions: 'They are bombing us. They probably think we are soldiers. Stay low, move down towards where the cows went. Leave the path, and move one at a time.' We ran to the closest banana plantation, dragging our bags behind us. There were two houses in the middle of the plantation, but no sign of life. Both dwellings were locked. Uncle Henry came last, holding my grandmother up with his right arm around her waist; she could not run, so she tried to walk as fast as she could. The cows, having run into the plantation first, were huddled together standing still, as if waiting for us humans to make a decision what to do next.

A few minutes later, we reached the asphalt road: Kigali-Ruhengeri-Gisenyi. That is where we separated. Uncle Darius, his sons, my grandmother and the cows went one way, while Uncle Henry, my mother and I continued towards Gisenyi. I never understood the reason for that decision.

CHAPTER 14
Passing into a new era

The walk to Gisenyi was uneventful. We were part of a dwindling crowd. We stopped near the village of Gatagara and slept in the field on the side of the road. In that area, the fields are not tilled flat. They make large wave lines with crests on which the seeds are planted and the troughs trap and channel water, making the field look corrugated from a distance. We rested our backs against the soil heaps, with our feet in the troughs, and spent hours chatting as we struggled to fall sleep. I lay on my back, staring into the depths of the night sky, dark and stippled with so many bright stars, while Uncle Henry listened to his shortwave receiver, trying to tune in to Radio France Internationale, his favourite source of news. A woman read the news rapidly in French, announcing that the government of Zaire had ordered the borders opened to allow Rwandan refugees fleeing the RPF rebels to enter the town of Goma, and that two rockets had been fired across the border into the mass of refugees already crowding the streets of the small town, located north of Lake Kivu, killing many of them. The news also confirmed some semblance of normality in the city of Kigali, including the fact that they were already preparing to install a provisional government.

Uncle Henry sighed. Rwandans had fled across the borders as refugees and the country had been captured by rebels, both things thought completely impossible only a few months earlier. Though nobody said it, we knew that RPF rebels were advancing towards us, and that it was only a matter of time before they conquered the rest of the country. My uncle wondered if we would reach Gisenyi before they caught up with us. We woke up early and started walking; there were even fewer people on the road. When we arrived at what had been the administrative building of the commune of Mukingo, the tarred road heading to Gisenyi was flat and straight. But in the distance, it disappeared into the mist. It was eerily quiet. So quiet that my uncle felt suspicious and decided it was a bad idea to continue. He persuaded two other families that were with us to turn around – to return to Gatagara and wait. His intuition was confirmed when three armed government soldiers walked past, briefly interacted with us and decided to continue walking on the straight road to Gisenyi. Moments later, a gun fight erupted in the distance. Automatic fire from different weapons went on for a minute or two. Then it was quiet. Only one of the soldiers came back running, without his gun, removing his military uniform to reveal a grey tracksuit, with the word Suzuki on the chest.

We camped near the road in Gatagara village, and set up a fireplace for cooking. We were in front of a closed shop where a woman sat, back against the door, with a small plastic bag containing her possessions. But she was motionless. Curious, I approached her, and saw ants moving on her face, some even in one of her eyes that was not completely closed. Wondering why she was not brushing them off, I stared at her chest to see if it would rise and fall with her breath. It did not. I exclaimed: *'Uyu mudamu yapfuye!'* – This lady is dead! Who was she? How long had she been dead? Was she alone, or did her fellow travellers or family leave as soon as she died? Did she die of sheer exhaustion and hunger? So many questions in my head. My uncle, visibly disturbed, went to alert the closest group of people, and they discussed what should be done with her body.

The village of Gataraga had become a temporary stop for us and for a few other families who, like us, did not know whether we should move on towards Gisenyi and eventually Zaire, or if we should turn back and go to the capital city of Ruhengeri. Suddenly, at about 2 pm, heavily armed soldiers descended from the bush behind the shop, marching in a line that seemed to have no end. One after the other, they emerged from the clump of eucalyptus trees. Another line descended on the other side of the shop, and maintaining those parallel lines, they kept up a rapid pace as they marched down the short road that led to the tarred road. For me, it was exciting to see how different these soldiers were from the regular army. I had never seen such a uniform before; it had a much smaller camouflage pattern that was almost invisible from a short distance, so that the overall impression was of a dark green-brown dirty colour. On their feet they wore gumboots. They were heavily armed, some of them carrying AK-47s, others larger versions of the same weapon with a string of ammunition slung across their chests. Two of the soldiers were carrying short mortar launchers, and others had rocket-propelled grenades (RPGs).

Then a convoy of dark green 4x4 Mercedes Benz pickup trucks and SUVs with tinted windows flew past on the tarred road in the direction of Gisenyi. On top of the pickup truck in front was a large, mounted machine gun, a soldier holding it with both hands. Other soldiers were seated along the edge of the truck bed, facing outwards, fingers on the triggers of their guns.

My uncle, reading the situation very quickly, started calling all the people camped around us, encouraging them to move towards the tarred road to welcome the soldiers. He knew they were the RPF-Inkotanyi rebels taking over the area and moving towards Gisenyi. We all made our way to the road where more soldiers were marching in two lines, one on each side of the road. With all the onlookers on both sides of the road, we clapped continuously, forming a spontaneous guard of honour. One of the soldiers with a gun on one shoulder and a communication device in his hand stopped next to our group and looked at my uncle, who was cheering and encouraging others to cheer.

'You! You with glasses. Come here!' the soldier ordered. My uncle stepped forward, clearly worried. He looked different from the other villagers. He wore glasses and clean clothes that made him stand out. Nothing about him was rural. My mother was shaking. The soldier asked in a very harsh tone: *'Uri bourgmestre?'* – Are you the *bourgmestre*?

'No, I am not! I am just a normal citizen.'

The soldier then asked if he was the councillor in the sector. 'No! No! I am not a politician or a leader here. I am just a normal citizen, happy to see you!' my uncle replied, clearly shaken. One of the men in the crowd said loudly: 'No. He is just one of us. He is ours and he is not involved in government.' Other voices joined in agreement, almost drowning each other out with confirmations that my uncle was just a normal citizen like them. The soldier's bloodshot eyes swept across the rest of the small crowd, and then he started walking again. His comrades followed. A few minutes later, the vehicles that had just passed returned, passing us at the same high speed.

Shortly after the RPF rebel soldiers had passed through the area, we packed our belongings and began to walk back to my grandmother's place. A walk that was uneventful, until we encountered a truck full of soldiers coming towards us, labouring up an incline. The soldiers were chanting victory songs. Some, clearly enjoying the moment, shouted at us: 'Yoh! Do you need a lift to Gisenyi?' They were not threatening. But as we reached Musanze, approaching the city of Ruhengeri, we came upon another group of soldiers. Most were standing, one was lying belly down on the dry, grassy bank of the stormwater drain next to the road. Without sitting up, he talked to my uncle, wanting to know how old my mother was.

'She is 40. This is her son,' he said, quickly pointing at me.

'Leave her with us,' the soldier suggested. I was terrified. They could really do anything, and we would not have any help. My uncle turned around and looked at me. Then he started bargaining with the soldier, while his comrades listened in without reaction. My mother was wearing a green tracksuit around which she had wrapped an African fabric. Her eyes were open wider than usual, white, without blinking. It was tense.

'If you don't leave her, what will you leave?' the soldier eventually asked. My uncle rapidly replied, as if he had been expecting that question.

'My watch? It is a Seiko. I bought it in Germany,' he said. The soldier extended his hand, so my uncle took off his watch and gave it to him. They let us go. When we left the tarred road, another soldier hailed us from a distance. My uncle decided we should not stop. Instead, we ran off the road into the bush. It was already dark, but we kept running, calling each other softly to make sure we were still together. When we could not see much on the path, we stopped running but kept walking fast. We arrived at my grandmother's breathless. There we found members of the extended family who had come to seek shelter, but had found no one on the compound.

The following morning, the sun shone on us in a new country, a new era. On radio, we kept hearing news of more victories for the RPF rebels that were becoming the regular army of a government that was yet to be formed. The former army and government had fled into what was then Zaire. My little sister and brother, many of our cousins, uncles, aunts and family friends were among those who had managed to cross the border with them. A few days later, my uncle set a date for our return to Kigali, and my mother and I got ready for the long walk. Again.

Since we'd arrived at my grandmother's compound, those who had not managed to get to Gisenyi and cross the border had trickled back to the family home, including my grandmother, my uncle Darius, and a few cousins – and the cows. Uncle Henry listened to the news every morning to catch up on what was happening. A new government was in place that included Col. Kanyarengwe as deputy prime minister and minister of the interior, in addition to being the chairman of the RPF. Uncle Henry and my mother hoped that he would at least protect us if the new army or the new government we still feared were to be hostile in any way, as long as we could reach Kigali and let him know of our existence.

We didn't wake up early to start our long journey that day. It was a sunny morning. We took a little time to say goodbye to the rest of the family before we set off. We took only what we would need, some clothes and food, and set off at a moderate pace, knowing it was going to be a long walk (Cyuve to Kigali by road is some 100 kilometres).

It was still strange for me to see my uncle walking such a long distance – a man I regarded as wealthy, and who had his own car. He did not complain or swear. In fact, he and my mother exchanged jokes along the road, with long stretches of silence between in which all we heard was our own breath and footsteps on the deserted road, the wind sometimes whispering past our ears, and birds chirping from shrubs on the verges. It was discouraging to round bend after bend and look ahead to see yet another bend hundreds of metres ahead. The passage of time seemed inconsequential. We would stop wherever we came to at night, and sleep as best we could. Uncle Henry hoped our first stop would be at Gakenke village. Soon enough we were climbing the mountain passes toward the summit of Buranga. From there the views of distant hills and valleys of varying shades of green, almost blue as they receded into the distance, were spectacular. Several other elevated points on that Ruhengeri-Kigali road offered similar panoramic scenes. Without the fear of gunfire, we could at least appreciate the scenery.

But reminders of death were never far away. Occasionally as we walked, we were overwhelmed by a stench coming from a bush to the side of the road, an odour I had come to recognise: decomposing human flesh. Sometimes the body was not far from the road and we could see and hear the buzzing flies and carrion birds. Sometimes, the blackened shapes of legs and arms shattered the hope that it may not be a person. When we got beyond the nauseating smell, we would pointlessly debate how the person had died.

The sun had already set when we reached Nyirangarama, a village about 45 kilometres from Kigali that was famous for sheep soup and meat with *mandazi*, making it a favourite stop-off point for travellers between the capital city and Ruhengeri. Even then, under these strange circumstances, it was lively. Families dotted along the side of the road were cooking and enjoying the fire outside, in what looked like a temporary camp site, like so many we had seen in the preceding few weeks. There was a sprinkling of soldiers, and at least one shop and a bar were open. We walked slowly, looking for a spot to stop and rest. My uncle entered one of the shops, and came out moments later to signal that we should enter. Along the walls were small benches, one of them empty. The others were occupied by two civilians and three soldiers in uniform, AK-47s resting between their legs. It was a tight squeeze. The small room had barely enough space for the shop's counter and one bench, let alone several.

One of the civilians was a light-skinned young man who was extremely talkative, but no one seemed annoyed by him. The soldiers talked to us a little, and asked questions politely. They passed beer to my uncle, and then to my mother, but she refused, asking for a cup of water instead. They asked my uncle what he had been doing before the war, what he hoped to find when he got home, and what he thought of the new government. He answered candidly and slowly, obviously being careful with his choice of words. Then their attention turned to my mother.

'How old are you?' asked one of the soldiers.

'I am forty. This is my son, soon to be fourteen.'

'Where is his father if this man is your brother?'

'I was married to the *bourgmestre* of Gatonde, where Col. Kanyarengwe comes from,' answered my mother, hesitantly. She had to mention Kanyarengwe. It was our power name.

'Gatonde? Do you mean you were married to Bourgmestre Kabalira?' asked one of the soldiers, 'Eustache Kabalira?' he added, looking surprised.

'Yes. You knew him?' my mother asked. 'Unfortunately, he died.'

'Yes! I know he died. Everyone knew him. I was young, and I knew you too; my parents spoke of you a lot.'

'Who are your parents?' my mother asked.

I was amused by the coincidence: my mother had known them

in the late seventies and early eighties, as they had often visited Mukankindi when they were neighbours in rural Gatonde. The soldier said that his parents, who were fed up with the side-lining and oppression of the people of Gatonde because of their association with Col. Kayarengwe, had decided to send him and his brother to the RPF, hoping that if they won, things would change. His brother had been killed in battle, and both his parents had died before the RPF took over the country.

The conversation continued until one of the soldiers decided it was time to go. They invited us to be their guests. We left the village behind and walked along the tarred road, our steps lit by a small torch, under a clear but indigo-dark sky with very bright stars. The talkative young civilian walked with the soldiers as if he was one of them; surprisingly, he was bragging to us about the cows, meat, milk, rice, tea and other goods that the soldiers had at their base, as if they were his own.

As we walked, I overheard my mother telling the soldier whose parents she had known that she was HIV/Aids positive. Hearing that made my heart sink; the soldier could only have been making unwanted advances. Most of the walk was silent, though, as a sense of tension and anxiety started to overshadow the relief brought by the offer to host us, as well as the discovery of a soldier my mother would have been justified in considering a protector in our circumstances.

Minutes later, we arrived at what was the Nyirangarama primary school, much of it deserted. A few classrooms had been turned into dormitories for the soldiers. In the front yard of the main school block, they had built a fireplace for cooking. I could hear cows shifting around and mooing, but I couldn't tell how many there were. Nor could we tell how many soldiers were on the base.

We shared a silent meal by the fire. While I was wondering where we were going to sleep, the civilian man stood up to leave, and offered to take me with him. I refused, but my uncle insisted, whispering in my ear: 'Go, we will be fine, go. If we are not, at least you will be.' I silently picked up my bag of stuff and followed the young man, who talked all the way up the hill and through the fields.

I was not focused on what he was saying. I was worried, imagining all sorts of scenarios, the worst being that my mother and my uncle might be hurt or even killed. I kept hearing my mother's soft voice in my mind, clearly struggling to convince the soldier that she was dangerously infected with HIV, triggering the worst fears of what could happen to her. My uncle too, I imagined, would die fighting them. But he had insisted that I go with the young man who wouldn't stop talking, in what I understood to be an attempt to save me if anything went wrong.

Our arrival at the young man's home, meeting his old mother, and everything else we did or said before going to sleep left little impression on me, as my fear took over. I didn't close my eyes, even in the dark, waiting for the sound of a gunshot from the valley.

But no gun was fired. When I woke up, I didn't know how long I had stayed awake. It felt as if I had slept for only a few seconds. I heard birds singing; it took me a few moments to remember where I was. As soon as the recollection of the night surfaced, I sprang up, demanding to go immediately. The young man took a few minutes to wake up and wash his face, before he walked me down to the valley. My steps felt heavy and the walk too long as we approached the school blocks, surrounded by the green bush gone wild all around.

When we arrived, all seemed quiet. My mother, calm, quiet and collected, seemed only to be affected by the morning chill, like the few soldiers who were up and about. She asked me if I had slept well, and I almost laughed at myself for stressing too much – but I didn't. It seemed so peaceful that I never brought myself to ask any questions about what had happened that night. I was just glad my uncle and my mother were alive.

Now we could see what the base was like. The school playground had become grazing for many cows (my uncle kept wondering where they were from). Our meal the previous night had been meat, and it would be meat again for breakfast. One of the soldiers tore open some tea bags and poured the contents into milk boiling on the fire in a large pot supported by three stones. My uncle asked him for another tea bag. 'You should not tear these up,' he said. 'This string allows you to put the tea bag inside the pot or cup and pull it out as you wish, but the little package is designed to keep the water clear of tea leaves,' my uncle explained in Kinyarwanda, as a few soldiers watched attentively.

'Oh,' one of the watching soldiers said. 'So we have been doing it wrong all along!'

'I made the same mistake in the beginning too,' my uncle said, humbly, in a submissive voice, so as not to offend. 'We all learn something every day,' he concluded. I was surprised the soldiers didn't know how to use tea bags, wondering where they had got them in the first place.

A few minutes later, the soldiers packed up some cooked meat for us, and two of them, including the one whose parents knew my mother, walked with us a few hundred metres along the tarred road, before they wished us a safe journey and returned to their base.

We spent one more night in an abandoned house in Shyorongi, a few kilometres outside Kigali. The city had fallen to the Inkotanyi rebels on July 4, the day after we had joined the mass exodus, not knowing if we would return. As I settled down for what I assumed would be our last night on the road, I reflected on the distance we'd walked – about 235 kilometres – and on what we had seen and survived. But there was no way of anticipating what awaited us when we got home.

PART 4
NEW RWANDA

CHAPTER 15
Hustling to survive

Shortly before 11 o'clock the next day, some three weeks after we'd locked it behind us, we stood again at the metal back door of our house. It had been forced open. But that was not as shocking as the words, written with white chalk: *iyi nzu yarafashwe* – this house has been taken.

My mother stood still, staring at the writing. It was just above a hole in the bottom half of the door, which had evidently been forced open with a very heavy object. With one hand on her hip, standing in the midst of scattered family photos and papers that made the back yard look like a dump site, she ran her hand through her thick hair, and then put her hand to her mouth, staring without blinking. That image of my mother remains imprinted in my memory, probably forever. Then we pushed the broken door hard, and took our first steps into our house – our house that someone else had claimed as their own.

When the RPF took over the country, many Rwandans who had been refugees in Burundi and Uganda came with them. As most residents of Kigali had fled, the new rulers allowed the repatriated population to take over people's land and properties. Most houses had that writing on them, even though they were still empty. Someone would come, search for a house, mark it, and then go back to fetch family and possessions before taking occupation.

Fortunately, we arrived the day before our house was occupied. When the Burundian man who had written on the house showed up, it took him some time to understand what my mother meant by the words 'I own the property'.

'But we came before you,' the man said in Kirundi, sounding agitated.

'No. What I am saying,' my mother said patiently, 'is that we lived here for several years. This is actually my family property.' With the words, she used gestures to get the message across. Finally, the man understood, and looked despondent. Typical of her generous nature, my mother offered for him and his family to stay in one of our annexes. He indicated that he would try to find another house and if he didn't, he would come back and take up my mother's offer.

That was not the last time someone claimed our property. Shortly after, I was home alone when someone opened the window of the house in front of us – Eric's family home. A military officer with one yellow square on each of his shoulder boards appeared at the window where Eric used to chat to me. As he gestured for me to approach the window, I felt nervous. I had never been that close to an army officer in the new Rwanda.

'Why are you here? he asked, as if convinced I shouldn't be.

'This is our home,' I said.

'No. That is my house, he said assuredly. Then, with a little more menace, he asked if there was an adult at home. I replied that my mother was not home.

'When she comes, tell her to come and see me.' I nodded. When I told my mother, she laughed nervously before going. It turned out the lieutenant was trying to help his family, who were about to arrive from Uganda. His search would continue.

Remarkably, three days after we got home, our dog Bobby showed up. I don't know how he survived with all that happened in the city during our absence. But it was comforting to have something familiar with us, especially as everything, even the sound of our neighbourhood, was different. Rwandans who returned from Burundi spoke Kirundi. Those who returned from Uganda spoke Rukiga and Runyankore – languages of the south of Uganda. In the surrounding houses, there were too few of those who'd been there before the war had reached Kigali. With no school, there were no learners around. There were also no vendors in the streets, and people walking to town were few and far between. My mother responded to the call from the new authorities for public servants to go back to work. But there wasn't much work to be done.

Having discussed with my mother what it might mean for our family that Col. Kanyarengwe was now in a leadership position, my uncle got in touch with him and the colonel gave him a hand-written piece of paper with an instruction that gave him access to his old business office to salvage whatever was left of it. It had been looted and all he got out of there was one box of papers. When he came home, he made fun of it.

'Look what is left of my business. Just a few pieces of paper!' he quipped, telling us how the menacing soldiers blocking access to the business park in the city centre had looked at each other in surprise when they read the short note from *Raisi wa Kwanza*, loosely translated as 'the boss'. The soldiers stepped aside and let Uncle Henry search through the ruins of what had been his office. My uncle remarked that on paper, Kanyarengwe was powerful. In reality, it seemed that former rebel soldiers, who were now the military, were running the show.

When my mother eventually gathered the courage to visit Kanyarengwe's family at his residence in Kiyovu, an upmarket neighbourhood of Kigali, I was very excited. The whole time she was gone, I imagined what their conversation would be about. Would she talk about what happened to my father after Kanyarengwe had fled the country? Would he reassure her that he would protect us? When my mother came back, she brought a bag full of green avocados. There had been nothing substantial in their conversation. I was disappointed, realising that knowing Kanyarengwe would probably not change our reality. We, too, continued to depend on food donations.

Nigire was the first-born of one of our new neighbours, a friendly family. His mother Fiona, his sister Clarisse and little brother Alain lived in the house next door. His father had been killed during the genocide and buried in a shallow grave they later found. Nigire was very familiar with the new RPF army because his family had many friends who were officers. One of the soldiers often stayed with them, and when he smoked his cannabis joints, we could smell it from inside our own house. It was the first person I ever saw smoking cannabis, and I was fascinated by how his veins swelled and eyes turned red when he forcefully inhaled the smoke and held his breath for a few seconds.

Nigire taught me the language of the army, and the meaning of some of the words used, such as *afande* (superior) and 2IC (second in command), as well as some of the dynamics of the new army. Like how an officer's bodyguards will disappear into the background when his superior comes, because the superior officer's bodyguards take over protection. He often told me about his own reasons for not joining the army, but he had spent much time and many nights in barracks; as one of them, he was allowed to go anywhere and everywhere. His family spoke Congolese Swahili well, and Swahili was the language mostly used in the new army.

There were no schools open, and no children's street games. Most children from the old neighbourhood were displaced or were refugees; some were probably dead. Nigire and I would go together to collect relief food from Caritas at the Sainte Famille Catholic Church, until one day, something happened to change it all.

That day, it was chaos at the Caritas office. Before joining the queue, we had all registered our parents' names and how many people we were collecting for (you got five scoops of USAID-branded grains – a combination of oats, lentils and maize meal – per person). Since my proud uncle had been adamant that I should not count him in for food donations, I collected only for my mother and me. (My brother, sister and cousins were still in refugee camps in Zaire. At least, we hoped they were there, alive and well.)

But the Caritas staff were struggling to maintain order. People pushed and jostled to be in the front of the queue, driven by the fear that there would not be enough for everyone. The supervisor decided to stop the distribution until some order returned. I was in front of Nigire in the line. When I reached the front of the queue, I was ready for the staff, who all used identical large bowls, to drop food in my bag. My turn came. The woman dished out once. Twice. As she reached in for a third scoop, a strong female voice objected.

'No. Don't serve that one. *Ntabwo ari abarokotse.*' – They are not survivors.

I looked up, bewildered. It was the supervisor who was instructing staff not to serve me. I didn't know what to say, and everyone around went quiet, as if waiting to see what would happen. The lady serving me stopped dishing up and looked at her supervisor hesitantly. 'I said: don't give the food to that family. His mother is not a survivor,' she insisted, speaking slowly and loudly as if to underline her words. The staff member froze, and then asked me to move aside so she could serve Nigire, who was next in line. I was speechless, embarrassed and a bit tearful. In shock, I moved aside with the little quantity of grains she had already put in my bag, my mind racing with questions. I didn't even know that particular food aid station was exclusive to a certain group of people and not others. Survivors.

My mother is not a survivor? After all she was put through? No. She wasn't. The fact was that all I got as food donation was two scoops to take home, because the Tutsi supervisor decided that my Hutu mother was not a survivor. But how did that woman recognise me in the first place? Who was she? How did she know my mother?

I just wanted to leave that place as soon as I could; I could feel the eyes of people on me as I waited for Nigire. His bag was filled to the brim because he was collecting for everyone in his family. We started walking home, talking about what had just happened and debating the politics of 'survivors'. He was very upset, more perceptibly so than I was.

'Everybody has a stomach, everyone in this country suffered, and everyone has to eat. How can they do that?' he asked indignantly. Before we arrived home, Nigire insisted on giving me some of the oats he had in his full bag, all the while saying how sorry he was. It was not his fault, but he kept saying he was sorry. He insisted that I go with him on the next food collection date. He said he would add two people to his family tally, making sure that he collected for us too. When I told my mother about it, and described the supervisor, she said the woman was a former colleague, and that she had probably recognised the names I had put on the list.

Soon after, Octave, who was back in Kigali, came to visit; he had not managed to get to Zaire. He explained that he hadn't come back for us because his car had broken down. Now his small hatchback was an asset: on the door was a World Vision logo. Having a vehicle was a sure income because the many NGOs that arrived in the aftermath of the genocide needed cars and drivers. Octave was one of those lucky ones to earn in US dollars. When he visited, he left me RWF2 000.

I used the money to buy sweets and cigarettes, and became one of the first street vendors to sell at La Fraicheur after the war. My box was small and mostly empty, with a few packets of cigarettes and only one packet of sweets. Compared to cigarette and sweets vendors of before, whose boxes had been overloaded with different varieties of chewing gum, sweets, cigarettes and other small items, mine was tiny. But it was a beginning. A day later, one of the big box vendors joined me, and we set up our respective boxes on opposite sides of the road. It was while I was a street vendor that I started hearing of people going to school. But that surely had to wait. I was my family's breadwinner, and I was determined never to go back to queue for donation rations. The humiliation haunted me. Even at fourteen, I knew we were on our own. And I was determined that we would make it.

After our return to Kigali, positive news about our family lifted my spirits, and relieved my mother's continuous worry. When Albert had got separated from us in the throng on the road, he had followed the crowd to Gisenyi where, by chance, he had spotted his elder half-brother and was then reunited with the rest of his family. His father, my mother's brother Silvain, had led them across the border to Goma in Zaire, but just a few weeks later, instead of going further into the big refugee camps (which were later destroyed), he decided to return to Gisenyi, bringing my brother and sister with them.

We were elated to hear that they were at my grandmother's compound, so I walked back to Ruhengeri to fetch them. It was around 100 kilometres, so after a full day's walk I slept a few metres off the side of the road and set off again at daybreak, reaching Ruhengeri in the evening. I was so used to sleeping in the open that it didn't scare me anymore, and when we needed to get my brother and sister home, I didn't think twice about walking to fetch them. At the time, my brother was still twelve, my sister just six years old, and my cousin, ten. My plan was for us to walk home to Kigali and we had already set off when a soldier at the roadblock exiting Ruhengeri stopped us. He seemed shocked that I was going to walk so far with the children and ordered the driver of a big passenger bus to give us a lift.

When we got home, I heard more talk of schools opening, but aside from actually going there, I had no way of getting any information about my school, *Groupe Scolaire Officiel de Butare*. Besides, it was still far from my immediate focus: providing for the family. I gave my brother the box of sweets and cigarettes to keep selling, while I moved on to another challenge: making fried flour cakes. That meant I had to roam the city selling, instead of staying in one place. I went to major markets in Kigali that were opening up and soon made enough money to buy myself a bicycle. I found and bought one at a bargain. An old lady was disposing of the loot her son had left behind with her. She didn't know if he was in Zaire, or even if he was alive. They had been separated, and she had returned home.

My brand-new BMX bicycle had shiny, metallic handlebars with white plastic handle covers on each side, a bright silver frame boldly marked BMX, a red plastic seat at just the right height for me, white peddles and strong, light, reinforced white rims encircled with deflated red rubber tyres bearing a small brand name in white. The bicycle was the most precious possession I had ever had. It looked even prettier once I had inflated the tyres, and there could be no smoother bicycle ride than on my BMX. Other children rented it, so it made money for me too. Bought at fourteen thousand Rwandan Francs, it made me one thousand a day. In one week, I had saved half of what I had paid for it. But then disaster struck: exactly a week after I got it, a truck ran over my bicycle. Fortunately, the boy who had hired it for half an hour survived the hit and run. He was sure it was a 1621 Mercedes Benz army truck. I remember staring at my bicycle, other boys standing next to me, feeling nauseous with disappointment. I didn't know what to do or where to look. The bicycle represented a lot: from the past, the fulfilment of my father's promise; for the future, the potential it created; and the present, my pride. All crushed. I collected the scraps, salvaged what I could, bought some parts and put together another bicycle. But it was never the same.

I didn't want to go back to selling *mandazi*. They were labour intensive and walking all over town was extremely tiring. My cigarette business was no more. My brother had started smoking and had already smoked it away. I decided to do something else: thanks to a passing remark during a random conversation with a family friend, my mother and I jumped on an idea. My uncle supported it and I started another business.

It was becoming more common to see high school students around. Some schools were already opening, despite being out of phase with the normal school rhythm. But I still had to put bread on the table, so I made peace with abandoning school and focusing on my new business. The business was simple: I would go to rural community markets to buy fresh fruit and free-range chickens, and bring them to the capital to sell. I sold fruit in bulk and supplied chickens to restaurants. Sometimes, I left the fruit with my mother to sell while I set off for the next rural market for more. But although it was profitable, it brought about another major challenge: travel.

There were still military checkpoints all over. Every few kilometres, minibus taxis or pickup trucks I travelled on were searched, and passengers had to present identity cards. But I was too young to have an identity document. I was, however, too grown to be unnoticed while travelling alone. As schools were opening, the most common question I got from soldiers was why I was not going to school. If I were to pass as a student, I had to show a student card, which I didn't have. Also, because of the regularity of the weekly community markets, I had to pass through the same checkpoint several times a week, which meant I often encountered the same soldiers.

In partnership with my mother, I was managing to support the family, and I had found something that worked. When I shared my predicament, a friend advised me to register at an unremarkable school just to get the student card. I registered at Groupe Scolaire ADB (Association des Anciens de Don Bosco), a technical school, hoping to get a card and never return. Of course at roadblocks I would have to invent reasons for why I was not at school, but at least I would have a paper to show. Only, there was a problem: a delay at the school in issuing cards forced me to pretend to be a bona fide student for longer than I had anticipated.

Since I had been in the first year of high school before the genocide, I went back to first year, joining during the second semester. I enrolled in electronics – a class of about fifty boys and one girl. Some of the boys teased me frequently, making fun of the way I dressed. I had no sense of fashion, and I wore what I thought practical for my trips. Also a target of ridicule was my made-up bicycle, and arriving at school sweaty after a ride of several kilometres did not go unnoticed. Tired of the bullying, I decided to change to a class with fewer students. Second year *biochimie*. To my surprise, when I told the headmaster that my parents wished me to be in biochemistry and showed him reports of my first two semesters at GSOB, he agreed to the change. The class had just one boy and six girls.

Morning breaks were odd for me; I could not relate to any of the children. Many of them spoke Kirundi (from Burundi) and Lingala (from Zaire), and some spoke perfect French as a mother tongue. During the breaks, boys paged through *5 Majeurs*, a basketball magazine about NBA stars, and their conversations were all about Michael Jordan, Magic Johnson and Dikembe Mutombo. Pull-out posters of those superstars exchanged hands. Some of the boys from wealthy families wore FILA sneakers and wore their pants low on their hips so they hung down, baggy between their legs. The school's basketball court was not paved and just had a panel with a ring and no net. But it was the only activity in which I found myself comfortable. While I waited for my card, our French teacher often singled me out. She was the first to suspect I didn't really fit in, and she managed to get me to reveal that I wasn't there to stay. She encouraged me to change my mind. Soon after, the mathematics teacher told me I was brilliant. I enjoyed both subjects.

At home, a brief family meeting settled it all. Public servants, such as my mother, were starting to be paid in cash, not only food donations. My uncle had sold a house, and got a new job in a major corporation. He had just arrived to visit when we talked about it and the whole issue was concluded before he even sat down: I would stop worrying about feeding the family, and focus on school. My uncle would pay the school fees.

CHAPTER 16
Simmering stereotypes

My sister's favourite food was potato fries. We had them on special occasions, especially when we had visitors. She would insist on having them plain and without anything else. One Sunday, we had visitors for lunch; it was a feast. But uncharacteristically, my sister was eating without enthusiasm.

She tried to whisper in my mother's ear, but she rebuked her, saying: 'I taught you that if you can't say what you need to in front of people, you must wait until we are alone.' My sister, who had hardly touched her little plate of chips, continued to eat, but slowly. Then, moments later, she said loudly and firmly: 'I don't want to eat sharing with a Hutu.' Her words tumbled out, as if she wanted to finish saying them as soon as possible. Everyone froze for a moment, and the silence was only broken by my mom, shocked, inquisitive, asking: *'Ngo iki?'* – What?

My sister repeated the words, but this time, she added a name: 'I don't want to eat sharing with a Hutu, Nigire.'

Nigire, who I was beginning to call a friend, was one of our visitors that day. I looked at him, unsure what to do. He had a completely defeated look. My little sister had mistakenly called Nigire a Hutu, but it was the action of refusing to eat with him that was more shocking. As if sensing that everyone present needed an explanation, she gave details behind her decision. She told the story, hardly pausing to breathe.

'We were eating at their home, then *he* came, then he said he won't share with us because he doesn't want to share with *gipinga*, then Clarisse asked him why he eats at the Gashumbas knowing that they are Hutus, then he said that the Gashumbas are not Hutu, then Clarisse said that yes they are Hutu, and then Nigire said it doesn't matter he made his decision he will not eat from the same plate as a *gipinga*, then he went and dished out his own food on another plate. So me too, I will not continue eating with a Hutu.'

I was shocked. Nigire was my friend. We had met before I brought my sister back to Kigali. He had witnessed me being humiliated because I was not a 'survivor', and had expressed shock. So what had happened that day that he would do such a thing to my little sister? Everyone around the table, except my sister herself, knew what she meant to say. She was using words she'd heard during the incident at Nigire's home, with no understanding of what they meant. *Igipinga* is in fact a veiled reference to Hutus in the new Rwanda, meaning *opponent* in Swahili. Whereas Tutsis were known as *abarokotse* (survivors).

A few long seconds passed. Nigire sat frozen, saying nothing. My mother finally stepped in. 'No my child. You see, he is here, sharing with us. People change. He is a good child. You too can forgive him. Not so?'

My sister said nothing, as if pondering what my mother had said, lips pouted. She could sense the seriousness of the moment. She nodded slowly, planted her spoon in her little plate and started eating again. As if following my little sister's queue, everyone resumed the meal.

When we had finished eating, I went to my room, and Nigire followed me. 'Yoooo! I am so glad she got it all wrong, because I now respect your family even more. In my family, all the children know exactly who is what by the time they are four! For your sister, who is almost seven, to mix things up and call me a Hutu, that says a lot about your family. You don't really teach your children who to hate,' he added. I still didn't know what to say. I was aware that my sister's lack of awareness on ethnic identities was much more likely to be seen as naivety and

162

stupidity on our family's part. But that was my mother's choice.

Nigire went on: 'I feel so exposed now. Please present my apology to her? I feel even more embarrassed to ask your sister for forgiveness,' he added, closing his eyes as if seeing a picture in his head.

'Well, it is not necessary,' I said. 'You heard what Mama said, and I will talk to her later as well.' I felt a greater sense of closeness to Nigire through that conversation. This incident seemed to have broken down something between us. Some barrier was removed. The unspoken had been expressed, the ethnic wall destroyed. He opened his eyes, looked me straight in the eye, and we spontaneously locked right hands, and pulled each other into a brotherly embrace. We pressed our shoulders on each other, while patting each other on the back. We were friends.

I could tell that Nigire's comments were genuine. So much so that on a separate occasion, he stood up to his family. That day, he was having a squabble with his sister over soft drinks when Mama Kiki, a close family friend of theirs, entered the room, speaking loudly to their mother who was behind her: 'Yooo, Fiona! Fiona, what has happened to your children? They have become like Hutus! You stupid children, only Hutus squabble with each other like this. Has someone bewitched you to become Hutus?' she continued, before noticing that I was in Nigire's room, where it was all happening. The belief is that everything beautiful, dignified, orderly, wise and worthy is Tutsi. Ugly, rowdy, naive, unworthy . . . that is Hutu.

Nigire's squabble with his sister ended immediately. When Mama Kiki saw me, she cut her sentence midway and froze for a moment, before turning and walking out. As if my presence had forced them all to listen to Nigire, they kept quiet as he told them he was discovering that Hutus were not what they had taught him. His views were the complete opposite of what they would have hoped. His mother had a defeated look, clearly taken aback by Nigire's views. But she did not contradict him.

I had joined second year biochemistry in the second semester. At the end of the term, I was top of the class. To come first in high school for the first time should have been such a satisfying feeling, but long before we wrote exams I could see that I would achieve it: I had been getting the best marks for homework and tests. Despite the addition of Nick, a new classmate, the class was small and there was little competition to speak of. So when the French-speaking classmates started talking about a new school that was about to open, it caught my attention. It would be the high school section of an existing primary school that already had a very good reputation.

Children of the rich and powerful in our new country were at La Colombière. My classmates spoke of plans for tennis courts and a swimming pool, technology and other perks usually found exclusively at the prestigious Belgian or French schools reserved for expatriates and the select few who could afford them. My classmates could hardly string together a sentence in Kinyarwanda: for all practical purposes, La Colombière is where they belonged. As for me, it was out of my league.

When we reopened for the third term, my classmates were gone. Shortly after, Nick also left. One day after school, I cycled to the mighty La Colombière to see it for myself. As the primary school learners were leaving, it was chaos outside the gates. They were all wearing blue shirts and red ties, and the girls had darker blue skirts and the boys, shorts. Their parents or guardians waited in all kinds of luxury vehicles. When the high school learners started coming out, I spotted some of my old classmates. But it was Nick who saw me and approached for a warm greeting. He told me a little about the school, and about the learners. He pointed out the children of Paul Kagame – then vice president and minister of defence – and their bodyguards. This was definitely a school for the who's who. But Nick, in his usual nonchalant tone invited me: 'Come on man! You are a genius! They will love you here!'

I was flattered, but I thought the fact that my La Colombière peers did not have a uniform was bizzare, and it attracted more of my attention than what Nick was saying. However, he had planted a seed. When I flighted the idea of going to La Colombière, my mother responded with a loud no. My uncle also disapproved.

'This is a school for Kagame's children and all the powerful people. They only speak English and French. How do you think you will cope with that? Even if you do well in class, don't you think it will be difficult for you to fit in? Plus, it must be extremely expensive,' my uncle said, with the approving nod of my mother. It was a 'no' from them. But the following day, I went to see the headmaster at La Colombière. I will never know if it was because he was awestruck that a 'local kid' dared to approach him, but he was overjoyed at my request to join the school.

'We welcome great students here. Bring your school report, we will see!' he said. No procedures. No security background checks. No questions about my family. Just my school report.

A day later, I was a La Colombière student in the French section, and I had jumped yet another year to third, the highest grade at the time. As a new school, they had decided to start with only three of six high school grades. I would be part of the pioneers of the school for another three years to come.

My mother and my uncle knew nothing about my attendance at the school. I used savings I had kept from my business to register and buy the basics. I went to the feared school for two weeks before I revealed it to them. Then I wrote a five-page letter to my uncle in French, explaining that my primary motivation was self-expansion and a decent challenge. 'What good is it for me to start a year knowing I will finish first in the class? If they only speak French, I will learn. But I will be competing with the best,' I wrote. The letter was enough to get his nod. After all, he was going to be the one paying for school fees, which were just twenty per cent more than at ADB. He agreed it was worth it.

Once in the school, I dropped the use of my bicycle in favour of public transport, because it was much further away. As we had no uniform yet, I had to invest in new clothes. Only a handful of us had grown up in Rwanda; everyone else was speaking Kinyarwanda, or learning it for the first time. We had no sports facilities and there were no plans to build on that site.

While the La Colombière primary school looked like a set of actual classrooms, the high school looked makeshift; it was housed in a warehouse that would not have passed the minimum of any enforceable standards for a high school. But then again, this was war-ravaged Rwanda just after the genocide. Priorities were different. Or someone was just well connected.

The prestige of La Colombière was not in buildings and facilities – it lay in who attended the school and who their parents were. The learners could mingle with their peers who spoke mostly French or English, and achieve academic progress without needing to speak Kinyarwanda. La Colombière was necessary to the new elite of Rwanda, whose secluded universe needed a school of its own. Somehow, I had slipped into that universe.

From having lacked meaningful competition at ADB, I was placed twenty-eighth of fifty learners when I finished term one. But by the time we completed the year, I was eighth overall. Soon, a uniform was introduced: we became the first private school to have a uniform that differed from the ubiquitous khaki and blue. We wore dark blue trousers or skirts, and white shirts with stripes. The school introduced ties in high school, the first in the country. When I started fourth year, the high school was separated from the primary school. We occupied a vacant property that had once been the home of an education institute, sharing it with the national brass band. They took time to teach us the national anthem – most of the learners had grown up outside Rwanda – and helped us raise the flag at school assembly. I was chosen to lead the singing, while another learner would raise the flag. Occasionally, we swopped roles.

La Colombière was a different world from my reality at home. Not only because no one at school knew my home circumstances, but because each trip to school was a trip to another social class, another way of life, and another language. Some of my schoolmates, including in my own class, were children of cabinet ministers.

At home, it was a densely populated township where people turned in surprise to look at me wearing a tie. In the house, we had welcomed a cousin and a child of a family friend. But it was less crowded than just before the war. The biggest trouble was my mother's health. She suffered from anaemia, and needed transfusions a few times a year. One day, I walked her to the emergency section of the CHK hospital. When she came out, she was being pushed in a wheelchair, doctors convinced she could collapse anytime. After the transfusion, she had a bad reaction: parts of her face swelled up so badly that it was hard to recognise her. While in hospital, she enjoyed food I cooked, once claiming that she could recognise my cooking by the aroma. It made me proud. At school, I still had no friend close enough to share my struggles with.

Despite her health issues, when my uncle Silvain passed away, my mother welcomed all five of his children to come and live with us. The twins, Albert and Albertina, were teenagers like me, the two girls a little younger and the last-born boy, a year older than my sister. They were all in school, except Albertina, who found a job.

As La Colombière had no sports facilities of its own, I played sport in our neighbourhood. Basketball was my favourite. But my memory of going to play basketball was tainted by a traumatising event. Alone on a dirt road leading to Caisse Sociale where there was a popular basketball court, I met three uniformed soldiers as I jogged to a game, occasionally bouncing my ball and catching it. The soldiers stopped me. There was not a soul in sight.

'Where are you coming from?' one of them of them asked, looking me in the eyes and moving uncomfortably close to my face. 'Where are you going?' he asked, in a more menacing tone.

'I am going to play at Caisse Sociale,' I said, pointing in the direction of the court that was not yet in view, although we could all hear the sound of balls bouncing on the concrete court, and players calling each other. Because I was feeling anxious, my ball fell from my hand and rolled away. As I tried to retrieve it, the soldier who had asked the questions stopped me. My stomach knotted. He pushed me towards one of his comrades, who pushed me back.

The two soldiers moved closer. One of them put his hand across my face, grabbed my nose and shook my head hard.

'I hate your ugly nose! You Hutus are so ugly. Look at this nose!' he exclaimed. The other soldier approached, grabbed my arm and shook hard.

'Wishe abatutsi bangahe wa nterahamwe we?' – How many Tutsis did you kill, you Nterahamwe? I didn't reply. I was defenceless. I tried hard to remain calm. Then he pushed me hard and I fell on my back. A car turned the corner and came towards us, but it was still a distance away. As I stood up, the soldiers started assaulting me. One of them slapped me hard. The second one tried to hit me in the stomach with his knee, but he missed. As the white car got close, the third soldier, who had so far stood still, saying and doing nothing, finally spoke in Swahili.

'Hey! Stop. People are going to come and see us.' The car approached very slowly, as if the occupants were hesitating. I wished they would come. One of the two soldiers assaulting me pushed me hard, I fell again. As I stood up, I noticed that the car had stopped moving, and was hovering in the middle of the road. The occupants were looking at the scene as it unfolded. The three soldiers then casually walked up a dirt pathway, leaving me on the ground. In pain, I stood up and fetched my ball. I waited a bit to see if the car would get closer so I could thank them, but it turned right and disappeared into the neighbourhood. I went on to the court, told nobody about the incident, and played basketball.

The next day, I stood in front of the assembly to lead the school in singing the national anthem. But doing that was never the same again. My nose. What do they think of my nose? Are they thinking I am ugly? Do they think I am a killer? Do they joke about my nose?

When the Rwandan Patriotic Army (RPA) invaded Zaire in 1996, its stated purpose was to root out remaining perpetrators of the genocide, but it also coincided with the beginning of a rebellion in the vast nation that eventually resulted in a new political and military leadership, and the renaming of the country as the Democratic Republic of the Congo (the DRC).

Hundreds of thousands of refugees returned to Rwanda, among them some of our family members, friends and acquaintances, including my godfather's family. Many who had been in the refugee camps for more than two years came back to homes that were already occupied. This happened to close family friends from before the war. While they were looking for a new place to live, they asked us to host their eldest son, who was a year younger than me.

Slowly, returnees we knew shared some of their experiences with us. One story that stands out includes a remarkable coincidence: the mother of the boy we'd been asked to host gave birth on the same day as my godmother, who was in the same refugee camp. It was the day the Rwandan army started bombing the camp and the two mothers, who didn't know each other, had to run into the virgin forests of Zaire. Both families lived through horrors, and witnessed unspeakable acts – horrors that took them days to tell us.

This family was not the only one fractured by political upheavals; our home became a haven for others too and soon my mother had ten children under her care, just three of them her own. Despite being a brilliant learner, my brother had rejected the idea of school and instead decided to hustle, first becoming a barber, then venturing into other activities he kept more or less hidden from us.

By contrast, I was focused on my studies and, at the conclusion of fourth year, something beautiful happened. On the day we received our school reports, the headmaster came to our class to make an announcement: 'One of the parents has graciously given us a prize for the best student in senior classes at the school. And it turns out that one of your classmates is not only your best, he is also the best in the school: Pie-Pacifique!' Everyone applauded. The prize was a full computer course during the holiday months. The headmaster's other announcement was that after the holidays,

La Colombière high school would move to another location.

Meanwhile, my mother continued working, but her salary was nowhere near enough to take care of ten children. My uncle was helpful, and my brother began to contribute from time to time. Apart from her health issues, my mother was facing another challenge: alcohol. One day when I walked past her she smelt of alcohol, and she had just sent my youngest cousin to buy another bottle of Mützig, her favourite beer. It was the worst time for our family to have such a problem, not only because of her health, but we really needed to spend wisely. When I confronted her, what she told me just broke my heart.

With a dejected look on her face, she said: *'Wa mwana we, iki-ca umutindi nicyo kimukiza'* – Son, what kills a miserable person actually saves him. My mother was giving up. I argued with her about it, but eventually I accepted that she knew the dangers. She just wanted to drown her sorrow. What had precipitated that? I realised I didn't fully understand what was really happening, and what was making her suffer emotionally. Whatever was happening, it was a delicate time. And it worried me deeply.

But as I worried about her, she worried about us more. For some time, she had been saying she wanted me and my brother to leave the country to go overseas. She didn't have a preferred destination: we just had to leave Rwanda. My sister, my mother's health issues, and her beer drinking were the biggest reasons I had always rejected such a suggestion. I was determined to stay to make sure they were all right.

At school, sometimes I would be caught deep in thought. My classmates suspected something was going on. My grades dipped, and I ceded first place in one semester for the first time. Ntikanga came first. He was of mixed race: his mother was a descendant of old Rwandan Tutsi refugees in the DRC and his father, Belgian. Ntikanga and Clemence, another classmate, were calm and great listeners. They were the only ones at school I had started confiding in about some details of my life.

When we finished fifth grade, the school moved premises yet

again. This time, we rejoined the primary school, which had been relocated to a site owned by the founders. But there was a problem: the school was full. So we would have to hold high school classes in the afternoon, using the same classrooms the primary school used in the morning. This arrangement was a first in the country.

CHAPTER 17
Death and detention

In 1998, the war in the DRC resumed at the same time as insurgents, known as 'infiltrators' launched their attacks in Rwanda. Infiltrators were believed to be the remnants of the former Rwandan army and militias still hiding in the jungles of the DRC. The north-west of Rwanda, Ruhengeri and Gisenyi became dangerous, and there were frequent reports of massacres, and of casualties involving members of the new Rwandan army, the RPA.

The army regularly patrolled residential neighbourhoods, and on one of those occasions, I had a chilling experience. I was walking home at about 9 pm and a few hundred metres from home, soldiers on patrol stopped me and demanded to see my identity card. The soldier didn't even look at it; he just put it in his pocket and ordered me to sit, pointing at a spot on the side of the road. Thanks to Nigire, who had taught me what to call military officers and had warned me of this possibility, I immediately knew I was being drafted.

'*Afande*, I am sorry but home is just here,' I said, pointing in that direction. 'I am a student,' I added, but he ignored me. Thankfully, he didn't become aggressive.

'I am a student, a student at La Colombière,' I blurted loud.

'Where?' he asked, sounding surprised as he snatched the student card I was handing to him.

I lived in a poor, densely populated township, where the chances of finding a La Colombière pupil were slim to none. Pondering what I had said, the soldier stepped away and called his superior.

They both approached, the soldier still explaining to him in Swahili. The superior shone a torch in my face.

'You study at La Colombière?' he asked, now shining the torch on the student card.

'Yes, *Afande*. I am sorry I am walking at night, but home is just over there,' I said, pointing to a light in front of a shop near my home. At the same time, a car passed by, its headlights illuminating the side of the road as it turned a corner. I caught a glimpse of men huddled together on the ground, where the soldier had ordered me to sit.

'Where is La Colombière?' he asked. I told him. Then, agitated, he asked what I was doing out at night. Handing my student card to me, he gave instructions to the soldier in Swahili to escort me home. Then he shone the torch in my face again.

'You should not walk at night!' he instructed, leaving me to go with the soldier, who reached into his pocket to retrieve my identity card, and gave it to me.

When I told Nigire the following day, he rebuked me: 'I told you. Right now, you would be in Kisangani, training!' he added. Young people in Kigali were being forcibly drafted into the army. It happened to me once more. Again, this time with no trouble, my La Colombière student card saved the day.

Some of the former armed forces and Interahamwe militia that had fled from Rwanda when the RFP took power threw their weight behind the new DRC government under Laurent Kabila in its battle against rebels that were known to be supported by Rwanda, and bolstered by RPA soldiers. Zimbabwe, Angola and Namibia were also backing up Kabila's forces.

A cousin who was in the pre-1994 Rwandan government army had spent some time in Zaire as a refugee. Among many other soldiers in the same situation, the new regime forcibly repatriated and imprisoned him for being a former army officer. When the RPA-backed rebels invaded the DRC for the second time, the RPF took all the former soldiers, retrained them, and sent them back to the DRC to fight their former colleagues.

When my cousin got what they called a pass, he would come and stay with us for part of it. He told us of horrors he had witnessed, especially when facing the Zimbabwean army, whose air raids, he said, were the deadliest: 'Zimbabwean plane? If you heard them coming, it was too late to survive. So many died,' he told us. This was the kind of information you did not hear or read in the media; on the contrary, Rwanda denied being involved in the DRC war. My cousin told us of courage, fear, survival, luck, hope and hopelessness. Some of his stories were heartbreaking, such as one of his tent mates who couldn't handle it and shot himself in their tent.

During this time, my mother was drinking a lot of beer and often smelled of alcohol. But she never became an alcoholic: it may have been self-restraint, or perhaps simply limited means that prevented her from going over the edge with drinking. Still, I hated it that she drank beer, especially as she had other serious health issues.

It was August 14, 1998 that my mother received a letter from my godfather with shocking news. I arrived home from school that evening to find her looking distraught, her hands covering her ears. She stood still, eyes closed, tears rolling down her cheeks. I sat down. My uncle, who was there, invited me to sit next to him. He handed me the letter. As I started reading, he said, in French: *'Ton frère n'est plus.'* – Your brother is no more.

My stomach knotted. I looked at my mother who was still standing, but now looking up to the ceiling, without blinking, saying inaudible words. My brother had gone to visit my godfather and his family in the rural north-west of Rwanda; the letter said that when they woke up on the morning of August 2, RPA soldiers were rounding everyone up. They selected strong men who had not managed to hide or run, taken them to a nearby administrative office, and executed them.

'Your son was buried in the same grave as my son, with the utmost dignity and discretion,' the letter assured. It was no consolation. August 16 would have been my brother's sixteenth birthday. Imagining my active young brother dead was almost impossible. For a long time, I hoped it was a mistake, that it wasn't him they had seen. I fantasised that one day, my brother would just show up and surprise us all. It was years later that I met an actual eyewitness, the sister of a victim who was killed and buried with my brother. She was there when they took the men, leaving women, children and the elderly. Three days later, she was one of the first to arrive where they had been massacred. All the victims still had their arms bound by their elbows, unnaturally forced to touch behind their backs. Like most victims, my brother had been completely disfigured. She recognised him by his shoes. 'We couldn't tell if it was the birds that took their eyes or if they had been gouged out in torture. The scene still haunts me today,' she said.

The image of my mother reacting to the content of that letter was what was engraved in *my* mind. The next day, I went to school. I clearly remember we had a biology test. Ntikanga was the only friend I told what had happened. He froze for a moment, looked into my eyes and asked: 'What are you doing here?' I didn't have an answer.

The RPA soldiers' atrocities seemed to know no bounds: we know about a baby that had been bashed against a wall and left for dead beside his murdered mother. The soldiers would randomly show up somewhere and kill people, sometimes just men, other times women and children too. This was the climate in which my brother was executed.

Unfortunately, the bad news did not end there. August 21 was my eighteenth birthday. Despite the recent terrible news, we wanted to celebrate. I had invited my uncle, who usually came to visit us after work, and normally arrived before 6 pm. By 7:30 pm, he was still not home. When his wife called to ask if he was with us, we knew something had happened. He had gone to work in the morning and never returned.

A day, two days, a month, three months went by . . . he and his car had vanished. We feared the worst. My mother held on. She tried to take care of us as best as she could. Until one day in December 1998, she went out to buy vegetables and returned with a group of army officers. I was getting ready for my afternoon session at school. They instructed me and others who were at home to sit in the living room as they searched it frantically. Thinking it was just a random search, I told them I needed to go to school. The senior officer among them instructed one soldier to watch me as I put on my uniform and picked up my books, then he escorted me to the bus stop where I would wait for our school transport. I don't remember much of that afternoon at school. I just remember getting home and finding one of our tenants waiting for me.

'They took her, but we know where she is: at the Muhima Brigade,' she said, almost out of breath, looking at me as if waiting for my instructions on what to do next. Muhima was the nearest detention centre, which was attached to a military camp. It was a huge relief that we knew where she was – especially in the light of my uncle's disappearance. It had been four months, and he was still missing.

I was only eighteen, in my final year of high school, with eight children to look after: my sister, six cousins and a family friend's son. I was the eldest, and with my uncle and mother out of action, the children were my responsibility. Naturally, I turned to the most powerful people I knew. First up was Col. Kanyarengwe. It helped that my school only started in the afternoon, so I spent mornings trying to pull strings I barely understood. My mother told me that in the last conversation she'd had with him, he had wondered how on earth I'd managed to get into La Colombière. He had said: *'Ntimubura ibyo muzira!'* Loosely translated, he was saying we create troubles for ourselves. Going to La Colombière was a sort of transgression.

The morning I went to see him, the first time I would meet him in person, it was less scary than I feared. He was no longer in cabinet, and had been pushed out of the RPF as chairman. He was just focusing on his entrepreneurial activities. We met on the roof of a multi-storey building still under construction next to his residence.

'They took my mother yesterday,' I told him.

'Oh. Do you know where?' he asked, not looking surprised.

'Yes.'

'And your uncle? Have you found him?' he asked. I didn't know that he knew my uncle was missing.

'No,' I replied. He nodded in silence, then asked about the children at home, and about school. Then he made me a promise.

'Anything to do with education, you must come and see me. Okay?' he said. He reached into his pocket and pulled out some money.

Another senior official in government we knew also gave me money, and wished me well. These men, to my surprise, could do nothing about my mother. They were powerless in these situations, and I had to deal with the fact that we were on our own.

Fortunately, my mother's pay cheque, some $70 a month, kept coming. But without the help of my uncle, it was nowhere near enough. So I had to make sacrifices. The first thing I gave up was school transport. It would save me RWF4 000, equivalent to the two bags of charcoal we needed. So I had to walk to and from school, which took up to an hour each way. My eldest cousin at home, Albertina, helped me a lot. She managed petty squabbles and distributed home chores. I was on cooking duty more frequently; we had to take food to my mother three times a day. That was a privilege, given how much worse it could have been.

My cousins' mother had been killed during the genocide because she was a Tutsi. While my mother was in jail, they could have gone to an orphan support centre for food donations, which would have been a huge relief for us. But they were told that because they were under my mother's roof, they would not be assisted. Were they not Tutsi enough? Were they not orphan enough? That day, they were shocked, and couldn't believe it was happening to them.

My mother was released after five months in detention. Surprisingly, she was released on the most revered public holiday in the country. April 7, 1999 would be the fifth commemoration of the Rwandan genocide. While in detention, she had picked up another habit: smoking. Fortunately, that didn't last long.

After a while, my mother told us some of her experiences, though

I suspect she withheld a lot. I have also always wondered why she was taken prisoner, and why she was released months later. No case. No trial. Those questions remain unanswered.

My mother's arrival was welcome. I focused more on school, and I had to. We were preparing for national exams, which determine your future in tertiary studies. But there was another reason why we had to do well: La Colombière was under the microscope from authorities. Kagame's children had long been taken out of the school to join a competitor created by those in power. Rumours had it that authorities were no longer so soft on La Colombière, and our system of afternoon classes had raised more than one eyebrow. So we, the first generation to sit for national exams, had to do well.

To my surprise, the school administration often solicited my views on how things could be better, and the headmaster, the great Genade Rutagorama, protected me in another special way. When I was behind on school fees, instead of calling me out in the assembly as he did to all the other learners, he discreetly put a piece of paper in my pocket during the afternoon break, which I would look at later. Such was the case for my very last payment for the final trimester of my last year. I owed RWF23 000. As promised, Col. Kanyarengwe made good on his promise. He signed and gave me a cheque for the amount of RWF25 000.

In class, I didn't realise how much my view was respected until I went to the administration to complain about something. I had borrowed a notebook of a friend who went to Lycée de Kigali, one of the most respected public schools in Rwanda. He was in the same year, about to sit for the same exams, but his class were far ahead of us in biology. Our biology teacher, who often seemed sickly, had missed yet another class. So I decided to study from my friend's notebook, and shared the information with my classmates. When I showed the head of academic affairs at our school, he agreed that we needed help, but he said nothing of what would happen.

The next day, he came to our class to announce that our biology teacher had been replaced. 'You have asked for the teacher from Lycée de Kigali. He will start tomorrow,' he said, to everyone's surprise. In our meeting, there had been no mention of this teacher, though I told him where the notes I was using came from – showing him only as evidence that we were in trouble. When the teacher, Ilunga, came to meet us for the first time, he brought good and bad news. The good news was that it was possible to catch up. The bad news? We had to put in at least three hours of class time on Sundays for the remainder of the year if we were to make it.

When it was finally time for the national exams, we were nervous. The exams were tough but we passed well. I was the only one to score 7.0, a distinction score placing me in the top 25 students in science in the country, and earning me a full scholarship at the University of Rwanda. Looking back, because of the leapfrogging I did as a result of the tumultuous circumstances in the country, and changing schools, it was an even bigger achievement than I allowed myself to appreciate at the time. In high school, I had done only two trimesters of first year before the 1994 genocide struck, and one trimester in second year at ADB before jumping to third year at La Colombière – a school I should never have dared to dream about. But I did, and I thrived.

CHAPTER 18
Leaving it all behind

My father praying is the overriding memory I have of him. On his deathbed, his last words were a request for a rosary to be put around his neck, the cross resting on this chest. When I was introduced to a group of nuns who practised most of the things my father did, I related strongly.

He had mentioned the preferred colours of believers: red, white, green and black; he had quoted William Kamm, aka Little Pebble, an Australian religious leader who lured masses to his way of practising Catholicism; he had pointed to how, in reality, the apocalyptic 'last days' were already unfolding, which included bloodshed, and neighbours killing neighbours . . . All these things were part of the message the nuns of the Movement for the Restoration of the Ten Commandments of God shared.

More importantly, the nuns told me of something else I longed for most: education. Not only was their leader educated in America but the movement also intended to send their young people to grand seminaries abroad. Although I had no intention of becoming a priest, I had always wanted to attend seminary. This was my chance. I joined the movement.

It was a relief for me to leave it all behind. The tragedies I had lived through were evidence of apocalyptic claims made by the movement. I would escape the world where I had witnessed how easy it was to turn into a killer, and how little value a human life could be given. It was a chance at taking a better path and learning to love rather than being drenched in hate and resentment, which weighed heavily on me. It was a place where the shape of a nose did not determine who was superior, and where, finally, I could believe God's love was for everyone. I would be educated to create more of that world. When we eventually discovered that my uncle was in detention in a special facility I spent the few minutes allowed with him to persuade him that this was my chance at grand seminary.

And so step after step, I became a devotee. We went to Uganda, where the movement was based, for the first round of purification at one of the many satellite bases they had in the country. Then, on the second trip, we were to go to Noah's Ark, the holy base of the movement. We lived mostly in silence, speaking to each other only through gestures. Cleanliness was a priority virtue. We always wore the chosen colours. Men were brothers, women were nuns. The base was on acres and acres of productive land in the middle of which were the dormitory halls, a church, a small chapel, administrative quarters, a row of rooms in which people with various skills served the rest, a primary school and a kitchen, surrounding a dirt courtyard where we congregated every morning to sing hymns, pray and to hear announcements. The self-contained community even included a tailor and a dispensary with nurses, two of them senior nurses.

They are the ones who recommended that I be sent back to Rwanda for medical treatment after contracting malaria because the dispensary was too basic and could not take care of me. When I returned to Rwanda wearing full uniform – green, black and white clothes, including a white gown – I felt proud. When I arrived in Kigali, I heard that my friend Nigire had followed in my footsteps. He had left for Uganda just days before.

My mother resisted my return to the base in Uganda so vehemently that she refused to give me the bus fare on the day I needed it, citing other financial priorities. She promised to help three days later. But while I waited, tragic news broke: all members of the movement who were at the base in Kanungu, reportedly hundreds of them, had perished when the church we prayed in caught fire. First reports were of a mass suicide, which I found hard to believe. There was no such thing in their teaching. Eventually, investigations ruled out suicide. It was a mass murder, the prime suspects being the two top leaders, who have never been found. And so, abruptly, my grand seminary dream died. But most heartbreaking was that my friend Nigire never came back. He is believed to have died in the fire.

The tragedy of Kanungu crushed my spirit. For months, I did not want to meet anyone who knew of my involvement with the movement, which was difficult given that I had been so public about it. I hated that most people called the movement a cult. I decided God did not exist. To my mind, if having survived all the horrors I had was somehow proof of God's faithfulness, Kanungu was stronger proof that He did not exist. I had pitied anyone who didn't believe in God, but then I stopped believing and pitied anyone who did. So when my uncle was finally released and his first stop was our house, I doubt I said 'Thank you Lord!'

My goal to attend seminary had died but I did not stop dreaming of tertiary education, so I said yes to my scholarship to the University of Rwanda. Although my mother had always wanted me to be a pharmacist, I was determined to study medicine and become a doctor. I had the marks. I had the brains. I had the scholarship. But there was a condition: all school-leaving students had to have an academic break for a year, during which they were obliged to take part in a two-month camp that was known as *Ingando*. At this gathering of tertiary education candidates, we were re-educated on the history of Rwanda, politics and patriotism. In a nutshell, what was taught before 1994 was bad, wrong and could only lead to a genocide, versus what we had to learn in the new Rwanda. In addition, however, we had to undergo military training, spending the full two months living as soldiers in training. Military uniform and gumboots, makeshift guns that were only replaced by real guns when we went to the shooting range, military drills every morning followed by hours of speeches and presentations from government and military officials. At the end, there was a fanfare ceremony with military drill demonstrations, and a certificate without which it was impossible to get a job or enrol at university.

As could be expected, a few hundred young people in a camp will develop some trends and words only those on the inside will understand. Ours was a simple word: *Ntawamenya*, meaning no one knows! It became so trendy that at some point, when a guest or a participant asked a question, a spontaneous *ntatwamenya* would be heard, sometimes followed by laughter or giggles. But when one particular question was asked by a young girl who identified herself as a Tutsi survivor of the genocide, not a single person slipped *ntawamenya* as a joke. That in itself was a measure of the heaviness of the moment.

'I must start by saying that I am a Tutsi survivor of the genocide,' the student said, her voice cracking as she choked back tears, prompting a stunned silence under the large marquee where we congregated for lectures. 'I also know that quite a few students here are directly affected by this,' she continued. 'Every year, we exhume more bodies of Tutsis killed during the genocide, to rebury them with dignity. The Hutus in this area where we are know where mass graves of their loved ones are, where their innocent people, killed by the RPF army are buried. Why are they not allowed to rebury them in dignity? Are they not worthy human beings? How do we expect the so-called reconciliation to take place with this kind of injustice?' Our *ingando* was taking place in Ruhengeri, in the North of Rwanda.

Tears rolled down her face as she held the microphone, and she was not the only one with wet eyes. The dignitaries took notes. Among them was Captain Jean-Claude Bizimana, who was serving as the representative of the army in the Rwandan national assembly. He had come to give us a lecture that was scheduled for that afternoon, but had arrived early and decided to join the last part of the morning session.

'In addition,' the student continued, 'the fund for survivors only assists Tutsi orphans of the genocide, but ignores Hutu orphans of the crimes of the RPF. Aren't they children? Aren't they orphans? And to make it worse, money is deducted without consent from the salaries of those who look after them, their adoptive parents or caregivers, to be put into the fund that assists only Tutsi children. How can we be talking of unity and reconciliation with a situation like that?'

You could have heard a pin drop. For a few seconds, it was as if everything was suspended. There were perhaps a handful of students who could have dared ask that question, and perhaps only her with such clarity and eloquence. The response from one of the dignitaries only served to increase the tension in the air. He was the president of the National Unity and Reconciliation Commission, the institution responsible for organising the camps bearing the same name: 'I cannot imagine myself spending one moment of my time honouring the enemies of our country you are speaking of,' he said, adding much more to justify his conviction. It was the last question of the morning, and the lunch whistle was followed by an uncomfortable murmur – mostly in admiration of the student and her courage.

As the afternoon session started, Capt. Bizimana revisited the last question of the morning, despite the fact that the dignitaries to whom it had been asked had already left. He used up all his time with his answer, which was as complex as the question was.

On other occasions, the *ntawamenya* joke emerged intact, even when the questions touched on serious, sensitive issues, such as when a student asked: 'We all know that people who manned roadblocks during the genocide, even if they didn't kill, are now in prison. So if things were to change, and another government asked us what we were doing here, in military uniform learning to shoot guns and fight guerrillas, what are we going to say?' She had to raise her voice to be heard above the laughter. She too, was laughing. And when she ended, there was just one answer from the audience, who responded in unison: *ntawamenya!*

Having done my time in camp, I finally got to university. Its motto, Illuminatio et Salus Populi, meaning 'the light and salvation of the people', highlighted the sense of responsibility that came with attending the tertiary institution. We were repeatedly told that the future was in our hands.

I enrolled in September 2000. As there were too few rooms in student accommodation, I had to live off campus in the academic capital, Butare. Although it was only a short walk away, I got myself a bicycle to navigate my new world. The buildings I had once admired while standing at the swimming pool of my first high school were now my immediate surroundings. First up was a language test. Lectures would be in English or in French, so those who had studied in French had to pass an English test and vice versa. Those who didn't pass or didn't sit for the exam had a compulsory year of learning the other language.

The auditorium was my favourite place. Every evening at 8 pm, there would be a screening of SABC Africa news on the big screen. I found it hilarious yet pitiful that the audience booed every time South Africa's president at the time, Jacob Zuma, appeared on the screen. Once, the viewers booed when a Brenda Fassie music video was played. The reason? The shape of her nose. This is a phenomenon that was once only understood by Rwandans, but now most people with some insight into Rwanda can understand. At the auditorium, they sometimes screened movies, big soccer matches and, mostly, they screened interesting documentaries. The library was massive. Some of the lecture halls were mini auditoriums. I was proud. I was capable. But one moment shook me.

While waiting for the allocation lists, Ntikanga and I had already started attending lectures in the faculty of medicine. We hoped to get in. But the competition for entrance into medicine was high because of one factor: we were competing not only with our peers but also the previous year's cohort that had just completed their language education year. We had opted not to do ours, and passed the English test. So the day the lists of medical students were published, it was an anxious wait. We were already outside the doors of the administration building when an official brought the lists and hung them up. All students above the line had made it. My name was the first below the line, and the only 7.0 distinction below the line. I protested to the vice-rector, to no avail. I could only speculate why I was excluded, but no official gave me a reason. I had no choice but to settle for what I had been given: Science B, which had a biochemistry slant.

When I went home for the holidays, I was surprised to find that my sister wasn't there: she was away at boarding school. It hit me that for the past few years, I had not had a chance to connect with her. She was only a baby when we had started receiving internally displaced cousins before the genocide. Then we had been separated for months during and after the genocide. Shortly after she and my brother returned to Kigali, the household grew from five to ten in a matter of weeks, and when I was the one looking after eight children, she was just one of many. Then when I became religious, I had moved away and the latest separation was for university. Now it appeared increasingly likely that yet another separation was soon to take place: my mother and uncle were pleading with me to leave Rwanda. 'You are now the family, Piyo,' my uncle said. 'Your mother has persuaded me to help you with the money needed, but I also think you should go.'

My uncle's word weighed very heavily with me. I respected him so much that the last thing I wanted to do was go against his advice. Given my recent incident with the religious group, I felt a sense of obligation to listen to him; I did not trust my own instincts anymore.

'My son, I love you,' my mother said. 'But there is nothing I fear more than the thought of losing you just as I lost your brother. It gives me so much pain to see you here, given all that we see,' she added. Then after a short pause, she added more arguments.

'Son, you will never be able to properly mourn your brother, because saying that he was killed would land you in serious trouble. Would you like us to have to feel the same way about you?' she asked, tears in her eyes. I did not respond.

'I love you. And I know that I would feel much more comfortable knowing that you are safe somewhere else than seeing you here every day, fearing for your life. Please go.'

It was no longer just about me; it was about the whole family. I was gradually convinced that leaving would be the right thing to do. A date was set, and arrangements were made. Other than my uncle, my mother and John – the man who would help me cross the border into Tanzania – no one else was to know where I was going.

PART 5
LEAVING RWANDA

CHAPTER 19
Another journey: destination unknown

I had packed very little, and told no one about my trip. I had been waiting for John since midday and spent the time thinking about what awaited me. I was interested to see what our first stop, Dar es Salaam, was like. Mostly though, I wondered how the journey to my ultimate destination, wherever that turned out to be, was going to unfold.

John arrived in the late afternoon. When it was time to say goodbye, my mother stood in the doorway. The afternoon sunlight picked out the brilliant greens and blues of the African-print shawl she was wearing over her shoulders, and gleamed on her face. She had a slight smile, but her eyes were sad. We didn't hug. It was as if we were both minimising the moment. I could see in her face that she was saying goodbye, but I didn't grasp the full importance of what was happening – that we would not see one another for a very long time. I was overwhelmed by the excitement, the uncertainty, and an intense sense of anticipation: I was finally going, something my mother had desperately wanted for several years.

John had discussed a few options with me: he said his contacts in Dar es Salaam could help me get to Canada, attractive because it was a Francophone country; I would have no difficulty continuing my studies in French. But it was encouraging to know that there were several other options, all of which John would help me with.

I could go to Europe, in particular the Netherlands, where John's contacts had connections. The other option was going to a French island in the Indian Ocean and seeking asylum there, which would give me access to France – with valid papers. All these were possible because I knew people who had successfully taken such routes to reach their destinations: cousins in Belgium, a friend in the Netherlands, and others I knew in Canada and the US.

The only option I had ruled out completely was South Africa. Although it was an advanced economy that I had been told many people chose as their destination, I had also heard that the Zulu people – whom I thought to be all the black people in South Africa – didn't like other black people from the rest of Africa, because they believed that they were taking their jobs. I had heard stories of them treating black immigrants really badly, including beating them up in the streets. I also feared racism from the whites. And the fact that I didn't speak fluent English made the South African option an impossibility in my mind. Yes, I had passed the university English exam, but I was not proficient enough to converse. All those thoughts kept me awake the night I spent at John's place, which would be my last night in Rwanda.

We spent the night at John's because we had to wake up at dawn and embark on a journey he did several times a year. First, public transport to the border with Tanzania. Then, once across the border, where John helped me to get a thirty-day stamp in my passport, we climbed on the back of a truck – a form of public transport. As we set off on the 420-km leg of our journey to Isaka, the green savanna of Rwanda and Tanzania melded into a picturesque horizon that slowly receded as the truck navigated the tarred road winding through the nature reserves of north-west Tanzania. After a full day's travel from Kigali, we arrived when it was already dark, and the next morning, we caught the Mwanza-Dar es Salaam train.

The first of many first-time experiences once I'd left my home country was seeing a real train moving; before that I had only seen trains in movies. When a cargo train rolled past, I wondered how such a heavy, long chain of boxes loaded with goods, each bigger than an entire truck, could actually move. It was also loud, so loud that it interrupted a conversation I had struck up, while waiting on the platform, with professor Kalembe, a maths teacher who had returned to the DRC to fetch his family – a pregnant wife and three small children – whom he was taking back with him to Mozambique, where he worked. In the Francophone system, a high school teacher is actually called a professor, and since he was from the Congo, I immediately assumed he was brilliant. In Rwanda, the best science teachers I'd had were from the DRC. I asked him if we could keep in touch and he gave me his contact details in Mozambique.

When the passenger train approached, the crowd that was waiting on the platform got ready. There was a commotion as people held their luggage and children ready to toss them onto the train. John yelled in my direction, reminding me what he'd already told me several times: 'The train will not stop. Just get on any of the cars!' When the train came into view, it was chaos. The front carriage passed. Then a few more, with closed doors. The train slowed down and people were poised: as soon as there were some carriages with open doors, they threw their luggage in, jumped on board and helped women and children to clamber in. As John had said, the train did not actually stop, it only slowed down. I leapt into a carriage, landing up in a different one from John, but we found each other. I wondered how the professor had managed to get his pregnant wife and three little children onto the train. The journey to Dar es Salaam would take three days and three nights.

Several times, I found myself thinking about a line from a Kenny Rogers song 'The Gambler' . . . *On a train bound for nowhere*. I had heard the song on a BBC radio programme that taught French and English through dissecting a topic and going through it slowly, with clear explanations. Now, on that train, I caught myself humming the beginning of the song as I thought about where I was going to land up. I still didn't know. I was on a train bound for nowhere. My intention was not to remain in Tanzania. Where would I end up? A few times, looking out into the darkness, I imagined an old gambler in front of me with words of wisdom. With reassuring certainty, I knew that wherever I ended up, whatever hand I was dealt, I would make it work. So I chose just two guiding objectives: to maximise my chances of success my destination country had to be French speaking. Then once there, I would enrol at university. The rest, I didn't really care about it.

Once in Dar es Salaam, John introduced me to Mzee Habara, a Rwandan businessman who had lived in Tanzania for many years and had helped John in his business trips. His connection to my family was that he had once been my father's co-accused in the treason trials of the eighties. He had known my father well. So he agreed to host me in his home in the densely populated neighbourhood of Buguruni. When John left, I realised he was my last direct link to my family. I was twenty, and I was truly embarking on a new and independent life.

In addition to Mzee's wife, one of their three sons, about my age, was in the house. I was taken aback at Mzee's treatment of his son: he was condescending and dismissive and clearly thought he was good for nothing. That was the opposite of how he spoke of his daughter, which he did often. She had apparently been lured away by a pastor, who invited her to do the work of God in Malawi. She spoke French and basic English, and was a devout born-again Christian – a good fit for the mission. However, the pastor had married her and cut all contact with her family. At least, that is what Mzee had heard. He wasn't sure which country they were in. Zimbabwe? Mozambique? Whenever he spoke about her, he was emotional. One day, he even wept at the dinner table.

Mzee helped me to receive the money that my uncle sent me for operation Canada. He sent me $2 300. Mzee activated his contacts, paid $2 100 to them, and arranged the trip. The plan was that his son and I would wait in a guest house. A car would fetch us and take us to a temporary UNHCR base where we would be mixed with refugees who had been selected for resettlement to Canada. All our details would already be there. Men were paid to coach us on what to say in all interviews along the way to Canada. The day arrived. I bought a little suitcase to take less luggage than I had on me, as per instructions. Mzee's son and I were dropped at the guest house at 3 pm. The car would come in the evening. We waited. No car came. At 1 pm the next day, Mzee showed up.

It was a scam. The money was gone. When I confronted Mzee with my suspicion that he was involved, he didn't deny it. At some point, he shrugged his shoulders and gave me a response I found so upsetting that I didn't want to spend one more night with them: 'The money is gone. Ask your uncle. He is rich. He will send you more.' I realised it was probably my fault for telling him my family's story; Mzee had got the impression that my uncle was very rich. Was he using me to get more money? Whatever the case was, the man I had respected as my father had stolen from me, and there was nothing I could do about it.

When John returned, he was shocked to see me. Mzee had told him and my family that I had gone to Canada. Eventually, he proposed that he and Mzee would give me money to continue my journey as I had decided. John gave me $200. Mzee gave $100. Before John returned to Rwanda, I asked him not to tell my family what had happened. 'I will tell them myself,' I added.

Promptly, I found the Mozambican embassy. I applied for a tourist visa using my university student card as a supporting document to indicate that I was on holiday. Then I left Mzee's home. Destination? Madagascar via Mozambique. At least, that was my intention. He was kind enough to take me to the Dar es Salaam harbour, where I boarded a ferry to Mtwara in south-eastern Tanzania, the closest town to the Mozambican border. I was heading for Mozambique because I thought there must be boats crossing from there to Madagascar. The ferry from Dar es Salaam would take about 27 hours. From Mtwara, I hoped to find a way across the border. I was encouraged by the fact that professor Kalembe was there. At least I would have someone to guide me once I got to Mozambique. Surely, I thought, he would know how I could get to my chosen destination.

195

The boat was full of merchandise, livestock, and people who all looked tired. It was not a 'get on board, pick up your suitcase and have a seat' situation. Unlike the train that had different classes, the boat seemed to have none. As it pulled away from the shore, rocking as if shaking its cargo to rearrange people and payload, those of us with no seats scrambled to look for support, while some of the merchandise rolled away from its owners. Women and men screamed, children cried. The ship's platform was solid metal, with rust in too many places to inspire confidence. Some metal beams were yellow. On the platform were benches where people were meant to sit. But it was overcrowded, with some people sitting on top of the massive bags of whatever they had procured, too few actually sitting in those rows meant for humans. Most benches were buried under boxes and bags of different sizes and shapes. A few minutes into the journey, the boat was no longer rocking but every few minutes, it felt as if it was sinking, then it rose again. These undulations were always accompanied by cries – from adults and children alike. The sound of a person vomiting, or chickens and goats making their presence known made me turn my head. But it was the overbearing smell of human sweat that forced me to move towards the edge, where my face was hit by a fresh ocean breeze. The ocean was a good seven to ten metres below. The roaring motors of the ferry made the platform vibrate under my feet, and the loud, grating sound was not of a new machine. I calmed myself by thinking that this was a daily scene and that the operators knew what they are doing. Many of the passengers seemed experienced, both in the way they were dressed, and simply how unconcerned they looked. On the faces of those I could see was just the frown of tiredness, some with beads of sweat on their brows. In my short-sleeved shirt and khaki chinos, with two clean suitcases, I certainly was not appropriately dressed for the journey. It was clear I didn't know how rough it would be. I even chuckled at myself when I recalled a vague expectation of stewards taking orders. No. It was no one's job to help. I was only glad the ocean became much smoother as the sky got darker. My fear subsided, giving way to the realisation that this was a one-way adventure, with no knowledge of where I would end up. Meanwhile, my mother thought I was already in Canada.

We arrived at the port of Mtwara the following day, early evening. Abdul, whom I had met on the ferry, helped me navigate the exit by speaking for me. He then suggested I follow him to the guest house he was going to use. We spent the evening in a restaurant where I briefly shared my story with him. He, too, shared his.

Abdul worked in Dar es Salaam, but his family, including wife and children, were in Mtwara. He made the ferry journey, both ways, every few weeks. He said he was amazed that I was so young and on such a big journey alone.

The following day, he helped me find the public transport going to Mozambique. They were pickup trucks. The one I had to board was clearly made of parts from different makes and colours. The front was an old khaki jeep, and the flat bed, dark green and rusty on the outside, was certainly from a different make. The fuel tank was a plastic container placed between the flatbed and the single cab. A man picked up my luggage and threw it, with little care, on top of other bags already on the flatbed. When I said goodbye to Abdul, he had a worried look on his face, which I had not seen the entire time we were together. I was never sure if he was worried about me because of what was ahead or because of the strange truck I was about to board. I climbed onto the back and sat on the edge, one arm holding the edge and the other a piece of metal on top of the cab. Abdul waited until the truck pulled away. And that was the last time I saw him.

The road was rough in places. We passed tall palm trees, the horizon lush with green bushes. Sporadically, there were villages consisting of grass huts. A few hours into the journey, the bush became sparser until there was no bush at all. Just a green swamp with patches of bush, and a progressively wet dirt road. It was the rainy season. A few times, the truck skidded sideways as the driver revved the engine harder. All the men would get off, push the vehicle out of a slippery hole, hop back on and the journey would continue. But at some point, the driver stopped because the truck could go no further. Fortunately, we were already in walking distance of the lone border post house, and we all had to negotiate what was left of the muddy road on foot.

Situated in the middle of the swamp, with no other building in sight, the border post was a modest construction that could have been mistaken for an abandoned house. It was only the officers in khaki uniform that made it look like an official government structure. Despite the fact that I had a visa, the Tanzanian border officials asked me to pay $50 – I did not know what for. Reluctantly, I paid. A few minutes later, a group of us were on a wooden boat crossing the Ruvuma river that forms the border between Tanzania and Mozambique. One man was in the middle of the boat with a bucket, bailing water, while one at each end punted us across to the other side. As I set foot on Mozambican soil, I thought, again, about my ever-increasing distance from home.

But there was no time to ponder. Ahead was dense bush and a few men waiting, who promptly picked up luggage and started walking in single file, penetrating the shoulder-high bush as we followed. I carried my small bag, with a strong man carrying the bigger one. It was me, a white couple who spoke perfect French, two men who looked Somali or Ethiopian, a Congolese man and other people I could not identify. We climbed a moderately steep path in the tall bush as we headed to the border post house, which was surrounded by tall trees. The porters asked for payment: one dollar each.

The Mozambican immigration officials also asked me for $50. To my surprise, the French-speaking woman, who was behind me in the queue, addressed them in Portuguese and the interaction quickly became heated. The officer angrily paged through my passport and stamped, still talking. I walked out without paying. Outside, the woman told me, in French, that she had threatened to report them if they had taken the money without giving me an official receipt, the authenticity of which she said she would verify in Mocímboa da Praia, the first town we would reach.

'I saw the Tanzanian officials do the same to you. I had to do something,' she said. I was grateful. We chatted all the way to the port town, sitting on the back of a much newer pickup truck, driving on a much better road. We exchanged email addresses as I jumped off at the post office to make a phone call at a public booth.

CHAPTER 20
Border crossing

The professor sounded surprised but friendly on the phone. He suggested a particular guest house, called a *pensão* in Mozambique, and then told me that, coincidentally, his wife and children were leaving for Pemba the next morning, where he had started a new teaching job. He said I should join them on the long bus journey.

When we arrived in Pemba, the professor checked me into another *pensão*, but didn't say how long I would be there. Naively, I had expected that he would host me. Accommodation expenses were exhausting the money I had left – less than $200. Although he had led me to believe he could help with my plans to get to Madagascar, it turned out he had no idea. What angered me more the following day was when I arrived at the *pensão*, after roaming Pemba on foot looking for information, he announced to the friends with whom he was drinking beer: 'Pacifique has a dream to become a scientist. He is going to Madagascar. Next round is on him!' accompanied by laughter that was surprisingly celebratory.

That day, while asking around for information on getting to Madagascar, Senegalese vendors in a market told me I needed to get to Nampula first. So I found a phone booth and called Mzee Habara. 'You have done me a great injustice by stealing the money,' I said. He didn't argue. 'I respected you as my father. Now I am in need. I am stuck, and I don't think I have enough money. Please help.'

'Son,' he said. 'Unlike my son, you are smart. You will make it.

So I am going to help you. But I will do so on one condition: my beloved daughter is either in Zimbabwe or in a refugee camp in Mozambique. I will send you $100, but if you go to Maputo, you have to go to the camp and confirm if she is there,' he concluded. I was happy he was going to send me some money, but I found it unfair that he should attach a condition to it. I had no choice but to agree. I collected the $100 from Western Union and kept it separate from the rest of my money, hoping to use it only when I arrived at my destination. It was my precious note.

So that evening, when the professor jokingly asked for a round, I decided to leave him and his friends politely, went to my room and packed my bags.

The next morning's bus trip to Nampula was quiet. Next to me sat a very reserved man. When we stopped for a break, most of the passengers entered a shop to buy snacks. I stood there wondering what to buy. For the first time, it truly hit me that I was a foreigner; no one spoke a language I could understand. And, try as I might, no one understood any language I could try. No French. No Swahili. No broken English. I could do nothing but point to a piece of bread I wanted, but I didn't know how to ask where the toilet was. I was starting to feel sick. Then the man I sat with on the bus noticed I was having difficulty. He intervened, helping me to ask for what I wanted. He happened to be a Congolese teacher. Once back on the bus, we told each other a little bit about ourselves. He was an English teacher, on the way to a conference in Nampula. He was the first to categorically tell me I would not be able to go to Madagascar from Nampula, adding that my best chance was in Maputo, where I could check myself into a refugee camp in a place called Bobole. He promised to help me get transport to Maputo once we arrived in Nampula.

As the journey progressed, I began to feel worse. But trying to accept that I would not achieve my goal of reaching Madagascar, and having to consider going to a refugee camp instead, was even more challenging. When the bus arrived at the station in Nampula, there was more bad news. The once-a-week Nampula-Maputo bus had left the day before. I had to wait for another week. The teacher then tried to help me find a suitable *pensão*. As we walked there, he said in a serious tone: 'Waiting for a week, in a place where you can't even buy yourself food, will not only be difficult but you will use up all your money. I think it is better, if you have any money, to use it all and buy a plane ticket.' That would never have crossed my mind. A plane ride was something I had dreamt about once when my uncle commented on mist in a valley as we were driving. 'Yooo! That mist reminds me of seeing clouds from a plane!' he had said, continuing to talk more about his travels to Italy and Germany, where he had studied. In my mind, a plane was to go to Europe, Canada, America; a plane was for other people, for the rich, and for white people. It was the furthest option in my mind. But I had no time to process. The teacher continued his reasoning as we arrived at the *pensão*: 'If you could get to Maputo, you would at least have a chance to get authorities there to take you to Bobole, the refugee camp. It is the best option for you,' he said. The teacher assisted me with checking in, then helped me find the Mozambican airlines office, which was not far. But it was closed. 'You'll have to come back tomorrow. I am sorry I can't help any further. My colleagues are waiting for me. I have to run. But good luck!' he said, jogging across the road. He had given me everything he could in the time he had.

That night, I pondered on his words. The following morning, I sat across the desk from a Mozambican airlines employee who barely spoke English, even though hers must have been better than mine. Fortunately, in the broken English we shared, we understood each other. 'I am a student. I don't have much money,' I pleaded. She disappeared into an office at the back, came back with a smile, and asked for my student card. When I gave her my University of Rwanda student card, she stared at it, disappeared again, and came back. I was anxious. '$138 for a student,' she said.

'Yes!' I replied eagerly. Moments later, I was at the *pensão* packing for a same-day flight to Maputo. I was so excited that in the end I didn't have to use my precious $100 note yet. At the airport, everything I did was a first experience, so I remember every detail. Seeing my luggage disappear on the conveyor belt. Going through security. The moment I entered the plane. I wondered if anyone noticed the excitement. Taking off. The clouds below us! Landing in Beira. Taking off again. Landing again.

On the Beira-Maputo leg of the flight, I sat next to a white Portuguese man in his seventies. He was kind enough to speak English so slowly so that I could understand. That was before I discovered that he could speak French, though with great difficulty. So between broken English and French, we spent the whole flight talking. A second-generation businessman and Mozambican citizen – a surprise to me as I had never heard of white African citizens, except in South Africa – he told me something I had already heard in Rwanda and in Tanzania: 'South Africa is dangerous for you. The Zulus don't want other African countries' citizens, and they are violent. Don't go there. It is dangerous.'

He didn't have to convince me about South Africa. I was still resolute. I had admired Nelson Mandela. I had learnt the story of Shaka Zulu in schoolbooks written in French. I had prayed for South Africa in primary school morning prayer. But I remained terrified of what might happen to me if I went there. I reconciled myself to the idea of the refugee camp in Bobole.

When the taxi driver from the airport dropped me at a *pensão*, I had no idea how much I should pay him. He picked up my luggage, walked to the reception with me and asked me for the money. But the man behind the counter, who spoke a little English to welcome me, rebuked the driver. I had no idea what they said to each other, but the driver was upset, and the man at reception was not backing down. He was the one who told me how much to give to him, then he gave the cash to the driver who started insulting him as he walked out. I understood that the man at reception had just saved me from being overcharged. After checking in, I set off into the city of Maputo to look for an internet café. I had decided to tell my family where I was.

It was difficult to find someone even willing to talk to me.

Everyone I approached with an 'excuse me!' introduction just ignored me. Towards nightfall, feeling defeated, I opted to retrace my steps to the *pensão*. That's when I spotted a group of schoolgirls in uniform, and decided to approach them. They looked at me suspiciously, but I greeted them anyway and said: 'Looking for internet café. Internet café for email.' One of them replied: 'Internet café?' When I nodded, she turned and appeared to be persuading her friends. They debated for a few moments, then she asked me to follow them. As we walked, I tried to start a conversation: 'You speak English?'

'A little,' she answered, unsure what to do. Her friends had dropped behind us by a few steps. It was a short walk during which I heard that her name was Rica Cane, what year she was doing, and that she would study in Portugal. I also wrote down her email address. Then she pointed at a neon sign that read 'Didata'. 'There is internet café inside,' said Rica Cane, before rejoining her friends. It was already dark.

Inside the shop were rows of computers, some of which were occupied. I paid for only thirty minutes as I had my message prepared on a piece of paper. A stopwatch was started on my screen. When I glanced at the screen to my left, I saw French. I typed my message to Thierry, a friend who would tell my mother where I was. When my time had expired, I waited for my neighbour's session to expire so I could start a conversation. I couldn't wait.

Kimana Kalenga happened to be the right person to talk to. Not only could he speak French and English but he was also a UN volunteer who had lived in the region for six years. He knew all the ways migrants used to go to various destinations, including South Africa. And more importantly, he, too, ruled out Madagascar. 'You would need to fly to go to Madagascar,' he said. 'And after hearing about you, I don't think you should go to Bobole. No one will look after you when you are sick, and the conditions are really bad,' he said assuredly, citing numerous examples of friends and relatives. We exchanged contacts, and he directed me back to the *pensão*, agreeing to meet me the next day.

To my great relief, he showed up. In the time we spent together, he educated me about the region, South Africa and Swaziland in particular, told me more about the refugee camp, and numerous stories of migrants who are tricked, as I had been in Dar es Salaam. Since I remained adamant that I didn't want to end up in South Africa, Kalenga suggested Swaziland. Unfortunately, unlike the Mozambican embassy in Tanzania that had accepted my visa application, the Swazi officials, speaking to me via an intercom at the gate, refused to help: 'We don't consider applications from people from those countries,' he said, meaning Rwanda and Burundi.

'Why is that?' I asked.

'Because I say so!' he replied. I was not sure if he was being mean or if it was actually official that citizens of those countries were not accepted.

When I insisted, he said: 'Come next week.'

'But sir, my visa in Mozambique will have expired, sir.'

'That's not my problem,' he replied. It was a dead end. Kalenga was not surprised when I told him. He then told me the thing I wanted to hear the least: 'You have no choice now but to go to South Africa.' He explained that even though the police might mistreat me, they would eventually take me to Home Affairs offices because I had a genuine reason to apply for asylum.

'I will give you the number of my friend Clement. We went to seminary together. He is a good man, and he will help you.' And so I was persuaded, with Kalenga promising to come and help me with the first step of a long journey that he explained to me in detail.

Before I left Maputo for South Africa, I decided to keep my word to Mzee Habara and go to the refugee camp to check if his daughter was there. It was a long bus ride out of Maputo to an arid area with little vegetation. I asked around, if anyone knew a young Rwandan woman named Valentine, but no one did. Just as I was giving up and heading out to take a bus back to Maputo, I met some Congolese women coming into the camp, carrying heavy plastic bags that must have been groceries. One of them spoke to me in French: 'We heard that you are looking for a young girl named Valentine. We have no such here. But there is a Valentine. She is married though, not a young girl,' she said, before directing me to her camp dwelling.

As I approached the little house built with corrugated iron sheets, a little girl standing outside saw me approaching and ran inside the house. Moments later, a woman stepped out and stared at me.

'*Muraho!*' I greeted her.

'*Muraho neza!*' she replied, her eyes fixed on me, a mixture of curiosity and worry on her face.

'Are you Valentine?' I asked. She nodded.

'What is your surname?'

'Uwamariya'

I had no more doubts. It was her. But just to be sure, and to let her know where I was from, I gave her father's first name and asked his surname.

'Habara,' she replied, her voice breaking, as if she knew why I was there.

'Your father sent me. Your family still lives in Dar es Salaam.'

Valentine broke down, burying her face in her hands, crying. The little girl stared at the whole scene while shyly standing in the doorway. Valentine's husband was not home.

The following day, she came to town and we met at the post office, where I paid for a phone call for her to speak to her father. He was not at home but had left his mobile phone with his wife. Valentine and her mother did not say much. They cried more. I gave her space to have her time until the money I could afford ran out.

The day I left Maputo for South Africa, I prepared to travel light. As instructed by Kalenga, I had just one small suitcase. The rest, I gave to Valentine to take to the camp. When the appointed hour arrived, I made the phone call. Kalenga was ill. He had flu, and could barely hold a conversation with me.

'Son, you are brilliant. You will make it! Just do as I told you. Call Clement when you arrive in Durban,' he ended, wishing me good luck.

Kalenga had told me the information he'd given me about the method people used to go to South Africa was so precious that many would pay hundreds of dollars for it. I was about to find out. And it all unfolded as he said it would.

'Everyone is going in the same destination, you need not ask anyone. Keep quiet,' Kalenga had instructed. 'Only when you get on the South African side, get the police to arrest you.'

The moment of departure, the moment that would chart the course of my life, arrived. From then things happened one after the other; my focus was so sharply on the present that it felt as if this, and only this, was taking place in the world. Boat ride across Maputo Bay in a small motorboat with a handful of other people. Pickup trucks on the other side. Pay to get your name on the passenger list. Early evening departure. Police roadblocks, remember how much money to have ready. More driving. Our truck alone on the road.

When we stopped in a village after dark, two men from our truck went into a house and stayed away a long time. We were left wondering what was happening. When we started moving again, slowly, I saw that the sand, which was slowing our progress, was almost white. When we were finally told to jump off, my feet sank to halfway up my leather boots.

We walked for hours in the dark. And then the border fence, in the wild, in the middle of the night. Two men who were leading us climbed through the barbed wire first. Then we were ordered to go through one by one. Four men, two on each side, stretched the strong strands of the fence apart. Then, one at a time, we bent down, pushed headfirst between the wires, then torso, one leg, then the other. I shoved my suitcase through first, then I followed. Behind me was a woman with a baby on her back. She struggled through but the child got stuck. One man pushed her, while another pulled from the other side. The baby cried. The mother, also clearly in tears, screamed at the men as they forced. She insisted on pulling back and starting again. It got a bit tense for a few moments. Finally, baby and mother were through.

We walked some more on sandy soil. Then, still digesting the fact that I was in South Africa, I chatted to a man I had learnt was Burundian. He did these trips as a business. He would be sent by clients in South Africa whose friends and families needed to cross the border. He had figured out how it worked, and people paid him for it. On that trip, he had two young men to deliver.

'So where would the police be?' I asked in French. One of the men who was leading us heard me. Agitated, he turned around and shone his torch into my face.

'Police? Police?' he hissed. Then he continued in an African language I didn't understand. The man kept his light in my face as the Burundian translated.

'He says we are in a nature reserve with lions. If you say police again, we will leave you here,' the Burundian said, while everyone else, I suspected, was looking on from their spot in the dark, straining to hear.

Terrified and embarrassed, I didn't utter a word. The walk continued. I had no idea how long we'd been on foot since we'd climbed off the pickup truck on the Mozambican side of the border, but I guessed it was about an hour since we had crossed into South Africa. Soon after threatening me into silence, the leader flashed his torch into the darkness ahead. A car responded. It was our next transport to the town of Manguzi. That is what Kalenga had said. But that is where the script changed.

The pickup took us into a forest, to a compound with mud huts. We were shown where to sleep, men and women separated. At dawn, men with sjamboks and sticks raided our hut, shouting in a language I could not understand. They searched everything and everyone, taking money and anything of value. Thankfully they missed my $100 note, which I had hidden under the waistband of my underwear. All they got, when they searched me, was some cash I had in my pocket. When they tipped my clothing out of my suitcase, they simply turned away, disinterested.

Then it was the turn of the women, who we heard screaming as their hut was stormed. Just as we tried to settle down to rest again, the light of dawn broke through the trees and the gaps in the walls of the hut. I could hear cars, as if they were travelling on a highway; clearly the compound was near a major road. It was a few hours later that the men who had been leading us put us on a pickup truck and dropped us in the town of Manguzi.

By then, the Burundian man had persuaded me not to go to the police. 'There is a chance they will not catch you all the way to Durban. I do this all the time. If you know people in Durban, go find them first,' he said. I didn't know people in Durban, but I had a phone number: Clement.

PART 6
SOUTH AFRICA

CHAPTER 21
A humbling start

It was time to use my precious $100. In Manguzi, I entered a big supermarket – a novelty for me – and exchanged my dollars for South African rands. I received R350. As I didn't know the value of the currency, I had no way of knowing if it was too little; it was a supermarket manager who changed my money, so I hoped it was fair. I was happy that it was much more than the R70 I needed to pay for a taxi. The Burundian man asked me to lend him some money because his had been taken, and he was responsible for two other people. I lent him about R120. He promised to pay me back as soon as we arrived in Durban.

Although we were travelling at night, I was struck by the size of the roads. The highways of South Africa were just as impressive as those I had seen in movies. Nothing about it said Africa. In the moonlight, the view of the waves crashing on the beach along the coast was spectacular. We arrived in Durban at 1 am and stopped at a place I heard them call the Market. From there we walked to where the Burundian man said people who were waiting for them would give him money to pay me back. When we got to Point Road, I began to feel nervous: where were they taking me in the middle of the night? So when we walked in front of an obviously reasonable accommodation place that was open, I walked in, enquired about a room and asked if I could leave my luggage. I followed the Burundian man and his two companions until they entered a building with no electricity, smelling of alcohol, urine and marijuana. That was it. I had gone far enough.

'You know where I am, in that lodge. Please bring my money in the morning,' I said, running down the stairs, and going back to the lodge. They never paid me back.

In the morning, the first thing I saw was a sweeping machine with a driver mounted on it. In South Africa, they sweep streets with machines? Right across the road was the tallest building I had ever seen, and just metres away, a phone booth. I called Clement. At first he thought I was a fellow Congolese. He was surprised to hear that his friend Kalenga had sent me, but he listened attentively, his responses measured and kind. However, he had his own problems. 'Unfortunately, I can't do much for you. But I know the leader of the Rwandan community. We will go see him this afternoon,' he said, before explaining his situation. He had recently quit his job, taken his savings and put all he had into a bid to get to Europe from Johannesburg. Unfortunately, things had not gone as planned. He was caught and sent back, but all his money was gone. He was trying to rebuild. In the evening, he introduced me to the Rwandan community leader. He, too, could not do much for me, and I could see why.

The wife of the bearded, dignified-looking former politician was pregnant, and they had four other children. According to Rwandan custom, the parents were named after one of the children: in their case, Mama and Papa Juliette. They lived in a studio apartment, with just a curtain separating the toilet from the living area. Even so, Mama Juliette offered: 'Wherever you end up, you must come wash your clothes and eat here. The only thing we can't do is host you, as you can see.' Then Papa Juliette took me to Point Road Manhattan building, where many Rwandans lived. Two young people, one of them interested that I had just been at the University of Rwanda, where he had studied before the war, offered me accommodation. I shared a bed with one of them.

The next day, Mama Juliette explained to me how to go to Home Affairs to report myself. I came back with a handwritten piece of paper saying: *This man had reported to Home Affairs. He will come back for his interview.* My very first document in South Africa, made official by the fact that it was date stamped.

Papa Juliette introduced me to various people, all of them warm and welcoming. One took it upon himself to introduce me to car guarding, which is what all refugees did to survive, no matter what their qualifications were. One of the young men hosting me was an accountant and the man introducing me to car guarding had been a senior military officer. Nurses, engineers and other professionals were all car guards. I felt it was degrading, but I had to override my ego and do the same to survive. The first place I stood at was Soldiers Way, behind a gym and across the road from the post office. On my first day, I felt embarrassed. I kept looking left and right, wondering how it had happened that I was now dependent on tips – often grudgingly given. To me, there was not much difference between that and begging. It was a shock.

I had planned to declare myself to the authorities, reveal that I was once a university student and, hopefully, get some kind of refugee assistance for subsistence, as well as a scholarship to keep studying. It soon became clear that I was naively optimistic. I realised I was on my own and would have to fight for what I wanted, while simultaneously hustling to survive. I hadn't expected that.

I gradually got over the shock of my new reality. At least I earned enough money to buy food – I made between R20 and R70 a day, and later, depending on the place, more than R100. Being given R5 was rare and I received R1 and R2 with so much gratitude. Most people just gave me loose coins, but together they made a few rands.

There were various reactions from motorists. A rare few would have a short conversation, which felt like a gift. Most avoided engaging with me, while others actually insulted me to my face in languages I couldn't understand – I could tell from the tone and expression that whatever they said was unkind.

When insulted or treated dismissively, I longed to tell them that I had been a university student. Back home, that carried some status. I even had an income from bursary allowances, which had

215

begun to feel like a salary. From that to being dismissed, or being pitied by motorists who gave me leftovers from a restaurant . . . It was hard. But I adjusted quickly and reminded myself it was a means to an end.

A month after I started car guarding, when I could afford to contribute to rent, I moved in with a young man named James, whom Mama Juliette recommended because he was serious and focused. He was also a car guard, mostly working night shift at the Pavilion Shopping Centre.

On top of trying to survive, I had to apply for refugee status. Then, somehow, fight my way into a university. It took weeks before a Home Affairs official interviewed me and I received an official document as an asylum seeker. With that, at least, I could apply for a library card, which I did with James's help. He made a point of taking me to the Durban City Hall Library and helped me to get a membership card to borrow books and VHS tapes of documentaries, to help me learn English.

James was short and slightly bulky, his skin was dark and his round face sported short facial hair. He always walked with confidence, his chest slightly puffed forward, and his strong arms swinging back and forth, a gap between them and his body, as if to avoid touching his torso. He seemed trained to elevate his chin while walking or interacting with others, reminding me of the phrase 'head held high'. James was always well dressed. His favourite shirt, the one I mostly associated with him, was grey, short sleeves. It fitted him well across his chest and exposed his muscular arms. Even in his car-guard uniform, khaki trousers and short-sleeved white shirt, James looked elegant. His leather shoes were always polished clean and shiny, and he spent considerable time ironing his clothes. Off duty, James always dressed as if he was going somewhere important. I noticed that he often held keys on a key ring in his right hand. In Rwanda, holding keys like that was a subliminal statement of control or status for men. It meant: the man has keys to a door – a car, a house, an office – whatever the door, the man is the boss and must be respected. James owned no car, house or office, but he knew how to be dignified and command respect. That was, in fact, why Mama Juliette insisted that he was the right single man to be my flat-mate.

James and I shared half of a one-bedroom flat on the first floor of City Heights in the city centre. Our beds were on opposite sides of the living room, mine close to the balcony that was a storage area. In the middle was a two-seater couch against a wall. By the opposite wall was a small TV stand on which stood a TV-VHS Player combo box. It all belonged to James. The bedroom was occupied by a family of three, a man, his pregnant wife and a toddler. We shared the kitchen and the bathroom. The family paid half the rent, while James and I paid a quarter each.

James and I had a few things in common. The first was a big surprise. He intimately knew the family that had hosted me in Dar es Salaam. Oddly, he was not shocked when I told him that Mzee had stolen my money. He shrugged and said: 'He is now a businessman. Businesspeople in those circumstances are different people!'

Anyone meeting James for the first time might have misinterpreted his dignified carriage, thinking it was arrogance. But the closer I got to him, the more I realised James was anything but arrogant. He was a dreamer. His biggest regret was that he had lost his proof of completing secondary school. James told me it was impossible to enrol at a university in South Africa as a refugee. But that didn't deter him from learning all the time. He read books and watched interesting documentaries on history and many other topics. He enjoyed political and intellectual conversations. He was deeply convinced that his car-guard circumstances were temporary, even though he didn't yet know of a way out. When he put on his uniform and shiny shoes, he did it with dignity. He was going to work. Off duty, he didn't carry himself as a poor car guard who lived off tips from shoppers. He lived, walked and behaved like a future somebody.

As roommates, we had very little interaction. He worked at night, I worked during the day. By 3 pm, he would be gone, coming back in the middle of the night. He spent most mornings sleeping. On his days off, James was generous with his time. He showed me around, and showed me what to do with the brown one, two and five cent coins that motorists usually gave us. James knew the supermarkets that accepted them, changing them or letting us use them to buy goods. In turn, the shops used them for small change returns at the tills. Inspired by James, I spent all the other coins except the yellow 10 and 20 cents, which I saved in an empty basmati rice cloth bag. I wanted to see how long it would take to fill up! His kind of discipline became mine. He may not know that, but James showed me that I could be a car guard and still be dignified. And that helped me to hold my conviction that our circumstances were temporary.

I had already realised that all I needed to successfully study was to listen and understand. So watching films in English and listening to talk radio became a habit. The SAfm station was my favourite. I got to hear the likes of Jeremy Maggs, John Perlman and later Nikiwe Bikitsha, as well as Rob Byrne, with his regular traffic updates.

I figured out that having my own car guarding spot was a trap. Most guards were territorial, and if I was to follow suit I would have to claim my place by being there, or I would lose it. That would have left no time for English, fighting with Home Affairs or making the many trips to the universities to enquire about bursaries. So I decided to be a floating car guard, working in other people's places when they had things to do, such as a Home Affairs run to renew their asylum seeker permits, which were valid for only three months. So I landed up at the beach front, South and North Beach, Victoria Embankment, various shopping centres, and around Kingsmead stadium on special occasions, such as big rugby matches. But the place I enjoyed most was outside the gates of the University of Natal. Besides the change I received, I appreciated having conversations with some of the students whose cars I was guarding. I was also close enough to hear the cranking of the turnstile as they swiped in and out of campus. I began to dream about having my own student card, and some day, be the one pushing those gates.

As I learnt more about refugees in South Africa, I began to think that if we were organised, we would achieve more. So I encouraged young refugees to be part of an initiative to create an association, but they were not interested. So I turned my attention to mothers working as car guards. I pitched the idea of a refugee women's organisation to a woman named Vestine, who responded positively. There were several occurrences that galvanised the women, but one of them could have been tragic. Refugee parents who lived on the second floor left their children at home when they went out to guard cars. One of their daughters fell from the second floor to the ground. Miraculously, she survived with no serious injury but the story sent shock waves through the community. The women decided their first project would be organising a child-care rotation system. Eventually, they even hired one of the women as a child minder and rented an apartment that became a crèche.

I attended their first meetings, encouraged them to become recognised as a non-profit organisation (NPO), and wrote their constitution. Since my English was limited, I wrote in French and used a dictionary to translate. Then I posted their documents to the Department of Social Development. They became known as the Union of Refugee Women.

CHAPTER 22
Banging down doors

I was guarding cars outside Osman's Cash and Carry when one of the customers started a conversation with me. His father owned a shop on the ground floor of City Heights. Hearing that my dream was to go to university, he promised to talk to his parents to see if they could help. So I stepped up my visits to Home Affairs in a bid to get my refugee status so I could at least register, then seek help from his parents.

I got my refugee status in November 2001. The very next day, I presented myself at the faculty of science seeking registration forms, only to be told that everything had to be done through the central applications office. James lent me the application fee, but not before teasing me: 'You don't even have the application fee! Why do you think you will succeed?' He was not the only one doubting.

Other young people told me it had been impossible for them. 'We have been here for years. We tried! There is no way. Why do you think you can?' they said, laughing. The woman who shared our apartment even went a step further, saying: 'If you succeed, tell me that my parents birthed *imbwakazi*,' which means a bitch (female dog). In Rwanda, that was one of the worst insults.

As soon as my application was accepted to be processed, I approached the man who had promised to speak to his parents. But when the parents saw me enter the shop, their demeanour changed. They were short and so dismissive that I didn't even hear them reply to my greeting. I asked for a loaf of bread, paid, and got out.

In January 2002, I had a muted celebration of the news that my application to the University of Natal had been successful. It was when the science faculty informed me that I had been awarded a student financial aid package that I screamed with jubilation. It was a study loan to be repaid after graduation. But the happiness did not last long.

Ms Moodley of the science faculty said I had been accepted, with the package. The student funding centre, however, said it had never given a financial aid package to a foreign student before, so the centre's Ms Pillay informed the faculty it was a mistake. The faculty insisted, saying I was a deserving student. So Mr Morrison of the student funding centre sent me to the university's finance department to enquire if there were any bursaries available. In a handwritten note to the faculty, someone from the finance department said: *In the sixteen years I have worked here, I have never seen a package given to a foreign student. Please consider any departmental bursaries available.*

'I am very sorry I gave you false hope,' Ms Moodley told me. 'But if you can find an alternative way to pay for the studies, your place will still be available.'

No. I wasn't going to give up. I was convinced that the university was missing something. I wasn't a citizen or a permanent resident. But I wasn't an international student with a study visa and a scholarship either. I was a refugee, and somehow there had to be a way. I approached the UNHCR for funding, but they refused. A letter they wrote to the university's international students office was of no help. So I decided to rejoin the queues at the student funding centre. Someone at the university had to hear my case.

All this happened over the course of a number of weeks. I was working as a car guard only over the weekend or in the evening and I was hardly making ends meet. But I had to give it everything, so I stood for hours in those queues. The staff who had sent me away saw me again and again. Eventually, fed up, Mr Morrison decided to end it once and for all. 'Come. Come speak to the director. He will tell you the same thing,' he said, ushering me through the corridor to Reverend Ngubane's office.

'Reverend,' Mr Morrison said as he opened the office door. 'We told this student there is no financial aid for him, but he doesn't listen. He keeps coming back. Please tell him we are not lying!' he said, closing the door with me inside. I took a seat in the visitors' chair.

The exchange was calm and cordial. Rev. Ngubane was the director of the Centre and I was convinced that if anyone had the power to help, it would be him. 'Look, this is like a bank. The government gives me money that I must lend to South African students,' he said.

'Yes, but the same government guarantees me the right to study as a refugee under the protection of the South African Constitution. You would not be breaking any law if you assist me,' I boldly said, with conviction.

'No. Do you think you can go to any bank in town and ask them to give you a housing loan with your refugee status? If they do, come back, I will also give you a study loan,' he said.

'But now, I don't need a housing loan, Reverend. What I need is a study loan. But when I need to buy a house, they really will have no right to deny it to me on the basis that I only have refugee status,' I said, convinced that I was correct. 'Right now, what I need is to study. And I am entitled to the loans just like anyone standing in those queues.'

'I am sorry we can't help,' Rev. Ngubane said, standing up from his chair, signalling the end of the conversation. As he walked me to the door, he added: 'Look, the problem is that you are looking for funding for first year. If you had already finished first year and had good marks, we would see how best to assist with a second-year scholarship.'

I was crushed. Again. But at least then I knew that all I had to do was get enough tuition fees or a loan for first year, then I might qualify for a scholarship. That night, I didn't sleep. I studied the university hierarchy again to understand who was next up. From the director of the student funding centre, next was the dean of student services.

Mr Wills spoke softly, his chin often tilted down, eyes raised, almost as if he was looking through his eyebrows. By the time I arrived in his office, he knew who I was. We sat on one side of his big office, on opposite ends of a boardroom table. I was sweating, trembling a little, hoping that my poor English would not fail me. If he knew my name already, I thought it was because I had caused a stir. Perhaps too much. So I was nervous. But I was determined to go all the way to the vice-chancellor's office. So this was just a step on that path. But Mr Wills quickly diffused my tension by agreeing with me before I even made a statement.

'Look, you actually have a point,' he said, to my surprise. 'You are not a citizen yet. But you are also not an international student with a scholarship and a study visa. I think the problem is that our international students' policy doesn't include anything for you as a refugee.'

For the first time, someone at the university was acknowledging my issue. And, kindly, he used simple English, which I could understand. 'I will take it up at the next university council meeting. Come back next week,' he said.

'Thank you, sir.'

When I left Mr Wills's office, I was overjoyed. I went to the faculty to get a timetable. Lectures had already started and I had to choose what to study – something that would make me different and unique. I was sure that, as a refugee, employability would be a challenge. The less competition there was, the better prospects I would have. That was my reasoning when I took up applied scientific computing as a degree, signing up for chemistry, mathematics, physics, and computer science. The latter was difficult because the student computer local area network (LAN) had turnstile access gates and I had no student card yet.

So I went to the faculty. Ms Moodley was surprised to see me. I told her that Mr Wills was trying to help, but in the meantime, I needed to have access to the LAN because lectures and tutorials had already started. She disappeared into an office behind the counter, and came back a few minutes later with a piece of paper that she asked me to take to risk management services (RMS) in the Shepstone Building. The RMS were responsible for issuing student cards with the right access features. I was within reach of having that piece of plastic with my name and photo on it. I couldn't wait! The walk from the science building to Shepstone appeared so long. Minutes later, I had my picture taken, and my temporary registration card was printed. I could not hold myself still. I ran to the science building, climbed fast to the fourth floor and swiped the card at the orange turnstile gates of the LAN. Clack! Once. I pushed the gate. Clack! Clack! It clacked again as I passed through. Tears of joy in my eyes, I sat at one of the computers. My login details worked. Then out I went. At the main university exit gate, the famous gate I had heard clack and crank over and over again when I was a car guard, clacked and cranked again. This time, it was me swiping. It was me pushing. It was me turning it, turning it from the other side.

The following Wednesday, I was at Mr Wills's office when he arrived in the morning. Before he even went inside, he told me he hadn't found a solution yet. 'Please come back next week,' he said, before disappearing into his office. I was so disappointed – my legs felt weak, my back slid down the wall of the passage and I found myself sitting on the floor, knees pressed to my chin. The situation was complicated. Attending lectures meant I was not working as a car guard anymore. But food and rent were not put on hold. So when Mr Wills told me bad news with no opportunity for discussion, it was as if the floor was taken from under my feet. I felt sick all day. The next day, I decided to go and tell Mr Wills the full story. He just listened.

'Mr Wills, I am a car guard. That means I have to spend time watching cars in the streets to have food and rent. But now I am attending lectures. By the time we get the financial aid package approved, I may have dropped out already,' I explained.

With a crooked smile, Mr Wills looked at me silently for a few seconds, then gesturing with his hands, palms facing up, he asked: 'What do you want me to do? The council has not considered the case yet.'

'I need a place in res,' I replied hesitantly. He was so surprised at my answer that the slight smile became a full one across his whole face. 'I haven't even managed to get a financial aid package for you yet!'

'But sir, by the time you get it approved, I will have fallen too far behind! I will drop out.'

Mr Wills continued to laugh silently. Then he picked up the phone, dialled and said: 'Sifiso, do you have a room for me?'

He was silent for a few moments, listening to an elaborate response. Then he looked up at me, still listening to Sifiso. 'Okay. Please assist the student coming through the door shortly. I will give you more details later.'

He put down the phone and looked at me in silence. I was holding myself from screaming with joy.

'Well, it seems you are lucky. Please go through that door and Sifiso will help. Welcome on campus!'

I stood up hastily, at the same time as Mr Wills. He walked back to his office chair while I walked through the door he had shown me, trying hard to contain myself. Sifiso did some paperwork, and confirmed my room number on the fifth floor of Towers Residence. When I stepped out of the main exit door of the student housing division, I found the same long queue of students I had walked past earlier, with no thought of ever joining it. I was that hopeless. Now I was a student in residence at the Howard College campus of the University of Natal.

I went straight downtown to City Heights, packed my suitcase, and picked up my basmati rice cloth bag full of ten and twenty cent coins. Then I sat and waited for the lady of the house to arrive so I could hand over the keys. Her husband and James had gone to do their nightshift at the Pavilion Shopping Centre. When she arrived, I considered reminding her what she had said: that her parents had birthed *imbwakazi*. But no. I could never. I understood where she was coming from. She wasn't totally wrong in thinking that this was impossible. I just handed in the keys and said: 'I am moving out!'

I lived on my ten and twenty cent coins while waiting for the financial aid package. Spaghetti, tomato sauce, tea, sugar and brown bread – that was my diet for weeks. When Mr Wills eventually confirmed I could go to the student funding centre and apply, I was overjoyed. Ms Pillay, Mr Morrison and other staff who had chased me away were now assisting me. I was dubbed Mr Wills's student. But that was not the end of my challenges.

As part of the application, I had to get a surety form signed. Being alone in South Africa, I had no one to sign such a document so I had to get a surety waiver. Then, when it was all approved, the university needed a bank account to give me allowances. Banks had refused to open a bank account for me. The university allowed me to apply for exemption, so I could be paid in cash. Eventually, I had my allowances. Soon, exams were coming. I passed well. Holidays came, and I had nowhere to go. So I applied for an exemption to remain in residence. Granted.

Noticing that I had challenges, Professor Jane Meyerowitz in the school of computer science suggested that I should go to student counselling. It was very helpful to have someone to speak to about all my challenges; I just found sessions too short.

In the second semester, I started getting income from research assistantships that supplemented my budget. And I had a girlfriend, Nomandia. She was a beautiful Zulu girl, so beautiful that other guys in our classes were envious. One of them decided that he would not speak to me in English. So when I asked him a question, he responded in Zulu. When I told him I didn't understand, he blurted out: 'How can you call yourself an African if you can't understand what I am saying?' He laughed, prompting others to join in.

'*Ubu se nkuvugishije mu rurimi rwanjye wowe wabyumva?*' I asked. It meant would you understand if I spoke to you in my language? He and his friends looked perplexed.

'You didn't understand that. Yet, I still think you are African,' I added, walking away.

Dating Nomandia was a challenge. I didn't have money to take her out. It didn't help that I wore shoes with holes in the sole so big that I had to stuff them with cardboard and plastic bags to avoid walking barefoot, especially when it rained. I had to hide that from her. Also, I had heard that women liked experienced boyfriends, so I was afraid she would discover she was my first. For both reasons, I thought I didn't deserve her. So when she asked me if I had a girlfriend back home, I said yes. Thus begun the problem with a lie: maintaining it.

Nomandia wanted to hear about me, and about my past. But I was not willing to expose that to her. I thought I would traumatise her if I told her the things I had seen. She probed. But it got worse when she asked me what having a girlfriend was like in my country. I made it up. Then, out of fear that it would go on, I decided to stop talking about it.

'Your girlfriend, what was she like?' she once asked. I told her she had died, and that I didn't like talking about it. She apologised for asking.

It did not sit well with me, so I brought this up in my counselling sessions. Why the need to lie? I then gradually realised that lying was a survival tactic. But beyond that, in Rwanda, what is not shared is often the most important. So much so that you can ask someone a simple question such as: *Uraho! Uturutse he?* – Where are you from? The answer might be: *Sinzi aho nturutse hariya haruguru.* – I don't know where I am coming from up there.

It is as if withholding information gives us some power over the other. But with Nomandia, I was also not willing to open wounds of the past. I thought I was damaged. I believed that there was no way I could remain normal, having seen the things I had. So if she knew, she would run from me. But equally difficult was intimacy with her. The moment I wanted to tell her, 'You are beautiful,' in my head I heard the same words the men had said of the dead girl. Anything intimate I tried just took me to that moment, and I froze with fear. I feared I was being violent. Unfortunately, she took my hesitation personally.

'What good am I if I can't even satisfy a man,' she once said, sobbing.

No Noma, I thought to myself, something is wrong with *me*.

CHAPTER 23
The tipping point

Although I had done really well in the first semester, I still had a deep conviction that something was wrong with me. I feared I was so damaged that nothing other than academic success would deliver me. Any sign of difficulty was amplified in my head, and I worked extremely hard to avoid failing. The more I feared, the less effective I was. That drove me to work even harder, but everything seemed like an uphill battle. That was the beginning of a downward spiral.

One memory stands out. I had a computer programming assignment that took me a long time to complete. Unfortunately, it was followed by a major test that would contribute to my exam mark. I studied hard, but my energy tank was dangerously low so I turned to coffee. From about 9 pm, I drank a cup almost every hour. I was determined to study until 4 am, sleep for about three hours and get ready for a 9 am test. I could sense my memory failing me; I could not recall things I had just studied. So I drank more coffee and went back to earlier sections. When I ran out of filter coffee, I turned to instant. At 3 am, I was still drinking coffee and studying. I pushed some more until just after 5 am. I was tired, but hopeful. I felt some palpitations in my neck. I stepped out for a bathroom break, then decided to take a nap. I wanted to rest until about 7 am, read a few things one last time, then get ready for the test. My life depended on my studies so I had to work hard to pass. As soon as I hit my bed, I fell asleep.

When I woke, birds were chirping, the light in the window was not very bright. The smell of coffee was everywhere. When I went to the shower, I was the only one there. When I went back to my room, there was even less light in the window. Perplexed, I checked my watch. It said 7. I still had time. I heard students cooking in the kitchen. Then I was confused. But soon, it started sinking in.

It was 7 pm. I had slept for more than thirteen hours but it felt like only a nap. The strong smell of coffee was coming from my bed: clearly I was so exhausted that I hadn't even woken up to go to the toilet. Ashamed, I started wondering if other students would find out. I kept thinking: Oh my God. Am I this sick? I spoke to my counsellor, looking for assistance. I was deeply afraid, wondering what other danger I might bring upon myself. But I refused to give up: university was my ticket to progress in life, and counselling could help me deal with the challenges along the way.

I continued to work myself hard, hoping to make extra money for treats and taking Nomandia out. One day, I insisted on working on a Wednesday afternoon, the only afternoon we were both free. When Nomandia expressed her disappointment, I was annoyed that she didn't understand.

'But Noma, I have to work. I have this research assistant job that helps me earn extra money. That could be good for us.'

'But I don't care about money or anything. I just want to spend time with you. I have been looking forward to this afternoon all week,' she replied, becoming tearful.

Despite her emotional response, I refused to be swayed; I was convinced I was doing the right thing. On my next pay day, I bought myself a brand-new pair of black leather shoes. I was so proud. The next day, Nomandia came to see me in res. It was a Friday afternoon. She didn't sit down.

'Pie-Pacifique, listen to me,' she said, with a serious face.

'I have a surprise!' I said, glowing, ignoring how serious Nomandia was.

'I am no longer your girlfriend. Please don't tell anyone again that I am your girlfriend.'

I was shocked. In disbelief, I acted as if I hadn't heard it. But she said it again, and I realised it was really happening.

'Noma! Noma! Please don't break up with me.'

Nomandia stood still, her back against the door of my little student room. I opened my wardrobe, pulled out the box of shoes and showed them to her. 'Look. I even bought brand-new shoes. I will look good for you,' I pleaded.

Nomandia shook her head slowly, eyes teary. Then she spoke again, her voice breaking: 'I am no longer your girlfriend. Goodbye Pie-Pacifique.'

She opened the door slowly and walked out, leaving me sitting on the edge of my bed. My heart sank. I knew I had lied to her. I knew I had disappointed her. I was afraid of losing her. And when it happened, I was caught by surprise.

I was restless the whole day, and paced up and down in our corridor. Then I took a very long, hot shower. Back in my room, I was irritated with everything. I began to clean up, throw items into my little bin. I had no energy to cook, so I ate bread with tea. Then I picked up my journal and wrote for a long time. It was a long, dark weekend. I hardly slept. All I did was watercolour painting.

On Monday morning, I arrived at the student counselling centre early and waited outside. A few minutes before my regular session, my counsellor, Jackson, came and sat next to me on the bench, and told me he needed to postpone. 'I am so sorry. I just received a call. I have a family emergency I need to attend to. Can we set up another time?'

I was boiling inside and I needed someone to hear me. But I understood. He had another priority. So I agreed to set up another session. In the meantime, I decided to use the time to see Ms Pillay at the student funding centre on an issue related to my second semester allowances. As I entered reception, I saw Ms Pillay go into an office. I approached the clerk at reception to say I needed to see Ms Pillay. Before the clerk answered, Ms Pillay shouted from the office: 'Tell him I am not here! I am busy!' But I heard it. Ms Pillay didn't want to see me.

Tired and disappointed, I dragged myself to my computer science lecture. Prof Meyerowitz was teaching. At the end of the lecture, I approached her, saying I really needed to talk to someone.

She continued packing her computer away. 'Unfortunately I don't have time now,' she replied, eyes still focused on her task. 'Can you go to the student counselling centre?' In my head, I wished she knew I had already been there. Then I went to my mathematics professor, who was a very good listener. But he wasn't there. I was exhausted. I thought of going to my room but I couldn't sleep. So I decided to go to the dispensary to get some sleeping tablets. At the clinic, I had to pay R5 for a consultation at the reception window, which was directly in front of the waiting area. As I approached, a nurse left the reception desk to go to another room. A second nurse was looking at the computer screen, while a third came forward to assist me.

'Hello,' I said. 'I haven't slept in three days. Could you please help me with sleeping pills.'

As if she hadn't heard what I said, the nurse named the amount I had to pay first.

'I need sleeping pills,' I continued, reaching into my pocket for five rand.

A loud voice came from another room: 'Don't. Don't take the five rand. Not sleeping pills. Don't take the five rand,' she shouted.

When I heard that, I felt dizzy. These nurses also don't want to help me, I thought. No one on campus will help me. No one wants me . . . My vision became blurry, and I felt weak as if all the energy was being sucked out of my body. The last thing I saw was the nurse in front of me jumping as if startled, and another nurse springing out of her chair towards the door on my left. I blacked out.

When I regained consciousness, there was cold water running off my face and head. People I didn't recognise were in front of me. All women. Then I remembered that they were nurses. One patted my cheek: 'What is your name? Can you hear me?'

'Pie-Pacifique. Why? Why is everyone refusing to help me? Why?' I wailed, starting to sob. Tears mixed with water in my face.

'What happened?' someone asked.

'My girlfriend. She broke up with me. I just want to sleep.'

They listened as I recounted snippets of the weekend and that Monday morning.

'Jackson. I wanted to talk to Jackson. Why would he reject me like that?' I sobbed.

One of them offered to call Jackson; soon he appeared.

'Why? Everyone?' I said, sobbing. 'I just want to sleep. I want to sleep.'

I cried, as if a dam wall had broken, I let it all out. 'And my mother. Her legs are swollen. She is too sick.' I was referring to a letter I had received a few weeks earlier. I could not imagine my mother in such a state. I was frustrated because there was nothing I could do. The dispensary released me into Jackson's care and he took me to a psychiatrist at King Edward VIII Hospital. She referred me to King George V Hospital to be admitted for severe depression and anxiety.

We were only weeks before the second semester exams. For me, it was out of the question to drop subjects and be hospitalised. So Jackson took me back to the student counselling centre and arranged a call to my mother from his office. 'I will be well, son,' my mother said. 'This will be over soon. Don't worry. How are your studies going?' she asked, with no knowledge about my struggle. Hearing my mother's voice was reassuring. At the end of the call, she did her motherly thing: 'I hear it gets very cold in South Africa. Are you dressed warmly enough?' The call ended with my mother wishing me well for my studies, and instructing me to go home and put on a jersey. But I didn't tell her anything of the day.

A few days letter, I agreed to be admitted to hospital. Jackson came to visit a few times. During one of his visits, we discussed my upcoming exams. He suggested that I drop some of the subjects and apply for supplementary exams for the others, which would be written in January. Dropping subjects was inconceivable for me, but I had no choice. I was in the hospital for three weeks. During that time, I had a CT scan and, when explaining the result to me, one of the doctors treating me said it looked as if a part of my brain was shrinking. He wasn't sure what was causing it, but said I should prepare because at some point I would not be able to function normally.

When I asked how long it would take, the doctor said he didn't know. I was saddened by the news, but I don't remember having a strong reaction. Mostly, I was worried about what would happen when I could no longer take care of myself. With my lack of medical understanding, I believed it was all logical: my brain had processed a lot and it had had enough. It was unravelling.

The doctor discharged me a few days later, giving me two sets of pills. Two days after I arrived back in student residence, I had problems. First, I was aroused most of the time, and parts of my body were always tingling, especially the tips of my fingers. But what terrified me was that I was struggling to speak; I couldn't turn my head or keep my mouth closed and I was dribbling. I thought the doctor's prediction that my brain would stop functioning properly was happening. I made a distressed call to Libby Collins, the deputy director of the student counselling centre, who had taken over my case. Libby arrived in a small white VW. She suggested that we see another doctor for a second opinion. She took me to Parklands Hospital, where I was seen by Dr Barrett. After the consultation, she took me off the red pill and gave me a different prescription.

'Nothing is wrong with your brain. You have depression, but that is normal. You can treat it,' she said. I was relieved beyond words. And deeply grateful to a Rwandan family, Theophile, his wife Agnes and their two young daughters, who opened their home for me to recover in a safe and caring environment. I wrote the mathematics and physics supplementary exams and got distinctions for both subjects.

I returned to campus after the holidays and enrolled in second year. I continued on the prescribed medication for depression, and made some friends who had a huge impact on me. Andrew Kerr was one of them.

He invited me to his home, where his parents, a preacher and a teacher, received me warmly. Andrew was quiet, very intelligent and a devout Christian. In fact, he slowly influenced my belief about the existence of God. We had a prayer group that I found helpful, and spending time with the guys who were part of it was not only culturally educational but healing too.

As I began to feel more stable, I became involved in student leadership and created the Physics Society. I led excursions, organised talks and encouraged physics students to popularise the subject. I eventually ended up on the Science Students Council as president. That gave me exposure to student leadership courses being offered, and I applied for a place on one being organised by Marie Odendaal in Pietermaritzburg. On day two, I wanted to leave. I felt inadequate. I began to feel that I had stolen another student's place. I thought I smelled bad, and was therefore ruining it for others. I approached Marie about it.

'Well, it is your decision. But for what it is worth, I don't smell you, and no one has complained to me. Just by being here, you are adding a lot of value.'

'Yeah, but I hate the fact that someone here might be inconvenienced because of me,' I said.

'Well, consider that at the moment, no one has shown any sign of that. You are free to leave, but I have a personal request.'

I listened, annoyed that I wasn't being convincing enough. I wanted out of there.

'There is a workshop starting tomorrow. It is only two days. May I suggest that you stay just for that, and then leave if you still want to? After all, your place is fully paid for, you have nothing to lose,' said Marie.

'I am not really sure I want to stay any longer. The same problem will still be there,' I insisted.

'I don't want to share too much about it now, but I think this workshop will address some of the things you are worried about.'

Noticing my hesitation as I broke eye contact, fixing my eyes on the floor, Marie added: 'Maybe not the whole workshop. Stay just for the first day. And then decide.'

It no longer felt as burdensome. I could endure one more day of uncomfortable self-consciousness. Besides, Marie had made me curious, and out of respect for her, and to honour the investment in me, I agreed to make it just one more day.

The workshop was the Alternatives to Violence Project (AVP). It was more than just a workshop, and much more than what the name suggested. It was an exercise in listening, sharing and applying simple techniques that demonstrably diffuse tense situations or avoid them altogether. One of the first exercises was to tell your story – uninterrupted. We sat in a circle, listening to the one sharing his or her life story. I felt more and more nervous as my turn approached. I thought of slipping out. But I couldn't bring myself to disturb the sacred space, marked by just one voice sharing in a room filled with attentive silence. Details of the lives I was listening to were interesting, often emotional. Slowly, I began to feel my tension dissolve as nothing seemed too dirty to talk about. Nothing too violent or too shameful to be received. And tears were not hidden. There were sobs from those sharing, and some of the participants in the circle wiped away tears as they listened. Outside of my counselling sessions, I had never been in a space where it felt so safe to share my story. But this was a group of strangers I had met only days before. For the first time, I was going to share intimate details of my turbulent, violent past. As I spoke, I looked at some of the participants' faces in the circle as they all looked at me attentively. Umulisa. Scelo. Rose. Sizwe. Lindo. These are just some names of fellow participants who looked at me with expressions of surprise, shock and disbelief on their faces. But they were there. Present. They listened silently. I remember one of the participant's eyes were red with tears. I became teary too. But I kept sharing. Time was limited, so I didn't share everything. I shared enough, for the very first time, to experience the gift of being listened to. The invitation to speak about violence was in the very name of the workshop. But the permission I needed was in the circle. The act of sharing was the beginning of a search for an alternative within. A personal alternative to the violence narrative.

In the introduction to the workshop, the facilitators explained that it was created by Quakers, formerly known as the Religious Society of Friends. Initially, the workshop was presented in US prisons, and it was so successful in changing the lives of prisoners and their attitude to violence that AVP became a movement. Marie, a Quaker herself, had included the workshop as part of the week-long leadership course. Apart from the sharing of life stories, we learnt and practised conflict and conversation management skills, and a kind of bonding with strangers that involved looking another human being in the eyes, listening to their story without judgement, and feeling deep respect for them just for their humanity. This was a new discovery for me. Understanding and sharing one's feelings through using the pronoun 'I', which implies taking full responsibility devoid of any blame, was not only a skill I wanted to acquire, but also to teach. I could see how this could create the opposite of the violence I had lived through, from an individual point of view. But the fact that this was a leadership course strengthened it even more. Is there a place for non-violence as a legitimate leadership tool? Are there outcomes impossible to reach without violence? Is it naïve to think of political leadership without violence?

After the two-day AVP workshop, I no longer felt like a misfit, a human with an unacceptable story or a repulsive life. The feedback I received from others after the workshop was beyond affirming, it was healing – as was the opportunity to acknowledge other people's stories. I stayed for the whole leadership course.

CHAPTER 24
Top 100

Always on the lookout for opportunities to improve myself and advance my skills, when I saw an advert for the Brightest Young Minds (BYM) conference, I didn't hesitate to apply. My confidence had shot up since the AVP workshop, and I was sure that my student leadership activities would strengthen my application. I had enthusiastically shared with my friends the wonders of sharing one's story with strangers, the self-discovery I'd experienced in the AVP workshop, and my new-found belief in my own worthiness. I believed I could get anywhere.

I told my friends that my next adventure was going to be the BYM conference. One of them, also a refugee, chuckled. 'That will be a tough one! Pacifique, they are looking for only 100 across the entire country. Why do you think they would choose you over the many South Africans who will apply?'

'I don't know. I don't think they will care about that. There is a specific set of qualities they are looking for. I believe, they will look at those qualities first,' I said.

We discussed various challenges we faced as refugee students, and how uncertain our future remained. But I believed we were in with a chance. Since the AVP programme, I was convinced that it was possible to be seen as a worthy human being above all else.

My interview at the Howard College campus was brief but lively. A young man and young woman, both dressed in smart corporate clothes, took turns asking me questions. I don't recall the details, but the experience remains fresh in my memory. Because I was so excited about getting the interview, I dressed up as smartly as I could, wearing my best trousers and short-sleeved shirt, and my new polished leather shoes.

The BYM selection confirmation letter came as a surprise. I had been 'top' a few times in my life, but never of something so prestigious. The fact that I was in a foreign country made it even more special, and I allowed myself to see it as evidence that anything was possible.

Sharing my excitement with my counsellor was my only real celebration of the significance of the news. Bubbling with enthusiasm, I told Libby: 'They said in the letter we must take clothes for two black tie events. I don't even know what that is. But I am sure they didn't select me for my sense of style or my clothes. So it doesn't matter that I don't have black tie things.'

'It sounds like you have chosen to be philosophical about it,' she responded.

'Yes. What choice do I have? I am one of the 100 Brightest Young Minds, representing UKZN. Should I really complain about not having a black tie?'

'Well you don't really need a black tie. Any tie would do. And any suit; you would still look good for the event.'

'Well, I don't have a suit at all!' Not having a suit would not prevent me from boarding a plane for the third time in my life, flying to Cape Town and mingling and networking with the brightest young people, handpicked from across the country. I might look out of place, but that didn't change what they saw in me: a visionary, a dreamer, a future leader. Leader of what? I did not yet know. But that was academic; someone else believed I was among the best. It trumped my limited means, and I was sure I could impress in other ways.

The day after my counselling session, I received a call from Libby: 'Hello Pie-Pacifique. I have very good news for you!' I was attentive. Calls from the student counselling centre were usually about appointments, but by then, as the 'child of the student counselling centre', I didn't need confirmations anymore. This was rare and exciting.

'I spoke to the dean of student services, and he has made an exception to help you with some money to buy what you need for the black tie events. He is very proud of you, and he wants you to look your best while representing UKZN.'

I was overjoyed! The money was enough to buy a R650 suit and a pair of shoes in a shop in downtown Durban. I had worn a suit for catholic sacraments, but never as an adult. I could not wait for the occasion.

The BYM was a glamourous event. Big corporate sponsors, a great hotel room, flashy events and high-profile speakers who all put a lot of effort into convincing us that we were the future, that a lot rested on us. We had entrepreneurship challenges, opportunities to brainstorm a range of initiatives, networking and excursions to various sites. Then, the organisers chartered a plane, renamed the flight number 'BYM' and flew us from Cape Town to Johannesburg. More site visits. More CEOs' speeches. And finally, the last dinner, hosted at the Presidential Guest House in Pretoria by the then first lady, Zanele Mbeki. When I was getting dressed in my new suit, I could hardly contain my excitement. It felt as if I was in a dream – or in a movie!

When I handed my maroon refugee ID card to the presidential security staff, they passed it among themselves, and turned it over and over as if they were looking at something they had never seen before. I had to explain what it was. The event was as glamourous as one might expect from something being hosted at that venue. There were speeches, photo ops, and an endless supply of food and drinks. Two moments are engraved in my memory forever: one when my turn came to shake hands with the first lady and exchange a few words. When I told her I was from Rwanda, she said: 'Ah! I work with some Rwandans. We bring Rwandan university students to study here in South Africa.'

After telling her I actually knew some of the students, I passed my little digital camera to someone in the crowd to take a picture of me with Mrs Mbeki. Almost everyone was taller than her, but she did not seem overwhelmed, neither by our height nor by all the hands extended in the hope of shaking hers.

The other moment was when I approached one of the VIPs, Anne Pratt, with the intention of inviting her to Durban. Earlier in the week, Anne had spoken with such eloquence that I kept imagining her inspiring refugee women I had worked with in Durban. Although I was intimidated by the idea of inviting her, I walked over to her anyway. She said yes, then she gave me her business card.

The psychological effects of that BYM week were considerable. But more importantly, the BYM was a bridge to the big wide world of South Africa. Beyond my new-found belief in a successful future, where my nationality and status may not matter after all, I laid the foundation for building a supportive social network. Little did I know that the steps I took across the floor of the Presidential Guest House to engage with Anne would profoundly change my life forever.

The next Wednesday, Anne called to say she would be in Durban that week and asked if I could organise a meeting with the refugee women. She fetched me from my student residence and, as she drove downtown, told me she was actually from Durban. She showed no discomfort as we approached Point Road, and confidently drove to the entrance of the tall building in which the organisation and the school were based. A few of the refugee women were waiting for us on the pavement. Once inside, Anne sat among the women and told them about her life and shared a few stories to inspire them. She spoke about respect, vision, action, time management, courage and perseverance. Then she paused before adding: 'You know, some of the skills I am talking about now, I learnt them somewhere. There is a life skills training programme called More to Life that I think would benefit you. I will arrange for two of you and Pie to take part in the next training.'

When Anne visited, she kept her interactions with the women

casual and personal. It fired them up. By that time, I had been to numerous leadership and life skills training workshops and events, so I was not really keen on another one. But out of respect for her and the refugee women, I agreed to attend. Anne asked me to contact Joanne Walsch to make the final arrangements. I met her at a coffee shop in Glenwood, and she briefly told me about the course we were to attend. Joanne was one of the trainers, with Ann McMaster from Texas. Initially, I was sceptical; the name More to Life made me think it was some kind of kumbaya movement. I'd had an experience of a cult, so if there was anything reminiscent of that, I would run. Despite my positive experience at the AVP workshop, I was still closed off, so it would take a lot to get me to share my emotional pain with strangers. However, to honour Anne for her generosity in sponsoring us I decided to engage in the experience – with caution. It turned out to be anything but a workshop.

It was a safe space to share, openly and fully, what was burdening me, primarily so that I could do something about it. Instead of feeling sorry for myself and seeking sympathy – a trap I had fallen into before – it was a place where the substance of my life experiences could be used to help me grow and develop greater resilience. But first, I had to recognise the trauma and work with transforming the debilitating effect it was having on me. For the first time, I shared extremely difficult memories and received support and help in processing them. Because I had found this so helpful, I took part in more programmes organised by More to Life. One of them proved to be a massive breakthrough for me and for those who were there with me.

The training was about money, and was entitled Making Money Count. It seemed to be a completely unrelated topic, but somehow, with the extraordinary skill of the trainer, Briggy Kiddle, we found a way into my life. On day one, I shared my misconceptions about money: on one hand, I felt that money and wealth meant nothing. Making my case, I shared that as a boy, I had witnessed a man I considered to be wealthy being killed; a single shot had left

Muturanyi lifeless in the middle of the road. Why would money matter? I had gone on to witness people losing everything, and sometimes everyone they had, and still they survived. So why hold on to money? Why toil for it? It doesn't matter. When everything is torn down, and death comes knocking, it doesn't save you.

Then, there was another side: people had begun to invite me to share my story at small gatherings, saying it was inspiring; that *I* was inspiring. So I had begun to believe that unless I had material wealth to balance the darkest moments of my life, material wealth that would show I had made it, I would not be inspiring after all. What did I have to illustrate the success people associated me with? I needed money. I needed to give myself permission to make this 'meaningless' money. It would become, I thought, my power to inspire.

As I shared these two extremes with the trainer and participants, I began to realise that both were mental constructs I had created. Beliefs that I needed to drop if I was to build a healthy relationship with money.

Day two of the training began with pain. I had a cluster headache attack, the kind that would render me completely helpless. Intense pain, localised somewhere in the depth of my eye socket on one side of my head, so deep I could not massage it, so painful I could not even scream. I barely managed to get to the training venue. I was late, and when I arrived, some members of the training team suggested I should lie down while one of them went to inform Briggy. She asked them to take me into the training room. With my right eye almost closed, and dizziness behind the left, I entered the room where participants were sitting in pairs, sharing. After a brief exchange, Briggy asked me: 'Where is your pain?'

'Behind my right eye, through the side of my head,' I responded, placing my fingers gingerly on my temple.

'What were you sharing yesterday?' Briggy asked.

'About the man I believed was wealthy, the man I saw being shot dead.'

'I don't think it is a coincidence that you shared that emotional memory yesterday afternoon and you have a cluster headache attack this morning.'

I remained silent, wondering where she was going with this.

'I have a hunch,' she added. 'If you are willing, I would like to work with you.'

I trusted Briggy; I had seen her do amazing work with people, including me, on traumatic events in their lives. I agreed to engage. She called everyone together, and told them she was taking a detour but that she would later show us how it was connected to the topic. She described my pain to the participants and asked me to sit in her trainer's high chair, to close my eyes and take deep breaths.

Then she encouraged me to remember the scene I had described the day before in as much detail as I could. After a few moments, eyes closed, I was back there. Back in 1994, hearing the sounds, smelling the stench of the garbage nearby, seeing the colours of all that was happening around Muturanyi's shooting. As I recounted what I saw, my body froze when I shared one detail: the silence that followed the soldier's single bullet. That silence that seemed to suspend everything, including time itself. The silence that was interrupted only by the buzzing in my ears as I shivered with terror. The silence that followed death. Briggy zoned in on that silence, saying softly: 'I know about that silence. Stay there. Stay there, Pie-Pacifique. Hear the silence.' I tried. I tried to remain silent too, but I could no longer hold it all inside. I exploded in tears, the silent scene still vividly playing in my memory: the lifeless body of Muturanyi, fresh blood gushing out of the right side of his head and flowing onto the tarmac, the frozen faces of the people standing there, like me, the soldier briefly looking at Muturanyi's body, then slowly turning to walk away, in silence. All so slow. All so silent. Fists clenched, jaw tight, my whole body was tense as if ready to fight. Fight it all.

'Noooo.' I screamed. 'Nooo. This should not be happening . . .' Out of breath, I found it hard to inhale. I dragged breath into my lungs as if I was choking. Briggy whispered: 'Keep breathing. Hear the silence. See everyone. And everything.'

It was so clear. As if I was there again, but this time, it was slower. The terrible silence was harder, and it was longer. As I gasped for air, Briggy encouraged me to breathe. It was as if I was at the scene, yet somehow I heard her voice as if she was there with me, watching it all unfolding. In that silence and stillness, I heard her soft voice again: 'The silence. What do you want to do with it, Pie-Pacifique? What do you want to do?'

I hesitated, trying to ignore the question. But as if she had just given me permission to fill the silence, I began to scream loudly. Slowly replaying the scene again in my head, I screamed with each breath, each piece of the memory. Then I started shouting the same words I had heard Muturanyi say to the soldier. Only, I screamed at the soldier. At the soldier I had once decided I would become.

'Why are you doing this? Why? Nooo. Nooo. Why are you going to kill him? Why are you doing that! Stooooop. Stooooooop. Stooooop,' I shouted at the top of my lungs. 'Stoooooooop.'

I could also see the people who had stood there watching the same scene with me. People who were silent. Still. I started screaming at them: 'Why are you silent? Why don't you do something? Whyyyyyyy?'

But they were only in my memory, just like the soldier who was ordering Muturanyi to sit down, and getting his gun ready to shoot him. I wished the soldier could hear me. I wished he could know I was desperately yelling at him, my role model, who was about to kill someone pleading for his life, someone asking for forgiveness, forgiveness for what, I didn't even know. I screamed harder. I screamed again as I heard Muturanyi's last words: *'Mana yanjye wee.'* – Oh my God. Then the shot. Then the silence.

I stopped screaming as the silence asserted itself again, but not for long. I immediately realised it was my silence too. My silence to fill. So I filled it, screaming 'Nooooo. Nooooo. Nooooo. Stooooop . . .' as loudly as I could. As I struggled to find the voice to scream some more, I realised it was all happening again, just as it had before. The soldier was not going to stop. Maybe he never would have stopped, not even if he could have heard me screaming. As I kept trying to reach him, screaming, crying, writhing in the high trainer's chair, I lost my balance and fell, but Briggy held me safe and gently said: 'It's okay. Lie on the floor.'

Eyes closed, exhausted, sweating, tears flowing, my nose running, I went on screaming in a failing, exhausted voice. Under the weight of my own body, I slowly felt the tension dissipating . . . the heaviness in my head slowly disappearing. Eyes closed, a sense of calm began to wash over me. But when Briggy whispered in my ear: 'Can you say YES?' I began to shake my head, saying no. No! And then I said, 'No. No. Nooo. I cannot say YES to this.'

But I had heard the intention behind her question: it was an invitation to embrace reality as it is. So I replayed the memory again, and a sense of peace began to fill my body. It was happening. Yes. The soldier was going to shoot Muturanyi. Yes. Muturanyi was pleading for his life. Yes. The soldier ordered him to sit on the ground. Yes. He, who was clearly older and, in our culture, deserved the soldier's respect. Yes. Muturanyi sat down, called out to God. Yes. The soldier shot him. Yes. He fell on his back. Yes. Yes. Yes. The silence. Yes. The soldier turned around. Yes. Yes. Yes. I was there. Yes. So I said gently, slowly, as if the word itself was slowly filling every cell of my being. Yes. 'Yes. Yes. Yes.'

My heart filled with compassion for Muturanyi, my eyes were wet again, crying. But now they were different tears. I kept saying Yes. He was dead. Yes. I had heard his last words. Yes. They were a call to God. Yes. I had been scared for him, been scared with him. Yes. That part of him that was also in me, that had wanted to be as wealthy as he was. Yes. The day he died, that part of him in me that hung on to life, to the idea of life, pleaded, begged, till the end, calling God. It happened.

Then I turned to the soldier. Yes. As I kept saying Yes, I got back in touch with what it was about him that I had been captivated by as a boy. He had once been a thirteen-year-old boy too. He had had dreams, desires, a future to look forward to. Then he grew up, became the figure I admired for weeks, the figure in which I saw myself. Yes. Yes. Myself.

As I kept saying yes, tears of love and compassion filled my closed eyes. I could feel my heartbeat. My head felt much lighter, though my face was still warm. I felt sweat rolling down along my ribs. Then I started feeling hands touching different parts of my body as I lay down on my back, arms and legs outstretched. I heard the trainer whispering to more of the participants to gather around me. I felt alive. I was not alone. Yes. I felt safe. Safe. And in the scene that was still vividly playing in my memory, nothing scared me anymore. Not even that silence. The bystanders at the scene, witnesses like me, somehow merged with those who were in that training room with me. They, too, had just witnessed it all. Yes. Still holding the memory of the scene I had just revisited, I slowly opened my eyes. Through my tears, I could see peaceful faces. Faces of witnesses to my journey to freedom. To free Muturanyi, let him go. To free the soldier, let him go. To free the bystanders, let them go. I sensed peace and love filling every cell of my body in complete relaxation. I felt a kind of freedom I had never experienced before. Peace. I, too, was free.

Some participants were crying softly, others smiling gently, most doing both. Each one was urged by trainer Briggy to touch a part of my body. In that room, we all became one. Or perhaps we had always been, but we experienced it deeply together that Sunday morning. Their faces were lit with a kind of light I could find no words to describe afterwards. Simply graceful. Yes. I smiled as I said 'Yes'. Some smiled with me, with love in their eyes. I knew they were truly there for me. With me. I breathed easily and looked up at the faces over me, connecting with a few of them eye to eye. And in their eyes, I saw Muturanyi. In their eyes, I saw the soldier. And for both, as I met them again, I felt the same thing. Love. Love. Yes, love. Somehow, I felt both of them present in me, in each of us there that morning.

CHAPTER 25
Meeting Mandela

The first person I told, out loud, that I intended to apply for the most prestigious scholarship on the continent was Joanne Walsch. That's because, when I met her before attending my first More to Life training programme, she asked what I would do after my degree.

I said I wanted to do honours in physics and, when asked how I would pay for it, I replied, without hesitation, that I would apply for a scholarship.

'What is it?' she asked.

'The Mandela Rhodes Scholarship,' I muttered, with a mixture of shyness and resolve. Ever since I had read a call for applications, I was sure I had the qualities the foundation was looking for; the advertisement specified that the scholarship was for candidates who had demonstrated potential in leadership, reconciliation, education and entrepreneurship. Despite my struggles, including depression, I was convinced that they were calling me. The AVP project, in which I had become a facilitator, and the BYM conference had boosted my confidence. I felt solidly grounded when I set out to apply for the scholarship.

I accompanied my direct application to the Mandela Rhodes Foundation with a nine-page essay entitled 'My journey to education'. Joanne was kind enough to edit it for me. I poured all my heart into the application essay, and into every step of the process. My efforts were rewarded with the news that I had been shortlisted.

But that was just a step in the rigorous selection process. The next was to write a 700-word essay on the topic 'What does the legacy of Nelson Mandela mean to you?'

An interview followed. It was intimidating facing the panel of eleven, led by the foundation chairman, Prof Gerwel. They had read my essay and grilled me from it. I particularly remember Isaac Shongwe, a well-known South African businessman and Rhodes Scholar, asking me: 'Where do you draw your strength from?'

'My mother,' I answered. 'Without her courage and sacrifices, I would not be here.'

As I prepared to leave, one of the panellists asked: 'What do you think is the most important problem in physics yet to be solved?'

Again, I didn't hesitate. 'Dark matter,' I answered. 'We can only observe and therefore account for a very small percentage of the mass of the universe. When we finally know what dark matter and dark energy are, the discovery will be as important as Einstein's work, if not more important.'

The panellists just nodded, with no hint in their expressions showing how they would vote. I thanked them and left.

The next day, I received a call from Prof Rejoice Ngcongo, the scholarships manager, to tell me I had been elected to be one of the 2006 Mandela Rhodes Scholars. I felt emotional, and immediately shared my news with my friend Andrew Kerr, who, on the day of my interview had just heard of his selection as a Rhodes Scholar. He was so happy that he ran to tell his parents. His father invited me to join the family to celebrate the scholarships together at a special dinner in the upscale restaurant of the five-star Royal Hotel.

A few weeks later I received a phone call and the soft female voice sounded very formal: 'I am calling you from the Mandela Rhodes Foundation. Do you have a moment to speak?'

'Yes, yes of course.'

'Well, Mr Kabalira, we have the pleasure of informing you that we received confirmation that Mr Mandela will be available to meet the scholars in Houghton in January, and I would like to discuss with you the travel arrangements.'

'Oh my God! We are going to meet Nelson Mandela?'

'Yes you are,' replied the soft voice, clearly enjoying my response.

At the gate of the Nelson Mandela Foundation, we had to present our IDs and, as usual, the security detail looked perplexed when examining mine. Our group of fifteen scholars was ushered into the auditorium, where we found journalists, and TV equipment already set up. Two couches were set in front, beneath a Mandela Rhodes Foundation banner. While we waited for Nelson Mandela to arrive, I heard the familiar voice in my head: How did I get here? As I felt a lump forming in my throat, some of the events of my life flashed through my mind, most of them evidence of why I should *not* be there in that moment. Dusty streets of Muhima. Bloody streets of La Fraicheur. Displaced. Fruit boy. Journey to nowhere. Car guard. Depressed. As the memory flashes intensified, my eyes filled with tears. I was both excited and nervous. I could feel the tension in my face and jaw as I forced a slight smile. I was trying hard to appear composed. Normal. My lips trembled. But I held it together. Despite all that had happened, the car guard was now a Mandela Rhodes Scholar. In a few minutes, the moment I could only allow myself to dream of would become reality.

My reverie was interrupted by an announcement reminding the media that no flash photography was allowed while Mr Mandela was present. A slight commotion near the entrance to the auditorium could only signify one thing: the statesman had arrived, wearing his trademark smile. As he entered, he broke the spell, joking: 'I am walking without a stick!' People relaxed and laughed. As if in slow motion, he approached one of the couches in front. Before he sat, he spotted one of the journalists in the fourth row. He called her by name, and said: 'You are still using the pen!'

She nodded, basking in his recognition. Zelda la Grange, his personal assistant, helped him settle in the couch and Shaun Johnson approached the podium. After a short speech, he called the scholars forward one by one, introducing them as they took a seat next to Mandela and had a little chat with him.

My turn! As soon as Shaun called my name, it was as if time stood still, so I remember every second of it. While Shaun said a bit about me, I shook Mandela's hand and took a seat, still wondering what to say.

He took the lead: 'So, young man! I hear you are from Rwanda.'

'Yes, Ntate. I am from Rwanda.' I replied. It was much easier answering his questions than figuring out what to say or ask.

'Please remind me: who is the president of your country.'

'It's Paul Kagame, Ntate.'

'Oh! It is still that guy!' As he said it, he burst into laughter, and everyone, including me, couldn't help joining in. For the rest of the interaction, it was as if we had known each other forever. I was no longer nervous when I told him how much I admired him and his journey. When my time was up, Mandela said: 'Please, when you meet Kagame, pass my regards to him!' I laughed again, not sure if he meant it, or if it was another joke. Whatever it was, it was joyful. Somehow, with every scholar, he found a way to start the conversation that made it specific to the individual, light and enjoyable for everyone present. Charismatic is an understatement. After all the scholars had their moment to sit and converse with Mandela, we had a group photo, huddling around the great man as he remained seated. As I stood behind the couch, I looked at Mandela's grey hair from above, and a surge of emotion hit me. I fought back the tears while trying to smile for the camera, swallowing hard to ease the lump in my throat. I was glad I was one of fifteen around him in that moment, so no one in the audience or the media would notice my struggle. At the same time, I was acutely aware of how special the moment was.

⁓

I was still riding the wave of my conviction that anything was possible and that good things could happen when the ghosts of Rwanda rose to haunt me again.

My good friend Khanyisile, a law student with an incredible

sense of curiosity about the continent, came running up to me, slightly breathless and bubbling with excitement.

'Pie, Pie! I learnt a lot today – about Rwanda!' she said, eagerly. I was curious.

'I learnt that Hutus and Tutsis will never get along,' she said, still glowing. Shocked, I didn't probe, but she continued anyway.

'Also, I learnt that if I was in Rwanda, I would be *umututsikazi!*' she added, her pride almost infectious.

'Where did you learn all that?' I asked, perplexed.

'Serge and Paul, the post-grad Rwandan students,' she answered. These were the same students I visited on campus, and through whom I sent and received packages to and from home.

'Serge told me that he was engaged, but he broke off the engagement as soon as he found out that one of his fiancée's parents was a Hutu,' Khanyisile said.

When Khanyisile learnt that Serge and Paul were Tutsis, she asked them what Hutus looked like. Their answer, which she readily shared, shocked me: 'They asked me if I knew a student called Pacifique. Then they said: "look at Pacifique. That is what a Hutu looks like!"'

Weeks later, at a commemoration of the genocide, the same students were telling a packed audience on campus that Rwanda was peaceful. 'In Rwanda, there is no Hutu, no Tutsi, we are all going forward as one,' one of them said, while the other, also on the stage, waited for his turn to speak.

I challenged the statement, querying the veracity of what he had said by publicly relating to the audience that these students had made me 'exhibit H'. They both fell silent and a representative of the Rwandan embassy in South Africa tried to answer.

It didn't end there. Not long after, I was at the centre of further reverberations of the Rwandan ethnic and political problem. One evening, I received a call from one of the key leaders of the Union of Refugee Women, who began: 'Pacifique, I know you well, but I want to know if what they are saying about you here in Durban is true. Are you working for the Rwandan government?'

Perplexed, I had no answer! She explained that people had concluded I was a Rwandan spy because I had suggested that Rwandan refugees and students from Rwanda meet in a support group hosted by the student counselling centre. That was not entirely accurate. I had lobbied for a support group for *all* international students to be hosted and facilitated by the centre. But it was what my friend said next that shocked me the most: 'They are also saying that Mandela wanted to give money to refugees, and you blocked it. Instead, you took it yourself. Is that true?' she asked, genuinely curious.

Soon after, I was informed by several other people that my 'Rwandan spy' activities were a household topic around the Rwandan community in Durban. I could feel the suspicion when I visited some of them. The tension. The pregnant silences. I could sense they were uneasy in my presence.

Many years later, I had another experience that showed me just how much our society was in need of healing. During a CapeTalk radio interview, talk-show host John Maytham was speaking to me about the refugee crisis in Europe. To illustrate something, I related my own experience of leaving all and everything behind. The podcast of the interview was published and one of my La Colombière classmates found it on social media and shared the link on a WhatsApp group for alumni, to which I had been added a few months earlier.

He wrote: 'Hello guys. Just listen to Pacifique. Very eloquent. However, there are some dots I can't connect when you say that in 2001, the situation was precarious. Can you educate me on that as I did not experience that.'

The responses included: 'In 2001? Weren't we studying? What happened after your studies?'

And shortly after: 'I was troubled by what I heard and it's very dangerous to bring or share our political beliefs on this group! Some of us felt uncomfortable even though they don't say it, but let's just stick to things that bring us together instead! My 2 cents!' This message got a thumbs-up.

Their questions were intriguing. Of course, apart from Clemence and Ntikanga, with whom I had shared some details about what was happening to me, my classmates had had no clue about what was going on in my head, or in my life. For me, the strict separation of school world and home world was unintentional. But it served me well. The messages on the WhatsApp group revealed to me just how much I had alienated myself. It was as if I turned into another person when I walked through the school gates, switched on another brain, made my academic success about more than just doing well at school.

'Good question . . .' I began my reply on WhatsApp. But before I added anything more, another message popped up, pleading for the group to keep a focus on what brought us together, starting a hashtag #Bringus2gether. By then, one of the members, probably upset, had already left the group.

'Guys,' I wrote, 'some of you don't actually know what was happening in my life while we studied together, and some did . . . But it may be time to tell you?'

Promptly, another member of the group said: 'Please do Pacifique. But keep in mind that here we don't share any political views and don't feel offended.' Somehow, the fear that my story would be about 'political views' dominated. It was exactly like at school all those years ago; shying away from politics, or anything related to politics, seemed to be natural, and perhaps not accidental, either. These young people had been completely shielded. Shielded from hearing or talking about sensitive issues in our society. Shielded from some of the realities of our country, particularly politics. The feeling expressed in their request was familiar to me: anything but politics. We were all together as one, but only as long as we kept our political views silent, and discussed nothing of our past, ethnicity, war, genocide or anything that would hint at these uncomfortable subjects. We had lived our school life as if politics didn't exist. It was perhaps one of the reasons I didn't, or couldn't, share anything about my reality then, although we were spending so much time together. And perhaps it was the reason they had

254

not picked up any suggestion, any clue about the things that were happening to me.

I was conflicted as I decided to finally share my story with them. I knew they might hear 'politics', even when I wasn't talking politics. But I was clear that it was not my intention.

I felt sad. Sad that I had spent so much time with them, and had gone to some of their homes, studied, laughed, played with and befriended some of them and yet, somehow, my life had remained private. It hit me hard that we were so disconnected, so alienated from each other. I began to cry. I was in my car, parked on the side of the road as I sent another message.

'. . . And I do support #bringus2gether. I think I shared no political view . . . or standpoint [in the interview] . . . I do my utmost best to avoid that . . . as much as I can.' Of course, I did. But did I need to reassure them?

'Great. So go ahead,' one of them said, as if to give me permission.

By the time I started sharing, strangely, all members of the group were reading the messages instantly, which had never before happened on the group. All the messages I sent immediately got two blue ticks; everyone in the group from around the globe was tuned in, 'listening' to me. I paused. My heart filled with sadness, eyes wet with tears. I began to sob. I realised I was about to reveal the truth about my life, which might come as a shock to my classmates, shielded not only by the privilege of their social class, but also by the tight control on the flow of information in my country. It would be a revelation to some. Whatever the case, I was going to tell them that the boy they had sat with in class had another life. A life that could change what they thought of him, of the country and perhaps of themselves.

I summarised parts of my story they had no idea about, told only in short highlights, and then I ended with a message of gratitude: 'Friends, that's all for now . . . I hope that gives you some context to my comments [in the interview].' I paused. 'Being at La Colombière with you was a great blessing, and I can only say thank you! That school, including you all, has taught me a lot, but actually also kept me sane and safe,' I ended.

A minute later the first response came through.

'Woah. I am speechless. Had no clue all this was going on in ur (sic) life Pacifique. And I am so sorry.'

'I am too. So sad Pie! Courage and God is there for you. *Pole sana*,' another one said.

'Pie, I don't know really what to say. But life isn't always fair and glad you made it! And your mother is proud of the man you are now! Courage and forgive that's the best way to fulfil your life.'

Then a message from the one who started the whole conversation came through: 'It is really very sad Pacifique. I hope that the ones responsible will be punished. It is sad that we were not able to support you in those moments.'

As the responses came tumbling onto the WhatsApp feed, some decided to send me private messages, all expressing the same sentiments. I felt a mixture of sadness and relief, but somehow I was still shocked at the realisation that they really, truly hadn't known. The fact that there had been two countries in one. My home life was in one, while my school life was in the other. And I wondered if that would ever end.

CHAPTER 26
Another beginning

During my honours year, I began to have recurring episodes of severe depression. I feared having another crisis during an exam period, leading to supplementary exams and failure. The fear of failing became so strong that I had crippling panic attacks. But it was made worse by the fear of failing the Mandela Rhodes Foundation. I could not appear weak, I had to be strong. So I pushed myself harder, falling into denial about signs of depression. I stopped taking medication, believing that it was affecting my energy and my memory. I pushed through, but it got harder. Easy things took me a long time. I slept much less than I should.

When exams came, I was prepared. At least I thought and felt so. But the experience of one paper, statistical physics and classical theory, will remain with me forever. I had studied hard and had worked through all the past exam papers. Because of the recurring questions over the years, it was easy to see what was coming. At the beginning of the exam, I felt happy while reading through the paper. I had practised. So I started. Question one: after writing line two of an equation, I had a memory hole. I knew the third line, but it was not coming. Okay, I thought. It'll come later. Next. Question two, similar experience. My heart pounding, I began to feel uneasy. My hands were shaking. Close to tears, my face trembled. The more I forced myself to keep going, the less I remembered. Had I not studied well enough? Did I not understand? After a while, I came back to question one. Then jumped to another. This is a disaster, I whispered to myself. I knew I was messed up, but had no idea of the extent. It was so bad that before the exam was over, I was praying I would get enough to get a supplementary exam. When the time was up, I was blank. I had sat there, watching the clock tick, unable to leave because I wasn't finished, but also unable to continue. I knew the work, but it just wouldn't come out onto paper. It was over. I rushed back home, and cried myself to sleep. When I woke in the afternoon, I was very hungry. I ate something. Then I picked up a notepad and wrote down the equations that had eluded me in the exam. What had happened? Why did I black out? I decided to go back onto antidepressants.

When the exam results came, I was not surprised. I had not even got enough marks for a supplementary exam. Failing a core subject meant automatic exit from honours. I delayed the call to Prof Ngcongo, or Prof Rejoice as we called her. What was I going to say? My girlfriend, Tessa Meyer, consoled me. I had met Tessa on the More to Life programme. She was a good listener, disciplined and kind-hearted. She was also very successful at her job, and was being considered for a secondment to China as part of her leadership development.

I eventually plucked up the courage to make the call: 'I have very bad news. I have failed. I have failed the Mandela Rhodes Foundation. I have failed you. I have failed myself,' I said, tears rolling down my cheeks. I held the phone with one hand, the other scratching my head. I was not only angry with myself, I felt ashamed. After a moment of silence, Prof Rejoice responded calmly: 'Oh dear, Pie. I am sorry to hear that.'

'No. I am sorry. I am the one who let you down,' I replied, feeling very nervous about how she was going to take it. After another moment of silence she said: 'Dear Pie. You are precious. And we still love you no matter what.'

I could not believe what I was hearing. Prof Rejoice had to be disappointed. She had the right to be angry. I had messed up, and so, I thought, at the very least, she would be disappointed too. I gulped for air, eyes still wet with tears. I was very surprised by Prof Rejoice's response. I expected her to express shock and dismay. That is what I deserved. But she did not. She was sad. She was sad with me, holding what had happened with compassion. Then she added, in a firm yet gentle voice that left no doubt: 'Whatever happens, Pie, you are still a Mandela Rhodes Scholar. And you always will be.' I could not respond.

This was the first time I could remember experiencing unconditional love from anyone other than my mother. Tessa smiled with tears in her eyes when I told her what had happened. 'Everything is not lost, Pie,' she concluded.

In the few days that followed, Tessa helped me to brainstorm what I would do next. One option emerged most strongly: having a conversation with the faculty about what was possible.

I could have sworn that Prof Meyerowitz had expected that conversation because, without hesitation, she offered me a temporary job at the university as an assistant in the newly launched science and technology centre.

I was grateful for the work, and having a focus, but my mind was working on finding long-term prospects. Through the BYM experience, I had developed a curiosity about how corporates position themselves to recruit talent. So when I received an email notifying me of an Absa presentation about its graduate programme, I decided to go. In the presentation, the guests kept talking about how great Absa was becoming, particularly after being acquired by Barclays, which added a global appeal to its profile.

Coincidently, the morning of the presentation, I had heard on an SAfm news bulletin that the chairman of Barclays had stepped down, an event that caused the share price at the London Stock Exchange to drop. When it was appropriate, I put my hand up to ask, just out of curiosity: 'How does the fall in the share price of Barclays in London yesterday affect Absa today?' When the three presenters seemed confused, I asked again, more precisely: 'The chairman of Barclays stepped down yesterday. The share price dropped in London. I was asking how it will affect Absa today.'

There was silence. Then, before addressing the question, one of the presenters, in an excited voice, pointed to me and exclaimed: 'Ladies and gentlemen, that's what we are talking about! This is the kind of curiosity that we reward. The kind of curiosity we are looking for in young talent! What is your name?' I was sitting in the last row of the half-full auditorium and was slightly taken aback when everyone turned to look at me as I gave my name.

Then the presenters continued. I didn't really get much of an answer, and it seemed as if none of them knew of the Barclays news I was referring to. However, at the end of the presentation, one of them approached me, saying: 'Hello. I am Riana Cassiem. Thank you for your participation in the presentation.'

'Well, I was just being curious. It seemed Barclays was a big part of your presentation, so I wanted to understand how they are linked,' I replied, before she surprised me with a question.

'Would you please apply?' she said, looking me in the eyes.

Hesitantly, I replied with a question: 'Oh. But I am a refugee. How would that work?' We then had a short conversation about what being a refugee meant in terms of work in South Africa.

After I told her there would be no need to apply for a work permit, Riana handed me a business card, saying: 'Please don't send your application through the portal. Send it directly to me. I will do what I can to get you into the recruitment process.'

A week later, I sent my CV to Riana, and indicated my interest. She promised to forward my CV and, after some psychometric tests and a question about whether I spoke Portuguese, Riana called to apologise: 'I am so sorry. Absa Africa is full, no one else is looking for a non-South African graduate, unfortunately.' With that, I closed the Absa chapter in my head.

***

I was visiting my childhood friend Eric in Cape Town when my phone buzzed. It was an SMS from my sister, informing me that my mother had just collected her passport. 'Yoh! When your mother comes, I want to be there to see you receiving her!' said Eric. A promise was made.

My mother had told me in December 2006 that 2007 would not end before she came to visit me. I had felt it as pressure, but she assured me it was not.

My mother had converted from being Catholic to becoming a protestant – a move she credits for surviving a complex operation that cured her chronic anaemia, and for deliverance from alcohol dependence. She was healthier, happier and full of faith. 'This was a message from God!' she said. 'A promise I received through prayers.'

Until then, we had considered my mother's visit too difficult. She had been denied a passport, due to an administrative problem authorities had failed to help her solve. So when she said she would visit within a year, it felt too far-fetched to even entertain as a joke. But that afternoon, when I received that SMS, I, too, started believing.

I had no suitable accommodation, and I was not earning enough to host my mother. If she was going to visit, it would depend on many people. This would become my first experience of social capital.

First, Darrel. I had met him at a life skills training programme in which he had a profound breakthrough. At the end of the course, Darrel told me something I thought would never come to pass: 'If ever you want your mother to come and visit, I would like to pay for her air ticket. You have profoundly touched my heart,' he said. Darrel was referring to an occasion when he received bad news while we were busy with an exercise. I reached out and held him as he collapsed in tears. Just before, during the healing exercise, I had shared a bit of my story.

But that interaction had happened two years before; at the time, a visit from my mother seemed like a far-off dream so I did not think much about Darrel's offer. Now, when it seemed possible, I reached out to him, and he immediately responded.

'Please do let me know how much money I need to send to pay

for your mother's journey. My original commitment to you still stands and I look forward to seeing a photograph of you both together,' he replied in an email.

We had an air ticket. The next thing was to get a visa. I needed someone to invite her to come and visit South Africa. That is where Laurie intervened. I had met Laurie at the Manning Road Methodist Church, which Andrew had invited me to attend with him. One day, the pastor of the church asked me to share my story with the congregation, and among those who connected with me afterwards were Laurie and Abby. Together, they organised more talks for me, aimed at raising money to receive my mother. Laurie also volunteered to formally invite her. The visa was sorted.

What remained was the accommodation. As things turned out, I had a misunderstanding with my landlord and decided to leave immediately. It was October; I mentioned to a student that I was looking for accommodation and it so happened that she was moving out of a beautiful room in a large house, parts of which were used for student accommodation. The house was so beautiful that it had been featured on *Top Billing*, a lifestyle TV programme. I would rent the corner room, in which part of the outside wall was glass. My room would be right in front of a lapa, a thatched structure for private outdoor events, from which we would have a beautiful view of the Manor Gardens valley. The room had enough space for two beds, so I could comfortably accommodate my mother.

Everything was in order. At 9 pm on Wednesday, November 28 at Durban International, I would see my mother for the first time since March 18, 2001. Eric kept his promise. He came from Cape Town to help me welcome my mother, and was hosted by Lauri and family.

The evening of my mother's arrival was unforgettable. I invited some Rwandan families to join us at the airport, but only Kayijuka and his wife Catherine were available. Lauri drove me and Eric to the airport. I was bursting with excitement. When I said I felt like screaming, Lauri lowered the window on my side and said: 'Go ahead and scream! Scream! It is so exciting!'

'Whoooaaaaaaaa!!!!!!' I screamed at the wind that seemed to be pushing my voice back into my face. Lauri and Eric joined in. We screamed at the open highway, and then laughed so hard that I started sweating, out of breath. I was wearing my green African print short-sleeved shirt that had subtle white embroidery around the neck, sleeves and pockets, and a much heavier pattern down on along the chest. I paired this with black trousers and my treasured pair of light brown fancy shoes. I was dressed up to meet my mother. Her miracle had been realised. 'From now, should my mother say it's God's promise, I will not argue!' I said.

'You better not!' laughed Eric.

After flight SA 581 landed, I could not stand still. I was afraid something had gone wrong at one of the airports my mother had to pass through. It was her first ever flight. She had never been through customs and immigration before, let alone having to change flights at an airport as big as Johannesburg. I was restless. But to be fair, I had never been on an international flight either. I could only imagine what it was like for my mother, who could not speak English, to have to go through three airports, and interact with all kinds of officials and numerous hosts and hostesses.

Clutching the bunch of flowers I had brought, exclusively made of calla lilies, my mother's favourite flower, I tried to peer through to the luggage area every time the automatic door slid open, to see if I could catch sight of her. I was unsuccessful. But Eric, who is significantly taller than me, was luckier.

'Look! There she is!' he exclaimed. I felt tingling in my stomach. I stood on tiptoe a few times, but no luck. Then I saw a tall black woman hastily walking across the luggage collection area, but the sliding door shut before I could identify her as my mother. I was very nervous; all day, I had felt scared for her. But this was God's miracle for her. Nothing was going to go wrong. That is how I calmed myself. Kayijuka and Catherine stood together, camera at the ready, and Lauri couldn't stop grinning. Eric was calm, arms crossed. He was wearing baggy, dark blue jeans, a mostly white tracksuit jacket and, underneath, a black T-shirt with the iconic headshot of Che Guevara against a background of yellow flames.

We were standing near the end of the barriers, and I watched as passengers emerged, and singled out those who were waiting for them. Looking at people hugging, smiling, posing for pictures and hugging some more, I wondered how I would hold myself together when my mother came out.

Finally, the sliding door opened for the nth time, and there she was – wearing a red African ensemble, with a matching head wrap towering West African style, and a white necklace. She walked out, and stood still in front of the sliding doors, in the middle of the exit way. She looked right, left and forward. When she saw me, she pushed and let go of her trolley, letting it roll forward, knelt down and raised her eyes and arms towards the roof, surely heavenward, in prayer. I sprinted towards her, forgetting that the alley was only for passengers coming out. I raced past one or two people and their trolleys, then past my mother's trolley. I was only slightly aware that we were causing a scene, but I didn't care. I threw myself knees first on the ground, still at speed, and hugged my mother tightly. The stems of the flowers I held out to her got squashed between our chests, calla lilies towering past our ears and over our heads. She murmured words I don't remember as we held each other in a tight hug. She also murmured her thanks to God in Kinyarwanda while I started sobbing, spurting the word 'mama' over and over again. We both remained on our knees in the middle of the exit way. When I finally opened my eyes, I saw everyone standing still around us, staring, but I didn't let go. I will never know how long it took before we finally released each other and stood up. I introduced her to the people who were with me. She already knew Eric, whom she was pleasantly surprised to see there. After she greeted and thanked everyone – Lauri, Kayijuka and Catherine – she said she'd like time to pray properly before we left for a simple late reception tea at Lauri's house. She knelt down on the floor of the arrival hall once more and prayed aloud to thank the Lord for what He had done.

My mother and I hosted many friends who came to greet her. As the December holidays were in full swing, the visits became increasingly festive. Since Youth Day 2007 fell on a Sunday, the Monday was a public holiday, resulting in a long weekend. It turned out to be unforgettable, for a life-changing and unexpected reason.

On the Saturday afternoon, while braaiing meat for guests who gathered on the wooden viewing platform of our magnificent accommodation, my phone rang and I retreated to my room to answer.

'Hello. Is that Pie?' the voice said, pronouncing 'pie' in English.

'Pie-Pacifique. Pie-Pacifique is the name. It is French, not pie in English,' I retorted, cheekily.

'Oh, I am sorry. My name is Debbie. Debbie Marshall. I am calling you from Absa in Johannesburg.'

'Oh! Hello Debbie,' I replied, with a mixture of curiosity and surprise – especially because it was the Saturday afternoon of a long weekend in December.

'I happened to pass by the office, and I have your profile here in front of me,' she said as I paused, unsure how to respond. 'Tell me, are you still interested in joining the Absa graduate programme?' she asked.

I hesitated. 'But . . . I was told not to wait; that there was no more available space for me as a non-South African.'

'Who told you not to wait?'

'Riana did.'

'Oh. I work with her. I am her boss,' said Debbie. I started to feel excited.

'Tell me, what does it mean for you to be a refugee? Are you able to obtain a work permit?' she asked. I'd had this conversation several times already.

'I don't need a work permit. The status implies the right to study and the right to work,' I answered confidently, determined to sound knowledgeable and professional. I knew that this was a conversation that could change my life forever.

'I like your profile. A lot. If you are interested, I will organise an interview for you. Unfortunately, most of our senior managers are already on holiday, but I hope to find one who is in Durban to interview you,' she said. I could hardly believe it!

I met the senior manager at the Pavilion Shopping Centre, at a rooftop restaurant bar. At the end of my interview, the senior manager gave me a chance to ask him a question: 'I am a physicist. What do you think I will do best in a bank?' I asked, hoping his answer would help me choose a path to follow.

'You see, with the physics, we know you can think and solve problems. The banking, we will teach you. But there are three things we can't teach you. Thinking. Character. Attitude. We know you have the thinking. And we hope you have character and attitude. The rest, don't worry about for now.'

Then he picked up his mobile phone and called his assistant. 'It's a go. You may send the offer,' he said.

When I returned home, my mother was on her knees, praying. She had also been fasting for a few days. 'I got the job! I will start in the Absa graduate programme in January,' I proudly said.

My mother immediately raised her hands towards the sky and murmured prayers in Kinyarwanda. Then she gave me a long hug.

As my mother's visit was drawing to a close, my lease on the apartment was coming to an end. I, too, would soon have to leave Durban for Johannesburg. It was so coincidental that one would think I had planned it. My lease would expire on January 31, and my mother's return flight from Durban was on Sunday, January 27.

The day before she was due to leave, when we were being hosted by the Union of Refugee Women, I received an SMS from an Absa employee telling me I would need to be at the graduate programme launch dinner on the evening of Sunday the 27th. The message also indicated that they were booking my Durban-Johannesburg flight, and details would be emailed to me later. I started worrying about what would happen on Sunday. Would I go to the airport first or would my mother go first? Who would help me to take her to the airport? What would happen if I was not there? So many thoughts flew through my head.

When we got home that evening, I checked my email so I could start organising the logistics. I looked at my mother's ticket to compare the flight times; Absa had booked me on the same flight as my mother, a ticket we had booked months earlier! Flight SA 554 at 12:40 pm on Sunday, January 27, 2008.

That evening, I repeated to my mother that I would never argue with her about her belief in God's miracles, irrespective of my own beliefs. We were happy together, shared a meal, talked about my sister, and packed gifts for her to take back to Rwanda. My mother reflected on people and experiences in South Africa, and suggested that we say a prayer together.

The next day my mother would fly home, and I would fly to a new job. We had one hour to share that journey. Over the years, I have thought about that flight, wondering what roles we were playing for each other. While I was accompanying her on the first leg of her journey home, she was ushering me into a completely new world, just as she had when she took me to my first day of school, or when she travelled with me for my first day at boarding school. Judging from our conversation on that flight, dominated by questions about my readiness for the great city of Johannesburg, it seemed she was grateful for that hour to fulfil her role as a mother.

The whole morning, I'd been thinking about the odds of us being on the same flight. As the plane took off, and my mother and I watched the fast-receding ground through the window on our right, I shared with her a thought that came to me: 'If ever there is a book or a movie about my life, it will end here!'

EPILOGUE

I worked at Absa for just over three years. It was a great learning journey, in which I progressed a lot. I uncovered my abilities and limitations, but most importantly, it helped me discover what I was really passionate about: working with people, learning from life and passing on lessons, as well as maximising human potential.

In what may seem like coincidence, I transitioned into my second job in a similar way to how I'd been offered my first. I met my future employer and mentor at a presentation by futurist Graeme Codrington, held at the Gordon Institute of Business Science (GIBS). Again, during the presentation, I raised my hand to ask the presenter a question. At the end, Jules Newton, the founder and CEO of Avocado Vision, approached me. 'Young man, I know talent when I see it!' she said. It was the beginning of a conversation that led to me joining her company as an account manager, beginning to learn about business development and sales. Logically, my clients were in financial services.

I learnt so much at Avocado Vision that just by applying the simple principles they taught me, I exceeded my targets in my first year. The next year, I did something I will forever be grateful for. As there was no budget for additional support staff for the sales team, I decided to have faith that I would be able to afford one. I got Agnes onboard to work for me for two hours a day. Jules allowed her to use a desk, phone and internet for the rest of the day, which would help her to pursue her other interests. A win-win for everyone. Agnes managed the time she dedicated to me so well that I not only exceeded my targets the following year, but I made so much commission that I could afford to take a break for eight months. I was tired, not so much from the job, but more because, most of my life, I had had battle after battle. My spirit was drained, and I sensed a unique opportunity to take a step back, recharge and chart a way to live intentionally, creating what I want, rather than running from something.

When I asked Jules to allow me to do that, she gave me her blessing. The following day, she sent me a photo of an article she had written with the headline: 'Do you want talent? Let them go!' That captures Jules's generosity.

In those eight months, I travelled to Europe and the US, explored ways of processing my life events and learnt from them, seeking a way to empower myself and others. That's also when the first lines of what became this book were written.

As I stepped out of that break, I had already made a decision: Africa, the whole continent, would be my workplace. I was seeking an opportunity that would expose me to business realities on the continent, focusing on business development. I then started working as a consultant, first with the Inspirational Development Group, and then with Whitten & Roy Partnership. Now, I run my own consulting company, and I have been to 23 African countries and a few in Southeast Asia, mostly just doing what I love: business development by empowering people to be the best they can be.

Completing a circle, in recent years I have had the privilege, a couple of times, of sitting on the other side of the table at the Mandela Rhodes Foundation, working with the late Shaun Johnson and Judy Sikuza – former and current CEO respectively – and with Prof Njabulo Ndebele, the chairman, on the final interview panel to select Mandela Rhodes Scholars.

I have been profoundly inspired by many people, to whom I am deeply grateful. For example, James, my roommate who always lived as if his role as a car guard was temporary, and who didn't at first think he could get into university but enrolled a year after

I did. He seized the opportunity with both hands and became a doctor. There are many Jameses . . .

As is the pattern in most families, there are endings and beginnings. My grandmother and my uncles have passed away, and I have finally managed to find my half-brother and -sister, both of whom are now connected to our family. Boldly, my mother legally adopted a baby girl she had practically raised from birth. The baby is now a teenager. As for my little sister, well, she is no longer little. A few years ago, she and I had a pact: I would support her to study, and she would aim at becoming more educated than I am. She has already achieved that! She is working for a US university, while completing her MBA at the same institution.

If I am able to share what I have witnessed, and enter the depth of my traumatic experiences, it is simply because I've had the privilege of encountering people who gave me a safe space to express myself without being judged. I was able to make breakthroughs in some areas of my life, changing my relationships forever.

For example, the first time I saw a woman being undressed, I was thirteen. She was dead, her body being abused by men using words ordinarily reserved for an intimate setting. It took me years, but I eventually discovered why I froze in front of Nomandia, my first girlfriend, and the reason I ended up in a series of relationships with non-black partners: subconsciously, intimacy with a black woman took me back to that scene I had witnessed as a teenager.

There were complex layers of conscious and unconscious fears – mainly that I was terrified of being like those men I saw violating her. I feared the violence in me, thinking it might be disguised as intimacy. I feared myself. So I froze.

I spent years of struggle, swinging between two extremes: total withdrawal (to hide), or overcompensating (to mask), both of which pushed away those to whom I intended to show affection. Gradually I found myself, and I am still working at it.

I have made other discoveries about my relationships. With money. With work. With male and female authority figures. With news of violence. With any kind of ethnicity, even in foreign countries. With my own body. With my black-manhood. With myself.

The damage to a young mind growing up in a world of fear, and witnessing war and violence, is so great that it takes considerable time to heal. Yet, many fellow Rwandans may never have the kind of opportunities I have had to be listened to, to share, and to process. But there is hope.

So much has happened to convince me that when we take the time to reflect, even when we don't like *how* events have unfolded, it becomes clear that Life is *for* us.

Without doubt, I believe Life is *for* me. *For* you.

ACKNOWLEDGEMENTS

Every step of writing this book was challenging. But none more so than discovering my ever-evolving purpose behind the decision to publish. I had doubts, fear and moments of anxiety – prompted by uncertainty about what it would become, and its potential repercussions. This is why I am so grateful for the many deep conversations that shaped the 'why' behind the content of this book. A diplomat friend pushed me, saying: 'I learnt about Rwanda through you and other Rwandan friends, and read a lot about it. I want to ask you: through reading your book, will I learn something new?' Another friend said: 'Rwanda is now the best country in Africa. The president is my role model. Why rehash the painful past of a country that is clearly just moving forward?'

I have often wondered if it is necessary to make a choice between confronting our past for genuine healing, and economic development. I don't have an answer. I believe it is possible to have both, although I acknowledge that I have met many people who think otherwise.

Some I spoke to were concerned about my safety. 'Why would you put yourself and your family in harm's way by publishing, knowing the possible repercussions of accounts that differ from the official narrative?' a friend asked. Each time I had such a conversation, I was challenged to dig deep. And I confess that I gave up several times.

Yet, the conversation that stands out the most was with a young Tutsi man who shared his story with me. He has vague memories of witnessing his parents being killed in 1994, when he was only five years old. He grew up in a children's orphanage for Tutsi genocide survivors. 'All the time, many kids were crying, asking when their parents would come,' he began. 'To make us feel better, the adults who looked after us told us that there was no adult who had a mother. Until I left the orphanage as a teenager, I believed it, so it is still strange to me when you say that you will be visiting your mother,' he said, eyes fixed on mine. 'How can you have a mother as an adult?' he asked sincerely.

After we had shared trustingly, he revealed: 'I just wish the genocide would happen again, but the other way around. Now that I am an adult, I know what I would do to show them,' he concluded, eyes wet with tears. I had chills running through my body, memories of that bloody chaos flying through my mind. Unfortunately, he is not the only one.

I encountered an expression of the other perspective when I moved to Johannesburg for work, and a respected member of the Rwandan community summoned me. 'Son,' he said, 'you must be careful. Don't let Tutsis anywhere close. They want to suck you dry, and then betray you. They are really snakes. I beg you, son, stay away from Tutsis in this city.'

Although it is now often stated in Rwanda that there is no Hutu, no Tutsi, only Rwandans, these two are not the only Rwandans I have met, Tutsi and Hutu, with this mentality. It is the kind of mentality that is just waiting for the wrong trigger, and a convergence of circumstances, to lead to another disaster. Unfortunately, many Rwandans have little to no opportunity to confront their pain. Yet avoiding the challenge of untying and dealing with these emotional knots from our past doesn't make them melt away. In many cases, they become tighter, harder and deeper, and the world around us experiences the consequences.

Witnessing is an attempt to provide a true account of a boy growing up surrounded by rumblings of war and witnessing extreme atrocities. As one of my friends put it, I am placing the story on the altar. It will become a different experience for each reader. My hope is that at the end of it, it is no longer my story. It is our story. Our witnessing. And we, together, can make a collective and conscious choice about how we want to move forward in our world.

I would like to express my deep gratitude to the following people who have played a significant part in my writing and healing journey. The late Shaun Johnson, who witnessed the seed of this book being planted and helped me to nurture it. Prof Rejoice Ngcongo, through whom I had experiences of unconditional love. Father David Holdcroft, Carol Kioko aka CK, Suzanne Mabaso, Margot Uys, Daisy McDonald, Caoilfhionn van der Walt, Kirsten Thomson, Anna Koblanck, Mandi Mzimba, Mandi Smallhorne, Athambile Masola and all who offered their ears so I could hear myself through them. Briggy Kiddle, Ann McMaster, Richard Perry and Pascale Ascher for expertly holding the space for me to grieve and discover the world beyond. David Templer for your inspiration and generosity. Anne Pratt, Jules Newton, Joanne Walsch, Gustaaf Wolvaardt, Peter Alkema, Roy Whitten, Scott Roy and colleagues at WRP, who continue to mark my professional journey while I unshackle myself from the emotional bonds of the past. Edd and Tash and your fellow teachers in the South African dance community who created platforms on which I learnt to express myself through dance, and all who danced with me. You may never know how much dancing meant to me, especially when I first wrote the most painful parts of *Witnessing*.

Gill Moodie for believing in this book, Abdeah Davis for starting me on the publishing journey, and Na'eemah Masoet for your incredible patience and sensitivity to the story. Gillian Warren-Brown, your way of editing was such a profoundly healing journey that I have deeply enjoyed.

Rwanda: thank you for birthing and nurturing me. South Africa: thank you for hosting me. You have both shaped who I am becoming.

To my family: I have duly left out details you wished to keep confidential and private, but know that I am so grateful, and that I'm still in awe of your tenacity over the years as I shared with you the evolution of this work. Without your courage and generosity, there is no book. Without you, there is no me.

Thank you to you all. We created this together.

Pie-Pacifique Kabalira-Uwase is the Founder and Director of PEM Afurika, a business consulting firm specialising in business development and sales. Having served as the Head of the Business School of the Foundation for Professional Development, a private institution of higher learning based in Pretoria, Pie-Pacifique is currently an Associate Consultant with the Inspirational Development Group (IDG) South Africa, and a Consulting Partner with Whitten and Roy Partnership (WRP), both companies with global reach, where he focuses on people-related business solutions. For much of the year, Pie-Pacifique travels the length and breadth of the planet inspiring, coaching and training leaders and followers to create the best results they desire, through team work and purposeful partnerships.

In 2002, against all odds, he enrolled at the then University of Natal, where he was awarded the Mandela Rhodes Scholarship upon completion of his degree in Physics. He started his professional career in the banking sector as a Business and Systems Analyst in 2008.

In 2011, he was appointed Account Executive at Avocado Vision, a company specialising in large-scale community and workplace training programmes, including Enterprise Development. He initiated and managed projects that touched thousands of people in marginalised communities in South Africa, empowering hundreds of community-based micro-enterprises. Since 2013, through his consulting work with IDG and WRP, he has delivered Business Leadership Development programmes and worked on Business Development projects in numerous countries in all four corners of Africa, as well as in Southeast Asia.

Besides his Business and Leadership Development activities, Pie-Pacifique is currently a Board Member of Jesuit Refugee Service Southern Africa, as well as an international Keynote and Motivational Speaker. He lives in Pretoria with his wife.